READING POWER

Reading Faster • Thinking Skills
Reading for Pleasure • Comprehension Skills

READING POWER

Reading Faster • Thinking Skills
Reading for Pleasure • Comprehension Skills

BEATRICE S. MIKULECKY
Boston University

LINDA JEFFRIES

ADDISON-WESLEY PUBLISHING COMPANY

Reading, Massachusetts • Menlo Park, California
Don Mills, Ontario • Wokingham, England • Amsterdam • Sydney
Singapore • Tokyo • Madrid • Bogota • Santiago • San Juan

Acknowledgments

We would like to thank our friends and our families for their support and encouragement during the past year. We would also like to acknowledge the many friends and colleagues who talked to us about our project. Without the inspiration and encouragement of Steve Molinsky, we may never have finished it. Valuable feedback was also provided by Gloria Mason, Carol Anastasi, Rachel Goodman, Ellen Smith, Gary Cestaro, Howard Tinberg, and Sue Siegel. Thank you one and all!

A Publication of the World Language Division

Editorial: Kathleen Sands Boehmer
Manufacturing/Production: James W. Gibbons
Illustrations: Kathy Todd and Susan Avishai
Design: Dixie Clark Production
Cover Design: Marshall Henrichs

Credits: p. 15, L.A. Morse; pp. 42, 43, 45, *The New York Times*; p. 45, *The Boston Globe*; p. 128, Adapted from *Tactics in Reading II* by O.S. Niles, D.K. Bracken, M.A. Dougherty and R.F. Kinder. Copyright © 1964, 65 by Scott, Foresman and Company. Reprinted by permission.

ISBN 0-201-15865-5
19 20-CRS-97 96

Contents

To the Teacher

Reading Power is intended for students of English as a Second Language who have studied English for an average of 100 hours and have acquired a vocabulary of about 600 words.

In appearance and in approach, this book is quite different from other reading skills books. Most books are used in a linear fashion from beginning to end. However, in this book the four parts must be used concurrently, since each part focuses on a different aspect of reading instruction. This means that each class should include several different kinds of activities and exercises from the different parts of the book. Using all the parts together in this way is crucial to a successful reading program.

PART I. READING FOR PLEASURE

Recent research in both first and second language reading confirms that the key to reading improvement is extensive practice, as common sense suggests. *Reading for Pleasure* is therefore an essential part of this book. Students must begin to develop the habit of extensive reading. This can only happen if they are given the opportunity to select their own materials. Part I includes lists of appropriate fiction and nonfiction books available at bookstores and libraries. Though not intended for ESL readers, they are written at the fifth-grade level or below and are accessible to beginning-level students. Graded readers, some especially for ESL/EFL students, are listed in the Teacher's Supplement at the back of the book. Also in the Supplement are guidelines for integrating *Reading for Pleasure* into the reading class and setting up a classroom library.

PART II. READING COMPREHENSION SKILLS

Reading comprehension involves specific thinking processes. The units in Part II are designed to provide focused instruction in the reading skills based on these processes. Greater awareness of the relation between cognitive process and reading skills will help students apply the skills when they are reading. Each unit is organized as a series of exercises, simple at first and then gradually more complex. Every class hour should include some exercises from Part II, preferably with students working in pairs.

PART III. READING FASTER

Lack of comprehension is often a result of reading too slowly. The reason is simple: the short-term memory can only retain information for a few seconds. Students who read very slowly, word by word, often forget the beginning of a sentence by the time they reach the end. Thus, instruction in reading faster will improve comprehension.

PART IV. THINKING SKILLS

These exercises are intended to be used by the students at their own pace. As they work through this section of the book, students will gain proficiency in following the logical sequence of ideas in English. The exercises will also improve their ability to guess the meaning of unfamiliar words from the context and to recognize synonyms, antonyms and referents.

Complete directions for using this book are found in the Teacher's Supplement on page 279.

Introduction

HOW TO BECOME A BETTER READER

Why is reading important when you are learning a new language? Here are some of the reasons:

- Reading helps you learn to think in the new language.
- Reading helps you build a better vocabulary.
- Reading makes you more comfortable with written English. You can write better English if you feel comfortable with the language.
- Reading may be the only way for you to use English if you live in a non-English-speaking country.
- Reading can help if you plan to study in an English-speaking country.

This book will help you learn to read better in English. You will work on four things in this book.

1. Reading For Pleasure

Read as much as you can. Read books, magazines, newspapers, stories. Read anything you like. The more you read, the better you will read.

Choose a book from the list in Part I. Or find another book that is interesting to you. Your teacher can help you find one at the bookstore or the library.

Read your book every day. Time your reading. Keep a record of your reading rate on the chart on page 275.

Be sure to talk about your book with your teacher, your classmates, and your friends.

2. Working On Your Reading Skills

When you read, you use many different skills. You need to work on them one at a time. Here are six important skills you will work on:

- **Previewing.** Before you start reading, find out something about what you will read. Then you can start thinking about the subject. You will be able to read faster and with more understanding.
- **Asking questions as you read.** This keeps your mind on what you read. Asking questions helps you pay attention. It also helps you to remember what you read.
- **Guessing what new words mean.** It takes too much time to look up every new word. And if you stop, you may forget what you are reading. Use the whole sentence or paragraph to guess words.

- **Finding the topic and the main idea.** The topic and the main idea let you know what is important. To find the topic and the main idea, ask two questions:

  What is this about?

  What does the writer want to say about this?
- **Understanding patterns in English.** A pattern is a way of putting ideas together. If you find the pattern, you can understand more. You will also remember more.
- **Using signal words.** Some words are like signposts on a highway. They tell you what direction the writer is going. And they help you to follow the writer's ideas. Signal words also help you guess what you will read about.

3. Learning To Read Faster

Reading faster is very important because of the way your brain works. When you read slowly, your brain does not get enough information. You understand better when you read faster.

4. Learning To Think In English

You also need to work on understanding English sentences. Learn how to get the meaning of sentences. Find out how ideas follow each other in English.

HOW TO READ FASTER

Why read faster?

Reading faster helps you to understand more. This may be surprising. But, in fact, your brain works better when you read faster. Try reading this:

> Many students are surprised when the teacher tells them to read faster. But they soon find out that they understand more that way.

If you read slowly, you read one word at a time. You must remember many separate words. Soon you can get tired or bored.

But if you read faster, you can read groups of words together. Then you can think about ideas and not just single words. That is why you understand better and remember more.

Read the three short passages in this chapter. Time yourself for each one. After each passage, there are comprehension questions. You will have two chances to answer them. The first time, do not look back at the passage. See how much you can remember. Then answer the questions again. This time you may look back if you need to.

Your teacher will tell you when to start the first passage.

Read Passage A.　　　　　　　Starting Time _____

A

Rosebud is a small town in New Jersey. It looks like many other towns in the United States. On Main Street there is a post office and a police station. The drugstore and the library are down the street. There is also a shopping center. It has a supermarket and a department store. Rosebud is a quiet place, not very rich or poor. But the town is growing. There are new houses every year. It is a popular place to live because it is near New York City. Many people live in Rosebud and work in New York.

Stop! Write the time you finished reading: _____
Turn the page and answer the questions. Do not look back.

Circle the best answer.

1. This passage is about
   a. New York City.
   b. towns.
   c. Rosebud, N.J.
   d. a quiet place.

2. Rosebud is
   a. like many other American towns.
   b. not like many other American towns.
   c. a noisy place.
   d. a large city.

3. Every year Rosebud
   a. has fewer houses.
   b. is like other American towns.
   c. has noisy streets.
   d. has more houses.

4. Many people want to live in Rosebud because
   a. it is growing.
   b. it is a quiet place.
   c. it is near New York City.
   d. it is not rich or poor.

Go back and answer the questions a second time. You may look back at the passage. Write the answers in the boxes at the right.

Check your answers in the Answer Key on page 259.

Number correct: _____ .

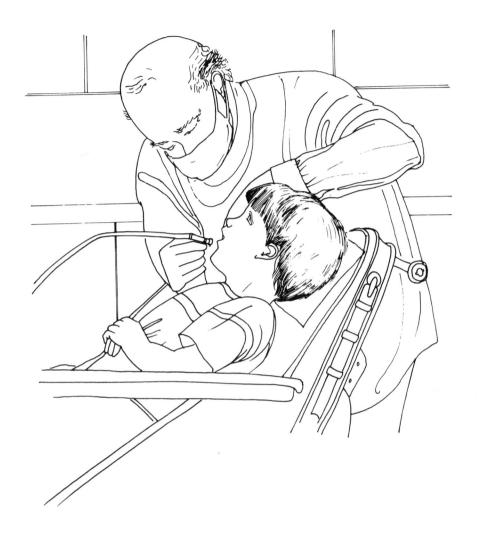

Now read Passage B.   Starting Time _____

B

In the middle of Rosebud, N.J., near the post office, is the office of Dr. Sam Diamond. Everybody in town knows Dr. Diamond. He's a very good dentist. He's also a popular person. He likes to tell funny stories to his patients. They forget about their teeth when they listen to him. On the weekends Dr. Diamond likes to go to basketball games. Sometimes he also watches sports on TV. But his favorite activity is fishing. Every Saturday in the summer, he gets up early in the morning. He and his friends spend the day fishing at Lake Massapog.

Stop! Write the time you finished reading: _____
Turn the page and answer the questions. Don't look back.

Circle the best answer.

1. This passage is about
   a. a dentist.
   b. what Dr. Diamond likes to do.
   c. Dr. Sam Diamond.
   d. fishing.

2. Dr. Diamond is popular because
   a. everyone in town knows him.
   b. he listens to his patients.
   c. he tells his patients funny stories.
   d. he likes to go fishing.

3. Fishing is Dr. Diamond's
   a. job.
   b. favorite activity.
   c. dream.
   d. patient.

4. Dr. Diamond likes to be
   a. with people.
   b. alone.
   c. quiet.
   d. a patient.

Go back and answer the questions a second time. You may look back at the passage. Write the answers in the boxes on the right.

Check your answers in the Answer Key on page 259.

Number correct:_____

Read Passage C.   Starting Time _____

C

Dr. Diamond is married to Susan Diamond. She is a scientist with a Ph.D in chemistry. She works in a laboratory in New York City. She and some other scientists are studying the air over the city. They want to find a way to make the air cleaner. Every morning, Susan takes the train to New York. She sees the dirty air. She also sees the dirt and garbage on the streets. She is glad she lives in New Jersey, and not in New York. The Diamonds' house has a back yard with trees and beautiful flowers. Susan's favorite activity is working in her garden.

Stop! Write the time you finished reading: _____
Turn the page and answer the questions. Don't look back.

Circle the best answer.

1. This passage is about
   a. Dr. Diamond.
   b. scientists.
   c. the city and the country.
   d. Susan Diamond.

2. Susan Diamond thinks New York
   a. is a nice city.
   b. is a clean city.
   c. is a busy city.
   d. has dirty air and streets.

3. Rosebud is
   a. dirtier than New York.
   b. cleaner than New York.
   c. crowded.
   d. not a good place to live.

4. Susan's favorite activity is
   a. taking the train to New York City.
   b. working in the laboratory.
   c. working in the garden.
   d. New York City.

Go back and answer the questions a second time. You may look back at the passage. Write the answers in the boxes on the right.

Check your answers in the Answer Key on page 259.

Number correct:_____

Now fill in this information. You can find your Reading Rate on the chart below.

Passage A

Finishing time _____ min. _____ sec.

— Starting time _____ min. _____ sec.

Reading time _____ min. _____ sec. = Reading Rate _____
(Words Per Minute)

Passage B

Finishing time _____ min. _____ sec.

— Starting time _____ min. _____ sec.

Reading time _____ min. _____ sec. = Reading Rate _____
(Words Per Minute)

Passage C

Finishing time _____ min. _____ sec.

— Starting time _____ min. _____ sec.

Reading time _____ min. _____ sec. = Reading Rate _____
(Words Per Minute)

Chart for Finding Reading Rate for Passages A, B, and C

Time (Minutes: Seconds)	Rate (Words Per Minute)	Time (Min: Sec)	Rate (Words Per Minute)
:10	625	2:10	46
:20	303	2:20	43
:30	200	2:30	40
:40	151	2:40	38
:50	125	2:50	36
1:00	100	3:00	33
1:10	86	3:10	32
1:20	75	3:20	30
1:30	66	3:30	29
1:40	60	3:40	27
1:50	54	3:50	26
2:00	50	4:00	25

You will find more passages for faster reading practice in Part III. (page 152)

- Read three to five passages every week.
- Do not skip any of the passages. Do them in order.
- Try to read a little faster than you usually read.

HOW TO THINK IN ENGLISH

If you want to read English well, you must think in English. These exercises will help you. In each exercise, the last sentence is not finished. Below the exercise, there are four endings. Circle the best ending. As you work,

    1. guess the meanings of new words.

    2. try to understand the way ideas work together in English.

Here is an example:

In the morning the language lab was full of people. Many students were waiting. Joe could not find a seat. He decided to come back later when the lab was

    a. closed.
    b. busy.
    c. more crowded.
    d. less crowded.

Why did Joe decide to come back later? Because the lab was full.
What is another word for "full"? Crowded.
Joe wants a seat. So he must come back when the lab is not full.
What is another way to say "not full"? Less crowded.
The correct answer is "d. less crowded."

Here are six more examples for practice. The underlined words may help you find the best ending.

1. Fruit is sweet, but candy is even
    a. nicer.
    b. worse.
    c. sweeter.
    d. less sweet.

2. Vitamins are very important for the health of young children. If children don't get enough vitamins in their food, they will
    a. get sick.
    b. be happy.
    c. get well.
    d. stay home.

3. Some people are vegetarians. They do not eat any kind of meat. One special kind of vegetarian will not even eat
    a. vegetables.
    b. carrots.
    c. fruits.
    d. eggs.

4. There are many kinds of coffee around the world. The Italians like their coffee strong and dark. Americans do not like very strong coffee. They prefer it
    a. stronger.
    b. weaker.
    c. for breakfast.
    d. black.

5. You can make tea from many kinds of <u>plants</u> and <u>fruits</u>. Some people drink tea from roses and other flowers. People also make tea from
    a. medicine.
    b. coffee.
    c. milk.
    d. apples.

6. Chocolate is popular around the world. In some countries, people use it in main dishes such as chicken. In other countries, it is used in <u>desserts such as</u> ice cream, pudding, or
    a. breakfast.
    b. soup.
    c. salad.
    d. cake.

Check your answers in the Answer Key on page 259.

If you made mistakes, look at the examples again. Try to find out why you did not understand.

In Part IV, (page 241), there are more excercises for *Thinking Skills*. Do one page of the exercises in every reading class.

PART I

Reading for Pleasure

Reading for pleasure is not the same as studying. You do not have to remember everything. There are no tests on books you read for pleasure. It is more interesting because you can choose your own book.

Reading for pleasure is very important for learning English. It will help you to

1. read faster in English.

2. find examples of good writing in English.

3. learn new words.

4. learn how English speakers use English.

5. learn about the culture of English speakers.

The first step is to find a good book. Look for a book that is interesting to you. Find one that seems easy.

Read some stories and novels. Read some books with facts and information. If you read both kinds of books you will learn English faster and better.

Read your book every day. Write down how many pages you read on the Progress Chart (page 271). Try to read your book very quickly.

After you finish your book, your teacher will talk to you about it. This is another way to learn more English. If you liked your book, tell a friend about it, too.

HOW TO FIND A GOOD BOOK

Go to the library. Find the Young Adults department. Many books for Young Adults are easy to read. They are in very easy English.

OR

Go to a large bookstore. Ask the clerk to help you find the books for Young Adults.

HOW TO CHOOSE A BOOK

1. Read the front and the back cover of the book. Do you think it is interesting?

2. How many pages are there in the book? It is better to begin with a short book.

3. Are there pictures in the book? Pictures can help you understand the book.

4. If you think you like a book, read one or two pages. Find out if you can understand it. You should read a book that is not too difficult for you.

5. The most important thing is this: **The book should be interesting to *you*.**

At the end of this chapter, there is a list of books. The books are easy to read. But they are not just for students of English as a second language. You can find these books at many libraries and bookstores.

HOW TO FIND YOUR READING RATE

Read this page from *Murder In the Language Lab.* You will learn how to find your reading rate.

Before you start, write the time: _____ min. _____ sec.

1 Against one wall there was a large machine. The sides
2 of the machine were made of black metal. The bottom half
3 of it looked like a large typewriter. The top part of the
4 machine was like a television set.
5   The man walked over to the tree. He looked up at the
6 hole in the roof.
7   The man called out, "Sally! Come down, Sally!"
8   After a short time, a face appeared in the opening. The
9 face had small, bright eyes. The mouth was very wide, and
10 the nose was flat. There were very big ears. The face was
11 covered with short brown hair. It was the face of a
12 chimpanzee.
13   The animal's lips opened, showing yellow teeth. It looked
14 like a smile. The chimpanzee made a happy sound.
15   "Come down here, Sally," the man said again.
16   Sally climbed down the tree very quickly. With her long
17 arms, it was easy for her to climb up or down very fast.
18 Sally looked at the man and smiled again.
19   "Do you want a banana, Sally?" the man asked.
20   Sally made another happy sound. She ran across the
21 room to the machine. She stood in front of the machine.
22 It looked like she was thinking very hard. She was study-
23 ing the part that was like a typewriter. There were many
24 more keys than are usually found on a typewriter. Also,
25 instead of letters there were little pictures or symbols on
26 the keys. There were circles and squares in different colors,
27 and many other symbols as well.
28   Sally looked at the keys with their symbols. She put out
29 her finger and pressed several keys. When she pressed
30 a key, that symbol appeared on the television part of the
31 machine. At the same time, words in English appeared
32 above the symbols. Sally finished pressing the keys. She
33 looked at the symbols on the television. The words above
34 the symbols said,

Write the time you finished reading: _____ min. _____ sec.
Turn the page and read the directions carefully.

To find your reading rate:

1. Count the number of words in three lines. There are __30__ words in three lines on this page.

2. Divide the number of words by three to find the average.

$$\frac{30}{3} = \underline{10} \text{ words on one line.}$$

3. Count the lines on the page. On this page, there are __34__ lines.

4. (Number of lines) × (words on one line) = words on a page.

__34__ × __10__ = __340__

YOU KNOW THAT THERE ARE ABOUT __340__ WORDS ON EACH PAGE OF THIS BOOK. NOW YOU CAN FIND OUT HOW MANY WORDS YOU READ IN ONE MINUTE.

5. How many minutes did you take to read the page? _____ minutes

6. $\dfrac{340 \text{ words on a page}}{\text{_____ minutes}}$ = _____ Words Per Minute

For example, if you read the page in 5 minutes,

$\dfrac{340 \text{ words on a page}}{5 \text{ minutes}}$ = 68 Words Per Minute

7. You can use your own book to learn to read faster. Just remember to time yourself when you read.

On the next page, you will learn to find your reading rate in your own book.

FIND YOUR READING RATE IN YOUR OWN BOOK

Book Title _____

1. Find a full page.

   Count the number of words in three lines. _____

2. Divide that number by three to get the average. _____

3. Count the lines on one page. _____

4.

   _____ × _____ = _____
   (number of lines)   (words in one line)   (words on a page)

   NOW YOU KNOW HOW MANY WORDS THERE ARE ON ONE PAGE IN YOUR BOOK. You can find your reading rate (Words Per Minute).

5. Read your book. Write starting time here.

   _____ Min _____ Sec
                  Write finishing time here.

   _____ Min _____ Sec

6. How many minutes did you read? _____ Min _____ Sec

7. How many pages did you read? _____

8. How many words did you read?

   _____ × _____ = words
   (number of pages)   (number of words on a page)

9. To find your reading rate, divide the number of words by the number of minutes.

   _____ words
   _____ = _____ Words Per Minute
   _____ minutes

10. Turn to page 275 and mark the graph. Write today's date on the bottom of the graph.

BOOK LIST

These books are easy to read. Many students in the United States enjoy these books. You can find them in many book stores and libraries.

Ban   Bantam Books
Col   Collier Publishing Co.
Dell   Dell Publishing Co.
NAL   New American Library
PB   Pocket Books

A Lantern in Her Hand   Bess Streeter Aldrich
The story of Abby MacKenzie Deal, who lived in the American West during the Civil War. NAL

Sometimes I Think I Hear My Name   Avi
The story of a 13-year-old boy who tries to understand his parents. Humorous. NAL

If Beale Street Could Talk   James Baldwin
The story of a young black American family. A man is in jail but he did not do anything wrong. Sad love story. NAL

New Burlington: The Life and Death of an American Village   John Baskin
How a village is moved because of a new lake. The people from the village tell their own stories. NAL

Paper Moon   Joe David Brown
This book tells the story of an 11-year-old girl in the American South during the 1930 depression years. NAL

The Incredible Journey   Sheila Burnford
Two dogs and a cat travel many miles to return to their home. Ban

The White Mountains   John Christopher
One hundred years from now Switzerland is the only free country. This is science fiction and a thriller. Col

Me Too   Vera and Bill Cleaver
A 12-year-old girl tries to help her twin sister. NAL

Where the Lilies Bloom   Vera and Bill Cleaver
Both of her parents die, and a young girl keeps her brothers and sisters together. Set in the Smoky Mountains in the American South. NAL

The Chocolate War   Robert Cormier
A student fights a secret society of other students and becomes a hero in the school. Dell

I Know What You Did Last Summer   Lois Duncan
A horror story about a secret. PB

Ransom   Lois Duncan
Five students take a strange and scary bus ride. PB

**The Autobiography of
Miss Jane Pittman**   Ernest J. Gaines

    The story of an American black woman born during the days of
    slavery. How she saw black people get freedom. Ban

The Miracle Worker (a play)   William Gibson

    The story of Annie Sullivan and how she helped Helen Keller. Ban

Cheaper by the Dozen   Frank B. Gilbreth and
                                       Ernestine Gilbreth Carey

    Life in a very large family, with twelve children and two very
    special parents. Ban

Morning is a Long Time Coming   Bette Greene

    A young American finds adventure and love in Paris after World
    War II. Ban

Summer of My German Soldier   Bette Green

    A friendship between a young Jewish girl and a German prisoner
    in America. Ban

The Friends   Rosa Guy

    A family moves to the United States from the West Indies. This
    story tells about the love and friendship they find. Ban

Ruby   Rosa Guy

    The problems of an 18-year-old girl as she tries to become a
    woman. Ban

Jazz Country   Nat Hentoff

    Life in New York City is tough for a young musician. Dell

This School is Driving Me Crazy   Nat Hentoff

    More about life in New York City. Dell

Siddhartha   Hermann Hesse

    A man tries to find truth and wisdom. Ban

The Son of Someone Famous   M.E. Kerr

    At 16, Adam wanted people to like him for himself, not because
    his father is famous. NAL

Night Shift   Stephen King

    Twenty horror stories to make you afraid of the dark. A best-seller!
    NAL

A Separate Peace   John Knowles

    What happens to two American school friends at the beginning
    of World War II. Ban

I Want to Keep My Baby   Joanna Lee

    A 15-year-old girl is going to have a baby. NAL

Very Far Away from Anywhere Else   Ursula K. LeGuin

    A young man wants to become a scientist, but his parents want
    him to be like everyone else. Ban

A Summer to Die   Lois Lowry

 The story of a young girl whose sister dies of leukemia. Ban

The Dog Who Wouldn't Be   Farley Mowat

 A funny story about an unusual dog. Ban

The Boat Who Wouldn't Float   Farley Mowat

 Another funny story by a very amusing writer. Ban

Edgar Allen   John Neufeld

 A white American family adopts a black child. NAL

For All the Wrong Reasons   John Neufeld

 What happens when teen-agers get married. Can it work? NAL

Island of the Blue Dolphins   Scott O'Dell

 An Indian girl lives alone for years on an island in the Pacific Ocean. Dell

The Upstairs Room   Johanna Reiss

 How two Jewish sisters lived with a Christian family during World War II in Holland. Ban

A Light in the Forest   Conrad Richter

 A white boy is raised by Indians in Pennsylvania. This book tells facts about early life in the United States. Ban

Gods, Heroes, and Men of Ancient Greece   W.H.D. Rouse

 Greek stories in easy English. Ban

Shane   Jack Schaefer

 A stranger helps a family in the American West. He teaches a young boy courage and self-respect. Ban

My Name is Davy — I'm an Alcoholic   Anne Snyder

 A lonely high school student drinks too much. NAL

PART II

Reading Comprehension Skills

In each unit, you will work on a different reading skill. The first exercises in each unit are easy. But then they become more difficult. You should do the exercises in order. Do not skip any of the exercises.

Be sure to read the directions before you begin to work. In some of the exercises, you must work with another student. Be sure to do that. You will improve your English that way.

The Answer Key for all units begins on page 259.

Previewing and Predicting

PREVIEWING

Before you start on a trip, you usually look at a map. It helps you plan your way. Then you know what to expect as you travel. This is a good idea in reading, too. Look before you read. Then it is much easier to understand.

That is what you do when you **PREVIEW**.

Read this passage.

> The first time you try it, ask someone to help you. You may fall if no one holds you up. It is a good idea to start on the sidewalk. The street may be dangerous. After you start, do not stop. Try to go faster. That will help you to stay up. Remember, even little children can do this. And once you learn how, you will never forget!

What is this passage about? _____

If you cannot tell, look at the picture on the next page.

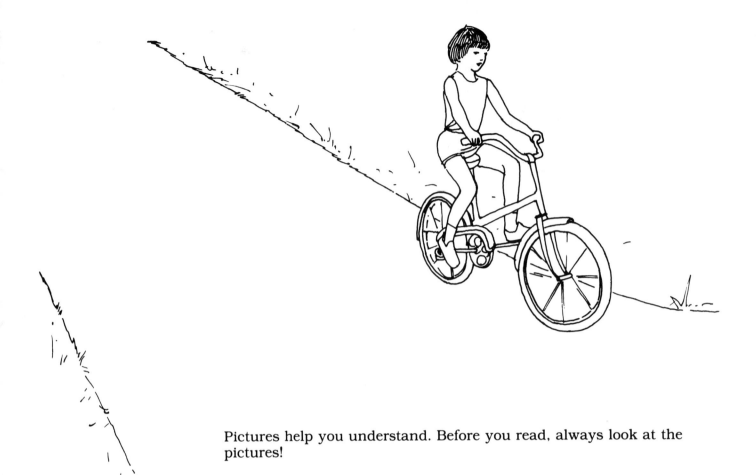

Pictures help you understand. Before you read, always look at the pictures!

How to preview a short passage:
1. Read the title.
2. Look at the pictures (if there are any).
3. Read the first few sentences in the first paragraph.
4. Read the first line of the other paragraphs.
5. Read the last sentence of the last paragraph.
6. Watch for names, dates, and numbers.

Read the passage on the next page. It will help you learn how to preview.

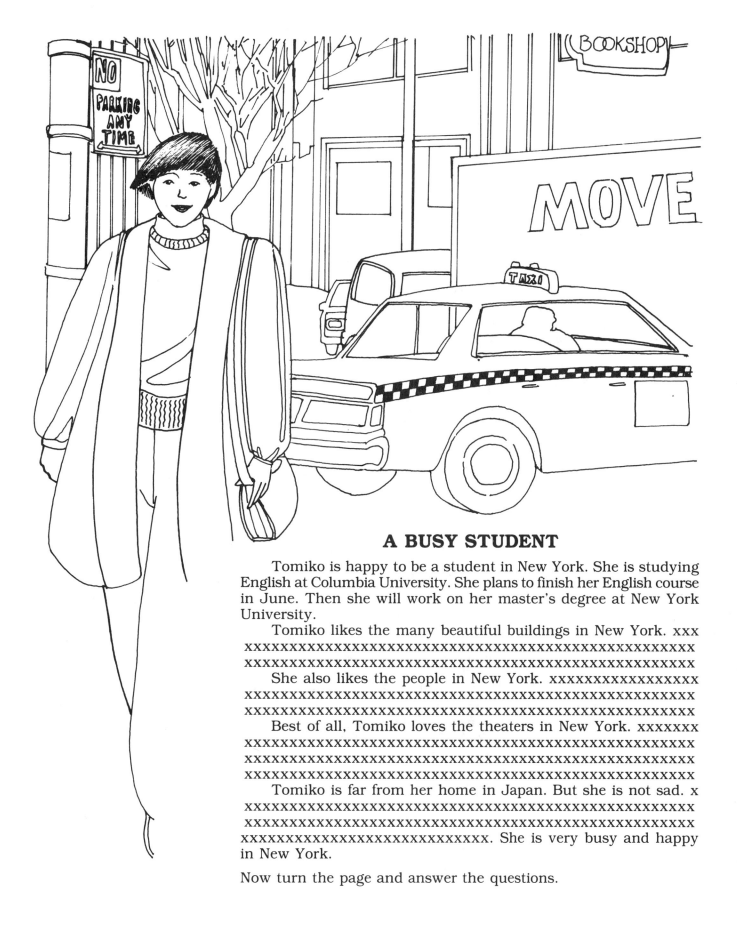

A BUSY STUDENT

Tomiko is happy to be a student in New York. She is studying English at Columbia University. She plans to finish her English course in June. Then she will work on her master's degree at New York University.

Tomiko likes the many beautiful buildings in New York. xxx
xxxxxxxxxxxxxxxxxxxxxxxxxxxxxxxxxxxxxxxxxxxxxxxxxxxxxxxx
xxxxxxxxxxxxxxxxxxxxxxxxxxxxxxxxxxxxxxxxxxxxxxxxxxxxxxxx

She also likes the people in New York. xxxxxxxxxxxxxxxxx
xxxxxxxxxxxxxxxxxxxxxxxxxxxxxxxxxxxxxxxxxxxxxxxxxxxxxxxx
xxxxxxxxxxxxxxxxxxxxxxxxxxxxxxxxxxxxxxxxxxxxxxxxxxxxxxxx

Best of all, Tomiko loves the theaters in New York. xxxxxxx
xxxxxxxxxxxxxxxxxxxxxxxxxxxxxxxxxxxxxxxxxxxxxxxxxxxxxxxx
xxxxxxxxxxxxxxxxxxxxxxxxxxxxxxxxxxxxxxxxxxxxxxxxxxxxxxxx
xxxxxxxxxxxxxxxxxxxxxxxxxxxxxxxxxxxxxxxxxxxxxxxxxxxxxxxx

Tomiko is far from her home in Japan. But she is not sad. x
xxxxxxxxxxxxxxxxxxxxxxxxxxxxxxxxxxxxxxxxxxxxxxxxxxxxxxxx
xxxxxxxxxxxxxxxxxxxxxxxxxxxxxxxxxxxxxxxxxxxxxxxxxxxxxxxx
xxxxxxxxxxxxxxxxxxxxxxxxxxxxxxxxx. She is very busy and happy in New York.

Now turn the page and answer the questions.

Circle the best answer. Don't look back at the passage.

1. This passage is about
   a. an American student in New York.
   b. a Japanese student in New York.
   c. a Japanese student in Japan.
   d. a Japanese man studying in New York.

2. Tomiko is
   a. unhappy.
   b. happy.
   c. lonely.
   d. not busy.

3. She goes to plays in
   a. large theaters.
   b. small theaters.
   c. New York.
   d. all of the above.

4. Tomiko has
   a. few interests.
   b. few friends.
   c. many interests.
   d. nothing to do.

Now read the whole passage.

Passage A   **A BUSY STUDENT**

Tomiko is happy to be a student in New York. She is studying English at Columbia University. She plans to finish her English course in June. Then she will work on her master's degree at New York University.

Tomiko likes the many beautiful buildings in New York. In fact, she plans to become an architect. Then she can build great buildings, too.

Tomiko also likes the people in New York City. There are many different kinds of people. They speak many languages. Tomiko has made new friends from other countries.

Best of all, Tomiko loves the theaters in New York. She goes to plays almost every week. Sometimes the plays are in theaters on Broadway. Sometimes the plays are in small theaters in other parts of the city.

Tomiko is far from her home in Japan. But she is not sad. She goes to classes every day. She visits her friends. She goes to see new places. And she attends many plays. She is very busy and happy in New York.

Check your answers in the Answer Key on page 259.

How many did you answer correctly? _____

You can learn a lot about a passage if you read just a few important sentences. This is the reason for **Previewing**.

Preview this passage. Read only the underlined sentences.
You will have 30 seconds to preview.

Passage B **LANGUAGE LEARNING IN
THE UNITED STATES**

Most people in the United States speak only one language:
English. They do not learn to speak a second language. High
schools teach languages. But very few students learn to speak
well. Why don't Americans speak other languages?

First, most Americans never travel to other countries. The
United States is a very large country. Americans can travel a long
distance and not leave the United States. They do not need to learn
a second language.

Second, one of the countries next to the United States is
Canada. Most people in Canada speak English. Some Americans
live near Canada. They travel there often. But they do not have to
learn a new language.

Third, many people in other parts of the world speak
English. If Americans travel to other countries, they can speak
English there, too.

Some Americans think that it is a mistake to speak only
English. They believe it is very important to learn a second
language. Maybe someday other Americans will agree. Then
more people will speak a second language in the United States.

Now turn the page and answer the questions.

Circle the best answer. Don't look back at the passage!

1. Most Americans never learn to speak
   a. English.
   b. a second language.
   c. to people in other countries.
   d. fluently.

2. Most Americans speak only English because
   a. they can't learn another language.
   b. they never travel to other countries.
   c. other languages are not important.
   d. they don't have language classes in school.

3. In other parts of the world,
   a. everyone speaks English.
   b. no one speaks English.
   c. many people speak English.
   d. everyone speaks a second language.

4. Some Americans think it is a mistake to
   a. learn other languages.
   b. speak only English.
   c. travel to other countries.
   d. go to school.

Check your answers in the Answer Key on page 259.

Number correct: _____

Here is one more passage to preview. Remember to follow these steps:

1. Read the title.
2. Look at the pictures if there are any.
3. Read the first few sentences of the first paragraph.
4. Read the first line of all the paragraphs.
5. Read the last sentence in the last paragraph.
6. Watch for names, dates, and numbers.

You will have 30 seconds to preview this passage.

Passage C

BODIES ON ICE

In very cold parts of the world, scientists study the past. They find animals frozen in the ice. The animals look alive, but they are not. They were frozen many years ago.

Russian scientists found a large animal called a mastodon in the ice. It looked like an elephant. But it was larger, and it had lots of hair. In fact, the elephant is the mastodon's younger cousin.

In 1984, American scientists were working near the North Pole. They found the body of a man frozen in the ice. This man went to the North Pole in 1846. He died, and his friends buried him in the ice. Today, his body looks the same. It did not change at all in the ice.

These facts interest doctors. They have some patients who are very sick. No one can help these patients. But some day there may be a new medicine for them. These doctors want to save people for the future. Maybe patients can be frozen until there is medicine to help them.

Answer the questions on the next page. Don't look back!

Circle the best answer. Don't look back!

1. Scientists are studying the past
   a. in the ice.
   b. in the laboratory.
   c. in 1848.
   d. in Russia.

2. Russian scientists found
   a. a man in the ice.
   b. a large animal in the ice.
   c. it was too cold.
   d. nothing interesting.

3. American scientists worked
   a. in Russia.
   b. in the laboratory.
   c. near the North Pole.
   d. with a mastodon.

4. Doctors think frozen bodies
   a. are too cold.
   b. are near the North Pole.
   c. are interesting.
   d. are mastodons.

Check your answers in the Answer Key on page 259.

Number correct _____

REMEMBER: always preview before you read!

PREDICTING

To *predict* means to tell what will happen. You will be a better reader if you *predict*. As you read, guess what will happen. You can use words and pictures to help you *predict*. Work with another student. The Answer Key is on page 259.

Exercise 1   USING PICTURES TO PREDICT

Find the right story for each picture.

Pictures

Names of stories

1. _____

a. Women in Science

2. _____

b. How Americans Shop for Food

3. _____

c. How Beavers Build Their Homes

4. _____

d. When Your Child Goes to the Dentist

5. _____

e. The Violin in the Symphony Orchestra

Exercise 2   GUESS WHAT WILL HAPPEN NEXT

Look at each picture. Predict what will happen next. Find the best sentence for each picture. Work with another student.

Pictures   **What will happen next?**

1. _____

a. Henry will play with his friends all day.
   OR
b. Henry will not go to school today.

2. _____

a. This family will buy tickets.
   OR
b. This family will meet a friend at the airport.

3. _____

a. They will stop and rest.
   OR
b. They will go faster.

4. _____

a. Mary will give the cat a nice dinner.
   OR
b. Mary will put the cat outdoors.

Exercise 3

Will you find these ideas in the story? Check *Yes* or *No*.

Boston: A Good Place to Live

	Yes	No
1. There are many poor people in Boston.		
2. The spring flowers are beautiful in Boston.		
3. There are many universities in Boston.		
4. Jobs are hard to find in the Boston area.		
5. Winters in Boston are cold and snowy.		
6. Boston City Hall is very beautiful.		
7. There are many famous old buildings in downtown Boston.		
8. People are not very friendly in Boston.		
9. The Charles River flows by the city. People like to walk along the river in the parks.		
10. Apartments are very expensive and hard to find.		

Exercise 4

Will you find these ideas in the story? Check *Yes* or *No*.

Modern Dentists: How They Can Help You

	Yes	No
1. Dentists hurt your teeth.		
2. Dentists have many new machines.		
3. Some dentists play the radio for their patients.		
4. Some dentists will pull out all your teeth.		
5. A nurse cleans your teeth at the dentist's office.		
6. The dentist's office is very comfortable.		
7. Dentists want everyone to have healthy teeth.		
8. A visit to the dentist is too expensive.		
9. The dentist may x-ray your teeth.		
10. Modern dentists must study for many years.		

Exercise 5   PREDICTING THE NEXT IDEA

EXAMPLE

Yesterday, there was a big snowstorm in Boston.

Which idea comes next?

a. It was a warm, sunny day.
b. It was very cold, but the snow on the trees looked beautiful.
c. Only one inch of snow fell.

The correct answer is b.
a. is not correct. It is not warm and sunny in a snowstorm.
c. is not correct. In a big snowstorm, many inches of snow fall.

Read the sentence. Then tell which idea comes next. Work with another student.

1. There were many good shows on TV last night. The Smith family stayed home.
   a. They turned off the TV and went to bed early.
   b. The only interesting show was about traveling by bicycle.
   c. They saw a play, a music show, and the news.

2. John and Alice Babson are not happy with the school in their town.
   a. Their children love to go to school.
   b. The classes are very crowded.
   c. It is a beautiful building.

3. The roads were covered with ice and were very dangerous today.
   a. Sam drove home very quickly.
   b. Sam took a long time to drive home.
   c. Sam enjoyed driving home.

4. Boston is a nice place to live in, but New York City is more fun.
   a. New York is a very dangerous city.
   b. There are many interesting things to do in New York.
   c. There are no good restaurants in New York.

5. Fly Happy Time Airlines! Take an exciting trip to Holiday Island.
   a. This trip is very expensive.
   b. Holiday Island has warm, sunny weather.
   c. Happy Time Airlines is never on time.

6. Alex had trouble falling asleep last night. He was awake until 3 a.m.
   a. This morning, he feels rested and ready to work.
   b. This morning, he is very hungry.
   c. This morning, he feels very tired.

7. Dr. Hammond was busy with his patients all day. He did not have time for lunch.
   a. He may not be hungry at dinner time.
   b. He had a very easy day.
   c. He will be very hungry at dinner time.

8. Judy and Alan moved to a new apartment near the university.
   a. Now they need a car to drive to class.
   b. Now they can walk to class every day.
   c. Now they will not be near the university library.

9. Max works all day in a shoe store. At night, he takes business classes at the university.
   a. Max wants to have his own business some day.
   b. Max has lots of free time.
   c. Max is not very busy.

10. "Eat at Joe's Diner! We serve breakfast from 6 to 10!"
    a. No one likes the breakfasts at Joe's!
    b. And the breakfast costs only $1.00!
    c. The food is cold and the service is slow!

Scanning

Look at the following shopping list to find out if you remembered to order bread:

Shopping List

milk
butter
ice cream
bread
bananas
broccoli
rice
potatoes
oranges

How many words did you read? *Bread* was the only word you needed to read. The other words were not important. This kind of reading is called *scanning.*

You usually scan: a telephone book
an index in a textbook
a list of movies in the newspaper
the ads in a newspaper
the pages of a dictionary

You usually *do not* scan: a mystery story
a textbook for an important course
important papers from a lawyer
a map for getting to a party
a question on a test

EXAMPLE

Scan the next page for the answers to these questions. Work as quickly as you can.

1. How many chapters are there in the book? _____

2. Which is the chapter on the computer in the classroom? _____

3. On what page can you read about games? _____

4. Which part of Chapter 3 is about having fun with computers? _____

5. Does this book have an index? On what page? _____

Contents

You do not have to read every word to answer the questions. You also do not have to understand every word. Scanning is helpful in finding information.

The next few pages will give you some practice in scanning. Do not try to read every word. Read *only* to find the answers to the questions. Try to work very fast. Your teacher will time you. The Answer Key is on page 259.

Exercise 1   **SCANNING AN INDEX**

Look for the answers to these questions in the index on the next page. Try to find the page numbers very quickly. Ask your teacher or another student to time you. Write down exactly how many seconds it takes to complete the page. (Hint: The index is in alphabetical order.)

Starting time _____

On what page(s) can you read about:

		Page
1.	*TOEFL*	_____
2.	taste	_____
3.	vocabulary	_____
4.	writing	_____
5.	sound	_____
6.	stereotype	_____
7.	*Time* Magazine	_____
8.	University of Illinois	_____
9.	Andrew Wright	_____
10.	Garry Trudeau	_____

Finishing time _____

Scanning time _____

Exercise 2   GOING TO THE MOVIES

Look for the answers to these questions on the next page. Try to find the answers as quickly as possible. Ask your teacher or another student to time you. Write down exactly how many seconds it takes you to complete the page. (Hint: The movie theaters are in alphabetical order.)

Starting time _____

1. What movies are playing at the Pi Alley movie house?

   _____

2. What is the address of the Beacon Hill Cinema?

   _____

3. What is the phone number of the Cheri Cinema?

   _____

4. How many movies are showing at the Allston Cinema?

   _____

5. What can I see at 9 p.m. today at the Village Cinemas?

   _____

6. Is there a show Sunday morning at the Copley Place?

   _____

7. Which theater is showing the most movies?

   _____

8. What is the name of the cinema on Stuart Street?

   _____

9. What movie is playing at the cinema in West Roxbury on Sunday? _____

10. Where can I go to see "Police Academy 2"?

    _____

11. When can I see "Secret Admirer"?

    _____

12. Can I see "Mask" in the morning?

    _____

                                    Finishing time _____
                                    Scanning time _____

BOSTON

Allston Cinemas, 214 Harvard Ave. 277-2140.
Lost in America (R), today at 1:15, 2:55, 4:30, 6:15, 8, 9:40 p.m.
Police Academy 2 (PG-13), 1:30, 3, 4:40, 6:15, 7:45, 9:20 p.m.

Beacon Hill, 1 Beacon St. 723-8110.
Code of Silence (R), due Fri. at 1, 3:10, 5:20, 7:30, 9:45 p.m.
Nine Deaths of Ninja (R), due Fri. at 1:30, 3:30, 5:30, 7:40, 10 p.m.
Mask (PG-13), today at 1, 3:15, 5:30, 7:45, 10 p.m.
Police Academy 2 (PG-13), today at 1:30, 3:30, 5:30, 7:30, 9:30 p.m.
Beverly Hills Cop (R), at 1:15, 3:15, 5.15, 7:30, 9:40 p.m.

Charles 1-3, 185 Cambridge St. 227-1330
Perfect (R), at 1, 3:15, 5:30, 7:50, 10:10.
Fletch (R), at 1, 3:30, 5:45, 8, 10:10.
Lost in America (R), at 1:15, 3:15, 5:30, 8, 10 p.m. (Exception: no show tonight at 8.)

Cheri, 50 Dalton St. 536-2870
Prizzi's Honor (R), due Fri. at 12:45, 3, 5:15, 7:45, 10 p.m.
The Goonies (PG), at 1, 3:15, 5:30, 7:45, 10 p.m.
View to Kill (PG), at 1:30, 4:30, 7:30, 10.
Witness (R), today at 1, 3:15, 5:30, 10 p.m.

Cinema 57, 200 Stuart St. 482-1222.
Brewster's Millions (PG), at 1, 3:15, 5:30, 8, 10:20 p.m.
Rambo (R), at 12:45, 3, 5:15, 7:45, 10 p.m.

Copley Place, 100 Huntington Ave. 266-1300. Following films have no morning showings on Sunday:
Witness (R), due Fri. at 10 a.m., noon, 2:40, 5, 7:30, 10 p.m.
Secret Places (PG), today at 10 a.m., 12:15, 2:30, 5, 7:30, 9:50 p.m.
Where's Picone?, at 10:30 a.m., 12:45, 3, 5:15, 7:50, 10:10 p.m.
Lily in Love (PG-13), at 10 a.m., noon, 2, 4, 6, 8:10, 10:10 p.m.
Allonsanfan, at 10:30 a.m., 12:45, 3, 5:30, 7:50, 10:10 p.m.
Streetwise, at 10:30 a.m., 12:45, 3, 5:15, 7:30, 9:45 p.m.
Gods Must Be Crazy (PG), today at 10:30 a.m., 12:50, 3:15, 5:30, 7:45, 10 p.m.
Camila, at 10:30 a.m., 12:40, 3, 5:15, 7:45, 10 p.m.
Purple Rose of Cairo (PG), at 10:10 a.m., 12:10, 2:10, 4:10, 6:10, 8:10, 10:10 p.m.
Amadeus (PG), at 10:15 a.m., 1:15, 4:15, 7:20, 10:10 p.m.

Nickelodeon Cinemas, 606 Commonwealth Ave. 424-1500.
Wild Duck (PG), today at 1, 2:45, 4:30, 6:15, 8:10, 10 p.m.
My First Wife, today at 1:20, 3:20, 5:20, 7:50, 9:55 p.m.
Pumping Iron II, today at 1:15, 3:25, 5:40, 7:50, 10 p.m.
Desperately Seeking Susan (PG-13), today at 1:30, 3:30, 5:45, 8, 10:10 p.m.
Private Function (R), today at 1:10, 3:15, 5:30, 7:45, 9:45 p.m.

Pi Alley, 237 Washington St. 227-6676.
D.A.R.Y.L. (PG), due Fri. at 1, 3:15, 5:30, 7:40, 9.45 p.m.
Secret Admirer (R) due Fri. at 1:30, 3:30, 5:30, 7:30, 9:30 p.m.
Code of Silence (R), today at 1, 3:20, 5:30, 7:50, 10:15 p.m.
Nine Deaths of Ninja (R), today at 1:30, 3:30, 5:30, 7:40, 10 p.m.

Village Cinemas, 547 VFW Pkwy, West Roxbury. 325-0303.
Police Academy 2 (PG-13), today at 7:15, 9 p.m.
Falcon and Snowman (R), Fri.-Sat. at 7, 9:15 p.m.; Sun-Thurs. at 7:30 p.m.

Exercise 3 LOOKING FOR AN APARTMENT

Look for the answers to these questions on the next page. Try to find the answers as quickly as possible. Ask your teacher or another student to time you. (Hint: The cities are in alphabetical order.)

Starting time _____

1. Are there any apartments for rent in Maynard? _____
2. How much is the cheapest apartment in Brockton? _____
3. Whom do I call about an apartment in Canton? _____
4. I want to live in Brighton near public transportation. Is there anything for me? _____
5. Can I have a cat at the Lakeside Village apartment in Easton?
   _____ _____
6. Is there parking near the apartment in Revere? _____
7. I want a three bedroom apartment. (3 bdrm) Where can I find one? (At least 3 towns) _____
   _____
8. What is the phone number for the Crane Realty? _____
9. Where is the apartment with the highest rent? _____
10. Where is the apartment with the lowest rent? _____
11. What is the rent for a studio (stu) in Somerville? _____
12. What is the rent for a studio near the beach in Lynn? _____

Finishing time _____
Scanning time _____

BRIGHTON, Spac. 2 bdrm., full kit., din. area, $460; Charming, clean 1 bdrm., secure bldg. $435; Spec. lux. studio, full kit., a.c., w&d $400; Lge. clean & sunny 3 bdrm., mod. k&b, $500, 876-5522

BRIGHTON, Houses/Bldgs. 1 rm. house, yd. $350+; sunny 1 bd., big kit., yd., $360+; charm. 4 rms., prkg., yd., $500+; 3 bd., prkg., $650+. 5 rm. condo, in gd. cond. prkg., $850. LORD REALTY 652-1122

BRIGHTON, Sunny studio, fresh paint, laund. $350; Charm. 1½ bed in house, $550 all utils; 2 bed in resid. area, mod. k&b, porch, laund., pkg. $625; DOWNTOWN R.E. 521-0021

BRIGHTON, Allston, BU. Stu. $325; 1 bd. $395, 2 bd. $500, 3 bd. $660, 4&5 bd + more, now & 9/1. 341-8003.

BRIGHTON, Brookline, unique find, mod. 2 BR, ww, a/c, d&d, avail. 5/1, $625, R.E., (617) 641-2019 or (603) 487-5558.

BRIGHTON, Near transportation. Extra lge. studio. Clean bldg. Good owner, $290 htd. Call 741-8800.

BRIGHTON, Off Comm. Lg. newly painted, 1 bed, clean secure bldg. $380 heated. Call 375-2323.

BRIGHTON, Brand new, 1 bed in house, d&d, yd. $450. R.E. 452-0667

BRIGHTON, Cozy 1 bedrm., with mod. K&B, lndry. & prkg., $365. 962-5431.

BRIGHTON, studios, 1 brs., 2 brs., 3 brs. Mod. K&B. Prices vary. R.E. 331-5876.

BRIGHTON, 3 BR in house, mod. kit, tile bath, lg BR's $795, unht. R.E. 286-3152.

BRIGHTON Gorgeous 2 BR in hse, lg LR, kit, pkg, now! $550 unht. R.E. 276-7432.

BROCKTON, Oak Park. Lg. mod. apts. w/D&D, heat, carpeting, balc., walk-in closet, pool, sauna, clubhouse, tennis court. Convenient to public transpt. & shop'g. 1 BR $475, 2 BR's, $535-$580. Equal Hous. Oppty. See our display ad Sun. ESSEX REALTY 598-8440.

BROCKTON, Oak Green Apts. on Stoughton line. Mod. apts. w/D&D, carpeting, prkg. & pool. Studio $410, 1 BR, $470, 2 BR, $560. Rent includes heat, h.w. & cooking gas. Equal Housing Oppty. See our display ad Sun. ESSEX REALTY 598-8440.

BROCKTON, lux. 1-2 BR, d&d, a/c, crptd., pool, tennis, incl. free heat, no pets. $379-$495. 876-2091.

BROOKLINE, Boston line, clean lge. studio, $380; 1 bdrm., hi ceils., h/w flrs., leaded glass winds., mod. K&B, $500, penthouse, 2 bdrms., w.w. mod. k&b, balc., frpl. $685. Others.
PARK CIRCLE R.E.
322-5550

BROOKLINE, Cool. Crnr., sunny 1 BR, frpl. $660. Village 1 BR, w/den, $725. CORNER REALTY 662-1120

BROOKLINE, 6 rm. 3 BR re-mod. k&b, redec. por. pkg. $795 unh. R.E. 776-1461

BROOKLINE (Vill.), 2 bd. in 3 fam., remod. $625/unhtd. R.E. 542-3200.

BURLINGTON, Ideal locale, neighboring mall and major routes, spac. 1 & 2 bdrm. apts., tennis, pool & more. Model open Mon.-Fri. 9-5, Sat. & Sun. 10-4. SIR WINDSOR APTS. 756-6422.

CAMBRIDGE, Som. line - 2 bdrm. lux. apt. in new brick bldg. ww crptg., c.t. bath, all elec. kit., balc. & assigned prkg. $625. incl. ht. Call Bonnie 355-4400 or 626-8181.

CAMBRIDGE, Shepard St., spac. 4 rms.-1 BR, lg. closets, porch. Ht. h/w, prkg, no fee. $684 5/1 341-8003.

CANTON, 2 br., eat-in kit., sunny, ww roofdk, priv. yd nr. shop. & trans., $575. May 1, call Susan 792-5670 or Mrs. Young 265-4147.

CHARLESTOWN, Bunker Hill St. nr. MDC pool, 1 BD htd., $425. 256-8622, aft. 5

CHARLESTOWN, Conterno. 1 BR condo, refin. flrs $450, R.E. 755-9219.

CHELMSFORD, Lowell line, nr. Rtes 3 & 128. Lrg. from $470 incl. utils, ac, ww, d&d, 745-5420.

CHELSEA, Lux. 1 & 2 BR apts.; nr. T, d&d, rf. deck, htd. $390-$450. 465-2881.

CONCORD Grn, 3 BR town-hse, pool, tennis, watervu $1050 htd. 532-0591, 7 pm.

DANVERS, Mod. apts., nr. beach & bay w/crpt., eat-in kit., prkg, heated. Studio, $355; 2 BR, $465. No fee. Equal Hous. Oppty. See our display ad Sun. ESSEX REALTY! 598-8440.

DORCHESTER, At Ashmont, nr. Carney. Studios $310-$350. 1 BR, $385-$400. 2 BR, $475-$500, htd. 983-4257.

DORCHESTER, 4 bdrm. w/heat in So. Boston style nghbd. Section 8 ok. $550/mo. Also mod. 1 BR $340 + utils. 983-5248.

DORCHESTER, So. Boston. New remod. 1 & 2 bdrm. apts. $360-$375. 1st, last & fee. 983-7330.

EASTON. Lakeside Village. Unique 1 & 2 bdrm. spacious townhouses. Just 30 minutes from Boston, convenient bus service available. Spectacular sports complex, private backyard. Small pets allowed & owner managed. Reasonable. 832-1186.

EASTON, 1 & 2 br. condos avail. Pool & tennis courts. Some with garages. Starting at $475 mo. Some include utilies. KINGSLEY PROPERTIES. 832-9501.

EAST BOSTON, 2 bdrm. condo, glass rm. & deck, overlooking harbor & skyline, all new, w&d, d&d, & disposal, ww crpt, $600 mo. Call Ed 754-0482.

EAST BOSTON, 5 rm., 3 br. lg. kit, new bath, rehabed, $525, no utils., section 8 ok., 754-2381.

EAST BOSTON, 6 modern rooms, 2nd floor, Call 755-6016.

LYNN, Newly decor. studio & $ bdrm apts. with ocean views. Rents from $350 inclu. ht, hw, stove, refrig., W/W, new kitchens & baths. 954-9876.

LYNN, Nahant line, steps to ocean, studio thru 2 br. mod. htd. apts. Some with all utils. From $275. NSP R.E. 954-4121.

LYNN, Ultra mod. ocean front stu. & 1 bdrm. apt., incl. new kit. & bathrm., w.w. crpts., many extras. $410-$675. 955-8653.

LYNN, Steps from beach. Completely renov. 1 bdrms. $325-$400. Studios $295. ht, hw, 1 hr. lease. HALL R.E. 954-2025.

LYNN, Studio, 1 & 2 BR apts. in beach area. Rents from $325 inclu. ht., hw, stove & refrig. 955-8887.

LYNN, 1 & 2 bdrm., newly remodeled starting at $325. Call 954-6217

MALDEN, Huxley Estates. Beautiful 1½ bdrm., w.w., mod. kit., ht., h.w., A/C, parking, pool, walk to T. No pets please. Avail. 6/1. 644-2281. M-F 9-5; Sun 1-5

MALDEN, Immac. 4 rms, 1 bdrm, nice loc. $336 unhtd. Baldwin R.E. 644-7562.

MALDEN, Lux. 1 bdrm., apt. prkg., a/c, w/w, $425 unhtd. 644-8026.

MALDEN, 3 rms., nr. T., ht. & htw, $400, avail. 6/1. Call 644-5137, after 6 p.m.

MALDEN, 2½ Rms., mod. kit., gd. loc. Avail. immed. $375. htd., Call 644-2053.

MATTAPAN, Mod. 2 BR, a/c, ww, $475-$550. Htd/unhtd. 288-5001.

MAYNARD, Immac. 2 br., lg. eat in kit., fully appl., w.w., $550 +, 781-5662.

MEDFORD, conven. loc., nr. Tufts, prkg., ldry. 2 BR, $425. No fee. 568-0028.

NASHUA or Salem N.H. Ocean Village Apts. are offering 1- 2 bdrm. Garden apts. Which feat. totally equipped kit, color coordinated bath, w/w, a/c, pool & tennis. 1 bdrm. from $475, 2 bdrm, from $525. Also has 3 bdrm. Townhouses avail. Sec. dep & last mos. rent are not reqd. for credit worthy applicants. Loc. on exit 1 on Rte 3 in Nashua, 683-812-2330.

NASHUA, N.H. Barbary Apts. Easy drive north or south, 2 min. Rt. 3. Lux. units start at $460. Incl. ht. & gas. Days 683-812-5875.

NEEDHAM, mod. apts. avail. 1 & 2 bdrm. Rents $495 to $825 + utils. Call 453-2986. Mon.-Fri. 9-5.

NEWTON, Lux. 1 bdrm. site, $650 w/all amenities. Pool, tennis, prkg, heat, h.w., on MBTA. No pets. Rental fee - $200. For Info, 256-5488.

NEWTON, Lg. sunny 2 rm. stu. mod. k&b, a/c, ldry, pkg. $425. R.E. 256-9753.

NEWTON, 5/1, lg. sunny 2 BR in bldg. nr. T. Hwd. flrs, Htd. $695. Own. 256-0011.

NEWTON, 1-2-3 br., various prices. Also Waltham. BARRY R.E. 255-9908.

NEWTON, 4-3-2-1 brs, stu., hses., etc. $250 up. R.E. 256-9775.

NEWTON, 6/1. Modern studio apt. Heated $395. Owner. 855-8037.

REVERE, Studio in newly renovated building. Heat. Parking. Near T. 455-7241.

SALEM, N.H., Spac. Studio; 1 & 2 bdrm. apts. w/ht. & many amenities. Loc. off 93, exit 1. 683-512-4682.

SOMERVILLE, Camb. line. New lux. apts. 1 bdrm. $490; 2 bdrms. $680. ht, ww, balc, prkg., no fee, no pets, 566-2991.

SOMERVILLE, Mod., clean 1 & 2 bedrm apts, ht & hw incl. No lease, no pets. $375-$800. 566-9465.

SOMERVILLE, sunny 4 rms.-1BR, closed porch, new kit., ht & hw, $500. No fee. 6/1. 565-0087.

SOMERVILLE, Immac. 2 Bdrm., mod. k&b. Winter Hill area, $400 unhtd. 566-9320.

SOMERVILLE, studio, separate kit., lg. clsts, ht. h/w, $360 no fee. 566-3025.

SOMERVILLE, Stu, $300 ht. 4 rm. $390-$475 ht. 5-6 rm. $425-$600. 566-7440.

SOMERVILLE, Lge. mod. $ bdrm., d&d, w/w, a/c, balc, $490 htd. 565-9116.

SOMERVILLE, Dunham Circle area, 1 bdrm., $425 unhtd. Samuels R.E. 566-1238.

SO. BOSTON, Dorchester Heights, 3rd flr., sunny, 1 BR, $350 unhtd., call Deb 372-5422.

STONEHAM, lux. Main Street Apts. Sunny 2 bdrm., fully appl. w/w., w.w., A/C, ht., h.w., pool, tennis, balcony. No pets please. Avail. 5/1. Close to 93 & 128. Call 758-2986. M-F 9-5; Sun 1-5

STONEHAM, Converted Vict. nr. Ctr., prkg. 1 BR. $375. No fee. 758-5019.

WALPOLE, unique 1 & 2 br. units in renov. historical landmark. All new interior features oversized livrm., din. area, fully applianced kit. w/designer cabs., ample closet & storage space. Immed. & future occup. From $500 mo. + utils. Ideal for commuters. Model open 7 days 11 am-5 pm, eves. by appt. Direc. Rte. 1 to Rte 27 West. KINGSLEY PROPERTIES 832-9501.

WALTHAM, West, 4 rm, 2 bdrm. apt. Pkg., nr. transp. $350 plus utils., no fee. PROPER REALTY. 885-2184.

WALTHAM, 1 br. apt., also 1-2-3 br. apts., condos, house rentals, $250-$700. 885-4220.

WALTHAM, 4-3-2-1 brs., studios, hses., twnhses, etc. $225 up. Also Wal. Newt., Bel. vic. R.E. 885-1629.

WALTHAM, 4 rm. apt., mod. k&b, nr. pub. trans., prkg. for 2-cars $600. 885-5205.

WALTHAM, in hse. Lg. ultra mod. 2 rm. studio, d&d, w/w, $380 htd. 885-8533.

WALTHAM, Conv. loc., pkg., ldry. fac., mod. 2 BR frpl. $525. No fee. 885-2040.

WATERTOWN & vic., 2 BR apt. $800. 3 BR apt. $750. Conv. to public trans.
CRANE REALTY
914-2811

Exercise 4   SCANNING A NEWSPAPER STORY

Scan the news story below to find the answers to these questions. Work fast. Ask your teacher or another student to time you.

Starting time _____

1. How many stores were damaged in the fire? _____
2. In which store did the fire (blaze) start? _____
3. What time did the fire start?_____
4. Where is the shopping center? _____

Finishing time _____

Scanning time _____

THE NEW YORK TIMES

14 Yonkers Stores Damaged by Fire

Special to The New York Times

YONKERS, Nov. 12 — A four-alarm-fire damaged 14 stores today in the Cross County Shopping Center, the largest shopping center in Westchester County.

Fire investigators said the blaze apparently started in a pile of cardboard cartons at the rear of a shoe store and spread through a utilities duct above the 13 other stores. The fire started at 4:40 P.M. and was declared under control at 6:14 P.M. The center is on the Cross County Parkway at the Gov. Thomas E. Dewey Thruway.

Two firefighters were treated at the scene for minor cuts. Lieut. John Carey of the Yonkers Arson Squad said the cause of the fire was under investigation.

Exercise 5   SCANNING A NEWSPAPER STORY

Scan this news story to find the answers to these questions. Work fast. Ask your teacher or another student to time you.

Starting time _____

1. How many people died in the typhoon (storm)? _____
2. On what day did the typhoon begin? _____
3. How many people lost their homes (were homeless)? _____
4. What is the name of the island that was hit worst? _____
5. What is the name of the typhoon? _____
6. How many people are missing? _____

Finishing time _____

Scanning time _____

THE NEW YORK TIMES

Philippines Sends Aid For Typhoon Damage

MANILA, Nov. 10 (AP) — The Philippine Air Force ferried medical teams and relief supplies today to provinces ravaged by Typhoon Agnes. The authorities said 515 people had died in the typhoon and more than 400 were missing.

An air force spokesman said more than 163 tons of food, medicine and clothing had been sent to the Visayan region, 300 miles south of Manila, and more aid was on the way.

The typhoon hit the region Monday.

The spokesman said helicopters were rescuing people stranded by floods that remained chest-deep today in some areas of Panay Island, which appeared to have been hit the worst. Most of the fatalities and missing were on the island, where 445,000 people were homeless.

The Philippine National Red Cross reported that 90 percent of the 86,000 houses in Capiz Province on Panay were destroyed. Many of the dead were children who drowned as 30-foot waves smashed into coastal villages.

Exercise 6   **SCANNING TWO NEWS STORIES
FOR INFORMATION**

Scan the two news stories to answer these questions. Work fast.

Starting time _____

1. How many astronauts walked in space? _____
2. On what date did this happen? _____
3. How much did the Palapa B-2 satellite weigh? _____
4. How many miles above the earth were the astronauts? _____
5. Who held the satellite for more than 90 minutes? _____
6. What is the commander's name? _____

Finishing time _____

Scanning time _____

THE NEW YORK TIMES

ASTRONAUTS SNARE ERRANT SATELLITE FOR THE FIRST TIME

AIM TO RETRIEVE 2D CRAFT

Major Obstacle Is Overcome by Wrestling 1,200-Pound Palapa Into Cargo Bay

By JOHN NOBLE WILFORD
Special to The New York Times

HOUSTON, Nov. 12 — Two space-walking astronauts boldly snared a satellite in orbit today and, overcoming a surprising and potentially serious obstacle, wrestled the large satellite aboard the cargo bay of the space shuttle Discovery.

It was the first salvage operation in space.

The astronauts plan to retrieve a second communications satellite Wednesday to complete one of the most ambitious and difficult operations in the shuttle's history. They are seeking to demonstrate the shuttle's overall versatility as well as to recoup some of the money insurance companies lost when the two satellites were misfired into useless orbits last February.

Just about dawn over the eastern Pacific, or 8:32 A.M., Eastern standard time, Dr. Joseph P. Allen flew away from the shuttle 224 miles above the earth, circling at a rate of 17,000 miles an hour. He moved toward the stranded Palapa B-2, a 1,200-pound drum-shaped satellite that was rotating slowly about 35 feet away.

THE BOSTON GLOBE

Shuttle snares disabled satellite

Crew wrestles orbiter aboard

Associated Press

SPACE CENTER, Houston — A free-flying astronaut snared an errant satellite in history's first space salvage yesterday, then he and a fellow spacewalker wrestled it aboard Discovery after a failed brace prevented use of the shuttle's robot arm.

"All right! We got it. We got it," called Dale Gardner after he and Joe Allen maneuvered the Palapa B2 satellite into the Discovery's cargo bay and secured it in place.

Allen had held the satellite for more than 90 minutes as Gardner attached a locking frame on the can-shaped craft. The work required Gardner to tighten nine bolts and Allen was forced to rotate the craft by hand at Gardner's directions.

"I can hold it wherever you want it, Dale," said Allen, grasping a rim at one end of the craft while Gardner worked at the other end to attach the locking frame.

The 5-foot-6 Allen was heard to gasp repeatedly as he strained against the inertia of the 21-by-7-foot cylindrical satellite, which weighs 1200 pounds on Earth. Allen held the satellite while he, the orbiter and Discovery made one complete orbit of Earth.

Several times Allen was cautioned by commander Rick Hauk and pilot David Walker, watching from inside Discovery's cockpit, to keep the satellite from banging into the side of the shuttle. And each time Allen was able to move the satellite slightly.

Exercise 7   SCANNING A NEWSPAPER AD

Scan the ad below to find the answers to these questions. Work very fast.

Starting time _____

1. Which computer has the lowest price? _____
2. What do you get free with the Process Partner? _____
3. What is the name of the computer store? _____
4. How many computer courses can you take at DSI? _____
5. Does the PaqComp run BIM programs? _____
6. What is the price of the Partner with 384K memory? _____

Finishing time _____

Scanning time _____

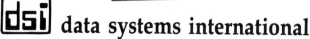

Guessing Word Meanings _____

You do not always know every word in a passage. But you can often guess the words you do not know. You can tell what *kind* of word the unknown word must be.

EXAMPLE

Read this passage. Then go back and guess a word to put in each space. Work with another student.

Henry had a wonderful birthday. His girl _____
(1)

bought him a new watch. His brother _____
(2)

sister gave him a party. Henry's mother _____
(3)

a special chocolate birthday cake, and all of Henry's good

_____ came to his house. _____ danced
(4)   (5)

all night. Henry really _____ his birthday.
(6)

Now check your answers:

1. *friend*   There is only one word you can put here. Someone who buys a watch for Henry.

2. *and*   There is only one word you can put here.

3. You could use a few different words here. The word has to tell what Henry's mother did with a cake. *made, baked, bought, brought, sent*

4. *friends*   This word must be some people, more than one because it says "all".

5. *they* This word tells who danced all night. If you say "Henry," you leave out his friends.

6. You could use a few different words here. The word tells how Henry felt about his birthday. You could use *enjoyed, liked,* or *loved.*

Exercise 1

Read these sentences. The missing words are all nouns. Write the best word for each space. The Answer Key is on page 260.

book   boots   bus   coat   window

1. Sara put on her _____ because she was cold.
2. Roy forgot his _____ so his feet got wet in the rain.
3. The teacher told us to read the _____ for homework.
4. My school is far away, so I have to take a _____ .
5. Tom did not close the _____ , so the room was very cold.

Exercise 2

Read these sentences. The missing words are all verbs. Write the best word for each space.

plays   runs   likes   cooks   calls

1. When Henry is late for school, he _____ all the way.
2. Bill's mother _____ his breakfast every morning.
3. Dr. Diamond _____ to go fishing.
4. Sometimes Jane is homesick, so she _____ her mother in London.
5. Liz takes piano lessons, and she _____ very well.

Exercise 3

A. Read this passage. Some words are missing. Guess what *kind* of word you need for each space.

If you need a noun or a pronoun (a person or a thing), write N. If you need a verb (*is*, *was*, or a word for doing something), write V. Work with another student. The first one is done for you.

THE STORY OF HELEN KELLER

Helen Keller was a famous American. She was a writer and a

speaker. She wrote ____N____ and articles about education and politics.
           1

She _____ to every part of the world. But the surprising fact about
    2

Helen Keller _____ this: she could not see and she could not hear.
        3

This blind, deaf _____ was a very special person.
        4

    Helen Keller _____ not always blind and deaf. She was all right
         5

when _____ was born on June 27, 1880. But she _____ very
    6   7

sick the next year. After that, she was not the same. Her parents

_____ her and _____ tried to take care of her. But it was not
   8   9

easy. Her _____ could not show her what to do.
      10

1. _____

2. _____

3. _____

4. _____

5. _____

6. _____

7. _____

8. _____

9. _____

10. _____

B. Here are the missing words:

books	traveled	is	woman	they
she	became	loved	was	parents

Go back and read the passage again. Guess a word for each space. Write the word on the line to the right.

Exercise 4

Read this passage. Some words are missing. After you read the passage, write the best word on the line to the right. Here are the missing words:

years	they	but	not	something
to	teacher	find	wrote	a	is

Show your work to another student. Do you agree?

By the time Helen was six _____ old, her parents were very
1

unhappy. _____ knew that Helen was very smart. _____
2   3

they could not teach her. They did _____ know what to do. But
4

they knew they had to do _____ .
5

When Helen was seven, they decided _____ find help for
6

Helen. They wrote to Michael Anagnos, a _____ in Boston. They
7

asked him to _____ a teacher for Helen. He _____ to them
8   9

and said: "I know _____ good teacher for Helen. Her name
10

_____ Annie Sullivan. I will send her to you."
11

1. _____
2. _____
3. _____
4. _____
5. _____
6. _____
7. _____
8. _____
9. _____
10. _____
11. _____

Mr. Anagnos worked at this school for the blind in Boston.

Exercise 5

Read this passage. Some words are missing. After you read the passage, write the best word on the line to the right. Here are the missing words:

wanted	what	beautiful	she	to
family	be	they	teach	not

Show your work to another student. Do you agree?

The Kellers were very pleased. They _____₁ a good

teacher for Helen. Then _____₂ could learn and they could all

_____₃ happy. The teacher could show Helen _____₄ to do.

She could teach Helen _____₅ read and to talk.

The Keller _____₆ lived in the South. They had a _____₇ house

in a small town in Alabama. _____₈ .were not rich, but they were

_____₉ poor. They could pay Annie Sullivan to _____₁₀ Helen.

1. _____
2. _____
3. _____
4. _____
5. _____
6. _____
7. _____
8. _____
9. _____
10. _____

Exercise 6

Read this passage. Some words are missing. But the first letter of the word is there. After you read the passage, go back and guess a word for each space. Write the word on the line to the right. Work with another student.

Helen was not always a nice child to be near. She did not know how to e _____ at the table. She made strange n _____ like
1 2
a bird. She sometimes hit h _____ mother or her father. She
3
often r _____ around the room and hurt herself.
4

I _____ was hard to know what Helen t _____ . She could
5 6
not see and she c _____ not hear. She could not k _____ the
7 8
world. No one knew how t _____ tell her things. And she could
9
n _____ tell things to anyone else.
10

1. _____
2. _____
3. _____
4. _____
5. _____
6. _____
7. _____
8. _____
9. _____
10. _____

Exercise 7

Read this passage. Some words are missing. But the first letter of the word is there. After you read the passage, go back and guess a word for each space. Write the word on the line to the right. Work with another student.

Annie Sullivan finally came to the Keller home. She came by train from Boston. Helen's m _____ and father tried to tell Helen
1
t _____ Annie was her friend. They could n _____ make her
2 3
understand.

Annie began to t _____ care of Helen. She tried to t _____
4 5
her. She showed Helen the names o _____ things. She wrote the
6
words on H _____ hands. But Helen did not understand.
7
A _____ began to feel hopeless.
8

1. _____
2. _____
3. _____
4. _____
5. _____
6. _____
7. _____
8. _____

Exercise 8

Read this passage. Then go back and try to guess a word for each space. Write the word on the line to the right. Work with another student.

One day, Annie was trying to teach Helen. They went for a walk, and _____ came to a well. Helen was _____ warm and thirsty. Annie put Helen's hand _____ the water. She took a _____ and gave Helen a drink. Helen _____ glad to have a cool drink.

_____ Annie took Helen's hand. She used her _____ to write "W A T E R" on Helen's _____ . Suddenly, Helen understood! She knew that _____ was telling her something. The feeling _____ her hand was the name for _____ !

Then Helen was very happy. She _____ excited. Now she could find out the _____ of everything. She took Annie's hand.

1. _____
2. _____
3. _____
4. _____
5. _____
6. _____
7. _____
8. _____
9. _____
10. _____
11. _____
12. _____
13. _____
14. _____

Exercise 9

Read this passage. Then go back and try to guess a word for each space. Write the word on the line to the right. Work with another student.

The next year, Annie Sullivan took Helen to Boston. They stayed with Michael Anagnos. _____ went to a special school. She _____ how to speak and how to "listen" with her hand. She learned _____ read books with her fingers. _____ she was ready to go _____ another school in New York. Annie went _____ Helen to New York, and they _____ to the Gilman School.

Soon Helen _____ nineteen years old. It was _____ for her to go to college. _____ took an examination to _____ to Radcliffe, a famous college _____ Massachusetts. Helen was a very _____ student. She passed the examination. Helen went to Radcliffe, and she _____ in 1904.

1. _____
2. _____
3. _____
4. _____
5. _____
6. _____
7. _____
8. _____
9. _____
10. _____
11. _____
12. _____
13. _____
14. _____

Exercise 10

Read the end of the Helen Keller story. Then go back and try to guess a word for each space. Write the word on the line to the right. Work with another student.

Annie and Helen stayed together. Helen wrote a book _____ 1

her life. It _____ 2 called *The Story of My Life.* She also wrote

_____ 3 other books. Some of _____ 4 books became movies.

Annie _____ 5 Helen traveled to England, Scotland, Greece,

and other _____ 6 . Helen visited almost every _____ 7 of the

world. She _____ 8 to help other blind _____ 9 . She also tried to

_____ 10 poor people and she _____ 11 to stop wars.

Helen _____ 12 that her life was _____ 13 because of Annie

Sullivan. She _____ 14 Annie, and she wrote _____ 15 book about

her called *Teacher.* _____ 16 is the name that _____ 17 used for

Annie all _____ 18 her life.

Helen Keller died _____ 19 June, 1968.

1. _____

2. _____

3. _____

4. _____

5. _____

6. _____

7. _____

8. _____

9. _____

10. _____

11. _____

12. _____

13. _____

14. _____

15. _____

16. _____

17. _____

18. _____

19. _____

Exercise 11

Read this passage. The <u>underlined</u> words may be new to you. Do not stop to look up the words you do not know. Try to guess. On the next page, you will have a chance to learn the meanings of these words.

BALLOONING

The first kind of air <u>transportation</u> was not a plane. It was a <u>balloon</u>. People traveled by balloon one hundred years before there were planes or jet <u>aircraft</u>. Those early days of ballooning were exciting, but they were also dangerous. Sometimes the balloons fell suddenly. Sometimes they burned. However, the danger did not stop the <u>balloonists</u>.

The first real balloon flight was in France in 1783. Two Frenchmen, the Montgolfier brothers, made a balloon. They filled a very large paper bag with hot air. Hot air is lighter than cold air, so it goes up. The Montgolfiers' hot air balloon went up 1,000 feet in the sky.

Later that same year, two other Frenchmen <u>ascended</u> in a basket under a balloon. They built a fire under the balloon to make the air hot. This made the balloon stay up in the air for a few hours. But their balloon was tied to the ground. So it could not go anywhere.

The first free balloon flight was in December, 1783. The balloon flew for 25 minutes over Paris. It traveled about five and a half miles.

Flying a balloon is not like flying a plane. The balloon has no engine, no power of its own. The wind controls the balloon. It goes where the wind blows. The <u>pilot</u> can only control the <u>altitude</u> of the balloon. He can raise and lower the balloon to find the right wind direction. That is how a good pilot controls where the balloon goes.

Very soon balloonists tried longer flights. A <u>major</u> event in the history of ballooning was the first long flight over water. In 1785, an American and a Frenchman flew over the English Channel. They left England on a cold, clear January day. After about an hour, their balloon began to <u>descend</u> towards the water. They threw out some <u>equipment</u> and food to make the balloon lighter. The balloon continued to fall, so they threw out almost everything in the basket — even some of their clothes. Finally, after about three hours, they landed in France, cold but safe.

During the 19th century, ballooning became a popular sport. There were balloon races in Europe. Balloons were also used by scientists to study the air and by armies in war time. After the airplane was <u>invented</u>, people lost interest in balloons. Planes were much faster and easier to control. But some people today still like to go up in balloons. High up in the balloon basket, they find quiet. They have a wonderful view of the world below.

A. The underlined words from the passage are in Column 1. The meanings are in Column 2. Write the letter of the best meaning after each word. You may look back at the passage. Work with another student.

Column 1

1. transportation _____
2. balloon _____
3. aircraft _____
4. balloonist _____
5. invent _____
6. major _____
7. ascend _____
8. control _____
9. pilot _____
10. altitude _____
11. descend _____
12. equipment _____

Column 2

a. important
b. distance above the earth
c. way of going from one place to another
d. something for travel by air
e. go down
f. person who flies a plane or balloon
g. special things you need when you travel
h. someone who travels in a balloon
i. go up
j. make for the first time
k. a bag full of air
l. make something do what you want it to do

B. Read the passage again. Then answer these questions:

1. The first kind of air travel was in a
   a. jet plane.
   b. aircraft.
   c. balloon.
   d. ship.

2. Many early balloonists lived in
   a. England.
   b. the United States.
   c. Italy.
   d. France.

3. The balloon will rise if the air inside gets
   a. colder.
   b. hotter.
   c. out.
   d. descended.

4. One way to control a balloon is to
   a. use the engine.
   b. find the right wind direction.
   c. ask the pilot.
   d. not change altitude.

5. People stopped using balloons for air travel because
   a. balloons are dangerous.
   b. balloons are not comfortable.
   c. it is not fun.
   d. planes are easier to control.

Exercise 12

Read this passage. The <u>underlined</u> words may be new to you. Do not stop to look up the words you do not know. Try to guess. On the next page, you will have a chance to learn the meanings of these words.

THE STORY OF PHOTOGRAPHY

In 1826, a Frenchman named Niepce needed pictures for his business. But he was not a good artist. So he invented a very simple camera. He put it in a window of his house and took a picture of his yard. That was the first photograph.

The next important date in the history of photography was 1837. That year, Daguerre, another Frenchman, took a picture of his <u>studio</u>. He used a new kind of camera and a different <u>process</u>. In his pictures, you could see everything very clearly, even the smallest <u>details</u>. This kind of photograph was called a daguerreotype.

Soon, other people began to use Daguerre's process. Travelers brought back daguerreotypes from all around the world. People photographed famous buildings, cities, and mountains.

In about 1840, the process was <u>improved</u>. Then photographers could take pictures of people and moving things. The process was not simple. The photographers had to carry lots of film and processing equipment. But this did not stop the photographers, especially in the United States. After 1840, daguerreotype artists were popular in most cities.

Matthew Brady was one well-known American photographer. He took many <u>portraits</u> of famous people. The portraits were unusual because they were very life-like and full of <u>personality</u>. Brady was also the first person to take pictures of a war. His 1862 Civil War pictures showed dead soldiers and <u>ruined</u> cities. They made the war seem more real and more terrible.

In the 1880s, new inventions began to change photography. Photographers could buy film ready-made in rolls. So they did not have to make the film themselves. Also, they did not have to process the film <u>immediately</u>. They could bring it back to their studios and <u>develop</u> it later. They did not have to carry lots of equipment. And finally, the invention of the small hand camera made photography less expensive.

With the small camera, anyone could be a photographer. People began to use cameras just for fun. They took pictures of their families, friends and favorite places. They called these pictures "snapshots".

Photographs became very popular in newspapers in the 1890s. Soon magazines and books also used <u>documentary</u> photographs. These pictures showed true events and people. They were much more real than drawings.

Photography also began to be a <u>form</u> of art by the end of the nineteenth century. Some photographs were not just copies of the real world. They showed ideas and feelings, like other art forms.

A. The underlined words from the passage are in Column 1. The meanings are in Column 2. Write the letter of the best meaning after each word. You may look back at the passage. Work with another student.

Column 1

1. develop _____
2. studio _____
3. process _____
4. details _____
5. improve _____
6. portraits _____
7. personality _____
8. ruined _____
9. immediately _____
10. documentary _____
11. form _____

Column 2

a. a way of doing something
b. what makes people who they are
c. completely fallen down, useless
d. showing how things really are
e. kind or type
f. a place for artists and photographers to work
g. change film into photographs
h. make better
i. small, important parts
j. pictures of people
k. without waiting, right away

B. Read the passage again. Then answer these questions:

1. The first photograph was taken with
   a. a small hand camera.
   b. a daguerreotype.
   c. a very simple camera.
   d. new film.

2. The story of photography
   a. began in the sixteenth century.
   b. began in France.
   c. is unknown.
   d. began in the United States.

3. Matthew Brady was well-known for
   a. inventing daguerreotypes.
   b. taking pictures of French cities.
   c. portraits and war photographs.
   d. the small hand camera.

4. The new inventions in photography made it possible for
   a. Brady to take pictures of the Civil War.
   b. anyone to be a photographer.
   c. only rich people to take pictures.
   d. people to use daguerreotypes.

5. Photography can also be an art form because artists can
   a. take pictures to show the real world.
   b. make documentaries.
   c. show ideas and feelings in pictures.
   d. copy old pictures.

Topics

A good reader always asks:

"What am I reading about?"
"What is the topic?"

EXAMPLES

1. Find the topic:

football	baseball	tennis	sports	skiing

The topic is **sports**.
The other words are names of sports.

2. Find the topic:

red	purple	color	green	yellow	blue

The topic is _____ .

The other words are names of _____.

3. Find the topic:

France	Germany	Italy	Europe
Belgium	Holland	Austria	

The topic is **Europe**.
The other words are parts of Europe.

4. Find the topic:

nose	ears	eyes	mouth	head
	cheeks		chin	

The topic is _____ .

The other words are parts of _____ .

Work on Exercises 1 — 11 with another student. Ask each other: "What are we reading about?"

The Answer Key is on page 261.

Exercise 1   FINDING THE TOPIC

In each group of words, circle the topic. Try not to use the dictionary. If you don't know a word, guess the meaning. Work with another student.

1. mother   sister   uncle   aunt   family   father
   grandmother   cousin   grandfather   brother

2. nine   sixteen   number   four   seventy-seven
   fifteen   eighty   thirty-two

3. dog   cat   elephant   lion   animal
   horse   camel   mouse

4. bedroom   bathroom   house   dining room   kitchen

5. table   chairs   refrigerator   oven
   kitchen   stove   sink

6. New York   Boston   City   Paris   Rome
   Moscow   Tokyo   Los Angeles

7. table   furniture   chair   chest
   bed   bookcase   sofa

8. bread   fruit   milk   butter   food
   cheese   meat   vegetables

9. music   food   people   party   laughing
   dancing   games   singing

Exercise 2   **FINDING THE TOPIC**

In each group of words, circle the topic. Try not to use the dictionary. If you don't know a word, guess the meaning. Work with another student.

1.
milk	cola	coffee	drinks	cocoa
orange		juice	water	tea

2.
shirt   clothes   skirt   suit   coat   pants

3.
dollar	quarter	half-dollar	nickel
money		penny	dime

4.
subway	metro	bus	airplane	jet
train	travel		boat	ship

5.
wheels   engine   windows   seats   doors   car

6.
river   lake   water   ocean   sea   well

7.
teacher	students	books	class	pens
notebooks		pencils	desks	

8.
doctor	nurse	hospital	beds	patients
rooms	X-rays		medicine	labs

9.
happy   sad   feeling   angry   nervous   proud

WORKING WITH TOPICS

Think of words for these topics. Write the words on the lines below. Work with another student.

1.   TOPIC: Good foods in my country

_____

_____

_____

_____

_____

2.   TOPIC: Important places in a city

_____

_____

_____

_____

_____

3.   TOPIC: People in our class

_____

_____

_____

_____

_____

4.   TOPIC: Good jobs

_____

_____

_____

_____

_____

Exercise 4   WORKING WITH TOPICS

Think of words for these topics. Write the words on the lines below.
Work with another student.

1.   TOPIC: Holidays in my country

_____

_____

_____

_____

_____

2.   TOPIC: Nice gifts

_____

_____

_____

_____

_____

3.   TOPIC: Reasons for learning English

_____

_____

_____

_____

_____

4.   TOPIC: _____
               (Now you write a topic.)

_____

_____

_____

_____

_____

Exercise 5 THINKING OF THE TOPIC

Write the topic. Work with another student. Try not to use the dictionary.

EXAMPLE

knife   fork   spoon   cup   plate   bowl
glass   dish   chopsticks

TOPIC: _____ kitchen equipment _____

---

1.   Venezuela   Mexico   China   Canada   Germany

TOPIC: _____

2.   hospital   factory   library   school   hotel   bank

TOPIC: _____

3.   table of contents   index   title page   chapters
glossary   cover   words   pages

TOPIC: _____

4.   French   Latin   Greek   Japanese   English
Arabic   Chinese   German

TOPIC: _____

5.   physics   chemistry   astronomy   biology   geology

TOPIC: _____

6.   cheese   milk   ice cream   butter   cream   yogurt

TOPIC: _____

Exercise 6   THINKING OF THE TOPIC

Write the topic. Work with another student. Try not to use a dictionary.

1. books   magazines   letters   catalogs   newspapers

   TOPIC: _____

2. morning   afternoon   midnight   noon
           dusk   evening

   TOPIC: _____

3. Colorado   New Mexico   California   Massachusetts
        Arizona   Iowa   Florida

   TOPIC: _____

4. homesickness   joy   anger   sadness
       happiness   fear   envy   regret   pride

   TOPIC: _____

5. Kennedy   Eisenhower   Truman   Nixon   Reagan
       Carter   Hoover   Lincoln

   TOPIC: _____

6. war   hunger   sickness   poor people   no jobs
       too many people   many people can't read

   TOPIC: _____

Exercise 7   THINKING OF THE TOPIC

Write the topic. Work with another student. Try not to use a dictionary.

1. captain   pilot   passengers   flight attendants

    TOPIC: _____

2. radio   computer   stereo   TV   calculator

    TOPIC: _____

3. arithmetic   calculus   trigonometry   algebra

    TOPIC: _____

4. Amazon   Ganges   Mississippi   Danube   Tigris
        Euphrates   Nile   Yangtze

    TOPIC: _____

5. doctor   orderly   lab technician   nurse
        secretary   patient   cleaner

    TOPIC: _____

6. swim   run   play tennis   bicycle   ski   walk

    TOPIC: _____

7. bridge   road   highway   street   tunnel
            turnpike   avenue

    TOPIC: _____

Exercise 8   THINKING OF THE TOPIC

Finding the Word That Does Not Belong

One word in each group does not belong with the others. Write the topic. Cross out the word that does not belong. Work with another student.

EXAMPLE

bicycle   motorcycle   car   ~~ship~~

van   bus   truck

TOPIC: _____Ways to travel on land_____

---

1. Boston   New York   Chicago   Paris
   San Francisco   Washington   Los Angeles

   TOPIC: _____

2. teacher   chalk   students   books
   ice cream   pens

   TOPIC: _____

3. hat   gloves   bathing suit   pants   scarf
   mittens   jacket   vest

   TOPIC: _____

4. February   April   March   January   Tuesday

   TOPIC: _____

5. ice cream   cake   carrots   cookies   candy

   TOPIC: _____

6. sailor   scientist   secretary   husband   doctor
   nurse   taxi driver   teacher

   TOPIC: _____

Finding the Word That Does Not Belong

One word in each group does not belong with the others. Write the topic. Cross out the word that does not belong. Work with another student.

1. legs   arms   shoulders   neck   top
              back   feet   stomach

    TOPIC: _____

2. red   orange   yellow   black   green   blue

    TOPIC: _____

3. nose   mouth   elbow   ears   eyes   chin   hair

    TOPIC: _____

4. bottle   cup   box   bag   pocket   table
                  package   basket

    TOPIC: _____

5. roof   wall   tree   window   door   floor

    TOPIC: _____

6. baseball   football   golf   tennis   swimming   basketball

    TOPIC: _____

Exercise 10   TWO TOPICS

Each list has words about two topics. Write the two topics. Then write the words under the topics. Work with another student.

EXAMPLE

ladder	concert	opera
movie	stairs	TV
elevator	play	escalator

Topic 1	Topic 2
Ways to go up	Things to watch for fun
ladder	movie
elevator	play
stairs	opera
escalator	TV
	concert

1.
Zimbabwe	Buddhist	Ethiopia
Catholic	Muslim	Jew
Nigeria	Christian	Zambia
	Kenya	

TOPIC 1 _____   TOPIC 2 _____

_____   _____

_____   _____

_____   _____

_____   _____

2.
nose	ears	red	yellow
mouth	blue	chin	purple

TOPIC 1 _____   TOPIC 2 _____

_____   _____

_____   _____

_____   _____

3.   dog   ocean   lake   elephant
     horse   cow   camel   river
     stream   canal   sea   cat

TOPIC 1 _____   TOPIC 2 _____

     _____   _____

     _____   _____

     _____   _____

     _____   _____

     _____   _____

     _____   _____

4.   California   Australia   Arizona
     Ireland   Washington   Oregon
     Scotland   England   Nevada
                  Canada

TOPIC 1 _____   TOPIC 2 _____

     _____   _____

     _____   _____

     _____   _____

     _____   _____

     _____   _____

5.   hour   bang   boom   second
     tick   minute   meow   thud
     roar   month   day   screech
     year   century

TOPIC 1 _____   TOPIC 2 _____

     _____   _____

     _____   _____

     _____   _____

     _____   _____

     _____   _____

     _____   _____

6. car   bus   shirt   dress
    pajamas   motorcycle   taxi   bicycle
    socks   pants   shoes

    TOPIC 1 _____   TOPIC 2 _____

            _____   _____

            _____   _____

            _____   _____

            _____   _____

            _____   _____

            _____

7. milk   math   reading   tea
    science   coffee   writing   history
    cola   water

    TOPIC 1 _____   TOPIC 2 _____

            _____   _____

            _____   _____

            _____   _____

            _____   _____

            _____

8. cold   windy   snow
    mountain   ice   hill
    river   sleet   valley
    lake

    TOPIC 1 _____   TOPIC 2 _____

            _____   _____

            _____   _____

            _____   _____

            _____   _____

Exercise 11

TWO TOPICS

Each list has words about two topics. Write the two topics. Then write the words under topics. Work with another student.

1. chair   table   book   bookcase
    magazine   newspaper   bed   chest
    desk   letter

    TOPIC 1 _____   TOPIC 2 _____

    _____   _____

    _____   _____

    _____   _____

    _____   _____

    _____   _____

2. noun   clouds   sun   stars
    adjective   verb   moon   article
    planet   pronoun

    TOPIC 1 _____   TOPIC 2 _____

    _____   _____

    _____   _____

    _____   _____

    _____   _____

    _____   _____

3. chest   arm   penicillin   leg
    aspirin   quinine   valium   shoulder
    tetracycline hip   neck

    TOPIC 1 _____   TOPIC 2 _____

    _____   _____

    _____   _____

    _____   _____

    _____   _____

    _____   _____

4. cotton   nucleus   wool
    silk   nylon   neutron
    proton   rayon   electron
    linen

    TOPIC 1 _____   TOPIC 2 _____

        _____   _____

        _____   _____

        _____   _____

        _____   _____

        _____   _____

5. jazz   classical   drum
    folk   trumpet   clarinet
    rock   blues   piano

    TOPIC 1 _____   TOPIC 2 _____

        _____   _____

        _____   _____

        _____   _____

        _____   _____

        _____   _____

6. see   sugar   honey
    hear   smell   maple syrup
    touch   taste   candy

    TOPIC 1 _____   TOPIC 2 _____

        _____   _____

        _____   _____

        _____   _____

        _____   _____

        _____   _____

7.   sunny   heat   photograph

      breezy   warm   showers

      painting   print   drawing

TOPIC 1 _____   TOPIC 2 _____

           _____   _____

           _____   _____

           _____   _____

           _____   _____

           _____   _____

8.   pencil   pen   beef

      chalk   pork   marker

      chicken   fish   typewriter

      lamb   brush

TOPIC 1 _____   TOPIC 2 _____

           _____   _____

           _____   _____

           _____   _____

           _____   _____

           _____   _____

9.   president   prime minister   bridge

      tower   mayor   dome

      skyscraper   chancellor

TOPIC 1 _____   TOPIC 2 _____

           _____   _____

           _____   _____

           _____   _____

           _____   _____

Topics of Conversations ⸺⸺

Read the conversation and answer the questions. Work with another student. The Answer Key is on page 263.

EXAMPLE

A. Was it a girl or a boy?
B. A girl. She's eight pounds and very healthy!
A. When will they come home from the hospital?
B. I'm going to bring them home tomorrow.
A. You'll have to come for a visit. What a nice change for the neighborhood!

What are these people talking about? *A new baby girl.*

Where are they? *Can't tell. Maybe at home.*

Which words helped you guess the topic? *hospital, eight pounds, girl or boy?, bring them home.*

⸺⸺⸺

Conversation 1

A. I like the color.
B. So do I. Red is my favorite color.
A. How many miles does it have on it?
B. Only 30,000. They told me it belonged to an old lady. She didn't use it very much.
A. How's the price?
B. It's really cheap.
A. Then I think you should get it.

What are these people talking about? ⸺⸺⸺⸺⸺⸺

Where are they? ⸺⸺⸺⸺⸺⸺⸺

Underline the words that helped you guess the topic.

Conversation 2

    A. Do you think Mom and Dad will be late?
    B. No. Air India is always on time.
    A. But it's raining so hard and the weather is even worse in New York.
    B. Don't worry. The airline agent will tell us if they're going to be late.
    A. You're right. Let's go have a cup of coffee while we wait.

What are these people talking about? _____

Where are they? _____

Underline the words that helped you guess.
_____

Conversation 3

    A. When did this happen?
    B. Yesterday. I was playing soccer and I fell down.
    A. Can you move it at all?
    B. Only a little.
    A. Can you walk on it?
    B. No. It hurts too much.
    A. I think we'll have to take an X-ray.

What are these people talking about? _____

Where are they? _____

Underline the words that helped you guess.
_____

Conversation 4

    A. Look at the long line! Do you think we'll get in?
    B. I think so. Some of these people already have tickets.
    A. How much are the tickets?
    B. Only $2.50 for the first show. I'll pay.
    A. Thanks. I'll buy some popcorn.

What are these people talking about? _____

Where are they? _____

Underline the words that helped you guess.
_____

Conversation 5

A. Well, what do you think?
B. The color is perfect on you.
A. What about the style?
B. It's a very popular style.
A. How does it look on me?
B. It looks great on you. It looks great on everybody.
A. You don't think I look funny in it?
B. Not at all. You look very nice.

What are these people talking about? _____

Where are they? _____

Underline the words that helped you guess.

_____

Conversation 6

A. Did you understand everything today?
B. No. I'm so confused!
A. So am I.
B. This test is going to be difficult.
A. Maybe we should go to the language lab this afternoon.
B. Good idea. I need more practice.

What are these people talking about? _____

Where are they? _____

Underline the words that helped you guess.

_____

Conversation 7

A. Where do you want to go?
B. To the train station. I'm in a hurry.
A. What time's your train?
B. In ten minutes!
A. Ten minutes! There's a lot of traffic now. But I'll try!

What are these people talking about? _____

Where are they? _____

Underline the words that helped you guess.

_____

Conversation 8

A. How many?
B. Two.
A. Do you have a reservation?
B. No.
A. Well, you're lucky. This is a quiet night. I think we have some tables. Right this way.

What are these people talking about? _____

Where are they? _____

Underline the words that helped you guess.

_____

Conversation 9

A. I can't believe that this is my last day here.
B. You're leaving us today?
A. Yes. I'm so nervous about this.
B. I'm sure it will be fine.
A. I don't know. It will be so different.
B. I thought you wanted a change.
A. Yes, I did. And I wanted more pay. But now I'm not sure it was the right thing to do.
B. Stop worrying. Everything will be fine.

What are these people talking about? _____

Where are they? _____

Underline the words that helped you guess.

_____

Conversation 10

A. This is one of the reasons I hate working in a big city.
B. I know. Every day, it's the same thing.
A. This is terrible! We may be here all night! I hope we don't run out of gas.
B. No, I think there's enough.
A. Let's turn on the radio. Maybe there's some good music.
B. Sorry, the radio's not working.
A. I think I'll take the train tomorrow!

What are these people talking about? _____

Where are they? _____

Underline the words that helped you guess.

_____

Topics of Paragraphs

The topic of a paragraph tells you what it is about. Ask yourself, "What is this paragraph about?"

EXAMPLE A

Mexico City is a popular place for tourists. Every year thousands of people go to Mexico City. They visit the old and beautiful buildings in this city. In the museums they learn about the history of Mexico. And in the restaurants they enjoy the spicy and delicious Mexican food.

What is the topic?

a. Mexican food
b. Mexico
c. Mexico City

The right answer is *(c) Mexico City.* It tells what the paragraph is about.

(a) *Mexican food* is too specific. It is only one part of the paragraph.
(b) *Mexico* is too general. It includes many ideas that are not in the paragraph.

EXAMPLE B

The food in Mexico sometimes surprises tourists. It can be very, very spicy! Mexican cooks use a special kind of pepper. This pepper is so spicy it almost burns your mouth. But most people start to like the spices after a while. They learn to like Mexican food very much.

What is this paragraph about? Check (✓) the best topic. Write "too specific" or "too general" after the other topics.

a. Mexican cooks _____

b. Mexican food _____

c. food _____

The right answer is (b) *Mexican food.*
  (a) *Mexican cooks* is too specific. The whole paragraph is not about Mexican cooks.
  (c) *food* is too general. It can include many kinds of food that are not in the topic.

What is the topic of both Example A and Example B? _____

Exercise 1 CHOOSING THE BEST TOPIC

A. Read each paragraph. Ask yourself, "What is this about?" Make a check after the best topic. Write "too specific" or "too general" after the other topics. Work with another student. The Answer Key is on page 263.

1

Mexico City is growing very fast. In 1970 the city had about nine million people. Now it has over 17 million. All these people are causing problems for the city. There are not enough jobs. Also, there is not enough housing. Large families have to live together in very small homes. Many homes do not have water. They also do not have bathrooms or electricity. The Mexican government is worried about all these problems. It is working hard to make life better in the city.

a. Mexican government   _____

b. large cities   _____

c. Mexico City's problems _____

2

Why is Mexico City growing so fast? Where are all these people coming from? They are coming to the city from the country. Life is hard on the farms in Mexico. Most people on farms have to live a very simple life. They have no extra money for modern things. People think life in the city must be better. So they leave their farms and move to Mexico City.

a. why people are moving to Mexico City   _____

b. how Mexicans live in the country   _____

c. life in Mexico today   _____

3

All around the world large cities have the same problem. That problem is air pollution. Mexico City has very bad air. The air there is dirty and very unhealthy. Cars are one reason for the dirty air. Many Mexicans now own their own cars and drive in the city. The factories in the area also cause air pollution. These factories put a lot of smoke into the air. It is not easy to clean up the air in a large city. The government has to make new laws and everyone has to help.

a. air pollution   _____

b. Mexico City's air pollution   _____

c. how factories cause air pollution _____

B. Write the topic for all three paragraphs. _____

Exercise 2   CHOOSING THE BEST TOPIC

A. Make a check after the best topic. Write "too specific" or "too general" after the other topics. Work with another student.

1

On American television there are many ads about kinds of soap. They show soap for washing clothes. They also show soap specially for washing dishes. Some ads show soap only for washing floors. Other ads are about soap for washing cars. Television ads show soap for washing people too. Often the ads tell about special soap for washing your hair. Other soap is just for taking care of little babies. American television seems very interested in cleaning!

a. soap in the United States   _____

b. soap for washing in the house   _____

c. ads for soap on American TV   _____

2

The evening news on television is very popular with many Americans. They like to find out what is happening in the world. On television they can see real people and places. They believe it is easier than reading the newspaper. Many people think television makes the news seem more real. They also think the news on television is more interesting. The television news reporters sometimes tell funny stories and even jokes. This makes the news about wars and crime seem less terrible.

a. why news programs have funny stories   _____

b. why Americans like television news   _____

c. what is happening in the world   _____

3

In the United States there are two kinds of television stations. One kind is commercial. About 841 of the television stations in the United States are commercial stations. These stations are businesses. They show ads to make money The other kind of television station is public. These stations do not show any ads. They get some money from the government. They also get money from the people who watch public stations.

a. the two kinds of television stations in the U.S.   _____

b. public television stations   _____

c. television in the United States   _____

B. Write the topic for all three paragraphs. _____

Exercise 3 CHOOSING THE BEST TOPIC

A. Make a check after the best topic. Write "too specific" or "too general" after the other topics. Work with another student.

1

Some of the largest trees in the world are in California. These are called redwood trees. Redwood National Park is a large forest of redwood trees. Visitors in the park can walk and drive through the forest to look at the trees. Some redwoods are hundreds of years old. These old trees are very tall. They are also very wide at the bottom. One tree has a large hole in the bottom. The hole is so big you can drive a car through it.

a. parks in California   _____

b. redwood trees in California   _____

c. the age of redwoods   _____

2

In many hilly areas of Scotland there once were large forests. Over the years the forests became smaller. People cut down the trees to use the wood for heating or building. They used the land for farming. But after a while the land was not good for farming. It became rocky because the earth was washed away by the rain. There were no trees to hold the earth in place. Now the Scottish government is planting new trees. These new forests look nice and green. They also will help improve the earth for the future.

a. the land in Scotland   _____

b. how trees hold earth in place   _____

c. forests in Scotland   _____

3

Large forests are important to us in many ways. They give us wood for building and heating. They are a home for many kinds of plants and animals. And for many city people, forests are a place to go for a vacation. People can learn about nature there. They can breathe fresh air and sleep in a quiet place. But there is one more reason why forests are important for everyone. The leaves on the trees in a forest help clean the air. Dirty air is a problem in many parts of the world. Without our forests this problem might be much worse.

a. the importance of forests   _____

b. taking vacations in forests   _____

c. large forests   _____

B. Write the topic for all three paragraphs. _____

Exercise 4   **CHOOSING THE BEST TOPIC**

A. Make a check after the best topic. Write "too specific" or "too general" after the other topics. Work with another student.

1

It is easy to make a good cup of tea. Just follow these steps. First, boil some water. Next put some hot water in the tea pot to warm it. Pour the water out of the pot and put in some tea leaves. You will need one teaspoon of tea leaves for each cup of tea you want. Then pour the boiling water into the tea pot. Cover the pot and wait for a few minutes. Now the tea is ready to drink.

a. good tea   _____

b. how much tea to use   _____

c. how to make good tea   _____

2

The first people to grow coffee beans lived in the Middle East. The Persians, Arabs and Turks were drinking coffee many hundreds of years ago. Then, in the 1600s, Europeans learned about coffee. They quickly learned to like it. Soon there were coffee houses in many European cities. Europeans took coffee with them when they travel-ed to new countries. That is how people in other parts of the world learned about coffee. Now coffee is very popular in North and South America, in Africa and in parts of Asia.

a. the history of coffee   _____

b. European coffee houses   _____

c. popular drinks   _____

3

In the United States orange juice is one of the most popular cold drinks. Most of the oranges for juice grow in Florida. In many homes around the country, orange juice is always served at breakfast time. It is also a favorite snack at any time of the day. When there is bad weather in Florida the whole country knows about it. Bad weather in Florida means fewer oranges. And that means more expensive orange juice!

a. cold drinks in the United States   _____

b. bottled orange juice   _____

c. orange juice in the United States   _____

B. Write the topic for all three paragraphs. _____

THINKING OF THE TOPIC

> **EXAMPLE**
>
> The first real bicycle was made in Scotland. It was built in 1839 by a man named Macmillan. His bicycle had two wheels like a modern bicycle. But it was much more difficult to ride. It was heavier because it was made of wood and iron. It did not have rubber tires like a modern bicycle. Instead, it had wooden wheels. This made it very uncomfortable on bumpy roads. But Macmillan was lucky about one thing: he could not get a flat tire!
>
> What is the topic of this paragraph? Think carefully about your topic. It should not be too specific or too general.
>
> Topic _____

The topic of this paragraph is "the first bicycle." If your answer is similar, that is okay too. For example, "Macmillan's bicycle" is also a good answer.

"Bicycles" is too general. "Bicycle wheels" is too specific.

Exercise 5   THINKING OF THE TOPIC

A. Write the topics. Be sure they are not too specific or too general. Work with another student.

1

Fog is really a low cloud near the ground. Fog and clouds are made of many little drops of water. These drops stay in the air because they are so small. You cannot see each drop. But fog can make it hard to see other things. It can be dangerous if you are driving, for example. Sometimes where there is a lot of fog you cannot see the road. Sailors also have trouble when there is fog. Boats may get lost and hit rocks or beaches in the fog.

Topic _____

2

When there is a heavy rain storm, you sometimes see lightning. It is a very bright light in the sky. In the past people thought the reason was religious. They thought it came from an angry god. In the 1700s Benjamin Franklin found out lightning was electricity. Storms with lightning really are electrical storms. But scientists today still do not know everything about lightning. They do not know exactly what it comes from. And they never know where and how it will hit the earth.

Topic _____

3

All clouds are made of many little drops of water. But not all clouds are alike. There are three kinds of clouds. Cirrus clouds are one kind. These are made of ice drops. They look very soft and light. Another kind of cloud is called a cumulus cloud. They are very large and deep and flat on the bottom. We usually see cumulus clouds on warm summer days. And finally there are stratus clouds, which cover the whole sky. These clouds make the sky gray and the sun does not shine at all.

Topic _____

B. Write the topic for all three paragraphs. _____

A. Write the topics for these paragraphs. Be sure they are not too specific or too general. Work with another student.

1

In the United States drinking water comes from a few different places. Many cities get their drinking water from special lakes called reservoirs. Other cities get their water from rivers. For example, the drinking water for New Orleans comes from the Mississippi River. In some areas, people get their water from the mountains. The water from mountain snow is delicious and clean. In other areas people dig deep holes in the ground for water. These holes are called wells. Outside of cities, most people get their water this way

Topic _____

2

Many American scientists are worried about the drinking water in the United States. They think that soon there may be no more clean drinking water. Dirt, salt and chemicals from factories can get into the water. Then it is not safe to drink. This is already true in some places. One example is a small town in Massachusetts. Many children in this town became sick because of the dirty water. Another place with water problems is Sacramento, California. The water near an airport in Sacramento is not safe to drink. Many other cities and towns have water problems, too.

Topic _____

3

It is very important to use water carefully. Here are some ways you can use less water. First, you should be sure you turn off the faucets tightly. They should not drip in the bathroom or kitchen sink. Second, you should not keep the water on for a long time. You should turn it off while you are doing something else. It should be off while you are shaving or brushing your teeth. It should also be off while you are washing the dishes. Finally, in the summer you should water your garden in the evening. That way you will not lose a lot of water. During the day the sun dries up the earth too quickly.

Topic _____

B. Write the topic for all three paragraphs. _____

Exercise 7   THINKING OF THE TOPIC

A. Write the topics for these paragraphs. Be sure they are not too specific or too general. Work with another student.

1

Finding a job is often difficult for a young person today. But it will be easier if you follow these steps. First, you have to decide what kind of job you want. Think about what kind of work you like to do. You should talk to your friends and your family about it. You can also talk to some people with different kinds of jobs. Next you need to write a resume. This tells about your education and your earlier jobs. It should be carefully typed. Then you are ready to start looking for a job.

Topic _____

2

The job of a young doctor is not easy. Doctors often spend many hours with a patient. There are usually more patients waiting. So doctors do not have much free time during the day. They often have to work all night in hospitals too. Or they may have to go somewhere suddenly when someone is ill. A doctor's decision may mean life or death for the patient. Even when doctors are very tired, they have to think very carefully.

Topic _____

3

The worst problem may be over when you find a good job. But you must think about keeping your job. You may lose it if you are not careful. Be sure you arrive at work on time every morning. You should not stop every hour for coffee. And you should not leave early too often. An important part of your job may be the way you work with other people. If you are difficult to work with, you may have trouble. Or you may have trouble if you do not make friends with the other people at your job. Remember these things if you want to keep your job!

Topic _____

B. Write the topic for all three paragraphs. _____

THINKING OF THE TOPIC

A. Write the topics for these paragraphs. Be sure they are not too specific or too general. Work with another student.

1

Galileo was one of the first modern scientists. He was born in Pisa, Italy, in 1564. At first he studied philosophy. But later he studied mathematics and astronomy. He was very interested in the way the earth and other planets move around the sun. He found out several important facts about our world. He also started a new way of working in science. Before Galileo, scientists did not do experiments. They just guessed about how something happened. But Galileo was different. He did not just make guesses. He did experiments and watched to see what happened.

Topic _____

2

Galileo is famous for his study of how things fall. He was the first person to do experiments about this problem. Before, people thought that heavy things always fell faster than light things. He found out that this was not true. He took a heavy ball and a light ball and he dropped them both from a high place. They fell at the same speed. This meant that weight is not important. This is the law of falling bodies. It is an important law for understanding our world.

Topic _____

3

The life of a scientist was not always easy in the 1500s. For example, Galileo had some trouble because of his scientific ideas. His ideas were not the same as the religious ideas at the time. Many religious people did not agree with him. During his whole life he had to worry about this. He even went to prison for a while. But no one could stop him from thinking. He continued to look for scientific answers.

Topic _____

B. Write the topic for all three paragraphs. _____

Main Ideas

The main idea tells you more about the topic. It tells you the writer's *idea* about the topic.

EXAMPLE A

Topic: *Elephants*

What are three different ideas about elephants?

1. Elephants live in Africa and Asia.
2. Elephants are killed for their skin and their ivory tusks.
3. Elephants can cause serious problems for farmers.

EXAMPLE B

Topic: *Supermarkets*

Write three different ideas about supermarkets.

1. _____
2. _____
3. _____

EXAMPLE C

    Bicycles are very popular today in many countries. Many people use bicycles for exercise. But exercise is only one of the reasons why bicycles are popular. Another reason is money. Bicycles are not expensive to buy. They do not need gas to make them go. They also are easy and cheap to fix. In cities, many people like bicycles better than cars. With a bicycle, they never have to wait in traffic. They also do not have to find a place to park. And finally, bicycles do not cause any pollution!

Topic: *Bicycles*

Write the topic beside the main idea of this paragraph.

    a. _____ do not cause pollution.

    b. _____ are better than cars.

    c. _____ are popular today for many reasons.

The correct answer is (c) *Bicycles are popular today for many reasons.* This is the writer's main idea about bicycles. All the information in the paragraph is about this idea.

(a) is not correct because it is too specific. It is only one part of the paragraph.

(b) is not correct because the paragraph is not about this. The paragraph does not say bicycles *are* better than cars. It only says that some people *like* bicycles better than cars.

Exercise 1

Read each paragraph. Ask yourself, "What is the topic? What is the main idea?" Write the topic beside the best main idea. The Answer Key is on page 264.

1

Clothes can tell a lot about a person. Some people like very colorful clothes. They want everyone to look at them. They want to be the center of things. Other people like to wear nice clothes. But their clothes are not colorful or fancy. They do not like people to look at them. There are also some people who wear the same thing all the time. They do not care if anyone looks at them. They do not care what anyone thinks about them.

a. _____ are colorful.

b. _____ can tell a lot about a person.

c. _____ always look nice on some people.

2

It is important to bring the right clothes when you travel. If you are going to a cold country, you should bring warm clothes. Be sure you have a hat and gloves, too. If you are going to a hot country, you need different clothes. You do not want heavy or dark clothes. In hot weather, light clothes are best. If you are going to a city, you may need some nice clothes. You may want to go to a special restaurant or a concert. It is different if you are traveling by bicycle in the country. Then you will want comfortable clothes. But one rule is the same for all travelers. Do not bring too many clothes!

a. _____ for warm weather are light.

b. _____ are important when you travel.

c. _____ can be heavy.

3

Clothes today are very different from the clothes of the 1800s. One difference is the way they look. For example, in the 1800s all women wore dresses. The dresses all had long skirts. But today women do not always wear dresses with long skirts. Sometimes they wear short skirts. Sometimes they wear pants. Another difference between 1800 and today is the cloth. In the 1800s, clothes were made only from natural kinds of cloth. They were made from cotton, wool, silk or linen. But today, there are many new kinds of man-made cloth. A lot of clothes are now made from nylon, rayon, or polyester.

a. _____ of the 1800s were beautiful.

b. _____ are made of man-made cloth.

c. _____ today are different from the clothes of the 1800s.

Exercise 2

Read each paragraph. Ask yourself, "What is the topic? What is the main idea?" Write the topic beside the best main idea.

1

Before the 1600s people were interested in chemicals. But they did not study them like modern chemists. These early chemists were called alchemists. Their kind of chemistry was called alchemy. They had some strange ideas. For example, they believed they could make gold. They thought they could mix together the right things and have gold. For hundreds of years alchemists tried to do this. Of course, no one ever made gold this way.

a. _____ never made gold.

b. _____ lived before the 1600s.

c. _____ studied chemicals in strange ways.

2

Antoine Lavoisier is important in the history of modern chemistry. In the 1700s, he began to use a new way to study chemicals. Before Lavoisier, scientists just looked at something and thought about it. But Lavoisier did experiments. He studied the size and weight of many different things. He found out something important. He found out that nothing really goes away. It changes into something else. For example, when water boils, it becomes steam. This was a very important idea for the future of chemistry.

a. _____ learned an important fact by doing experiments.

b. _____ studied the size and weight of water.

c. _____ lived in the 1700s.

3

Lavoisier is best known as a chemist. He learned some very important facts about chemistry. And he gave names to many chemicals. These are the same names we use today. Some of Lavoisier's other ideas were important, too. He used science to improve farming. He also worked on a way to improve France's banks and government. He helped to make the taxes and money the same all over France. Lavoisier was a great man in many ways.

a. _____ was a scientist.

b. _____ helped change the taxes and money in France.

c. _____ was a great man in many ways.

Exercise 3

Read each paragraph. Ask yourself, "What is the topic? What is the writer's idea about the topic?" Choose the best main idea sentence.

1

Cats and dogs are both popular pets. But cats are nicer pets in some ways. Cats are cleaner, first of all. They stay very clean and they do not make the house dirty. Cats are also quieter than dogs. They usually do not make a lot of noise. Cats are safer, too. Dogs sometimes bite people, but cats almost never do. And finally, cats are easier to take care of. You do not have to spend much time with a cat. In fact, many cats prefer to be alone.

a. Some people prefer cats as pets.

b. Cats do not make a lot of noise.

c. Cats are nicer than dogs in some ways.

2

Many children want to have a pet. But parents do not like the idea of a dog or a cat in the house. In fact, pets can be good for children. A pet means something to play with. This can be especially important if there is only one child. Also, children can learn a lot from a pet. They can learn about animals and the natural world. Children also learn about taking care of something. They cannot forget about their pet. This is an important lesson for all children.

a. Children usually want a dog or a cat.

b. Pets may be good for children.

c. Parents sometimes do not like pets.

3

Most Americans think of cats as pets. But not all cats are pets. Some cats help people and others are a problem. For example, on farms and in old houses, cats can help. They kill small animals such as rats or mice. But sometimes, people do not want cats around. Some people like to watch birds in their yards. Cats may kill the birds or scare them away. Cats are also a problem in cities. In Rome, for example, thousands of cats live in the streets and old buildings. They make a lot of noise, and they are dirty and dangerous.

a. Cats can be a problem.

b. Most Americans think of cats as pets.

c. Cats are not just pets.

Exercise 4

Read each paragraph. Ask yourself, "What is the topic? What is the writer's idea about the topic?" Choose the best main idea sentence.

1

The earth is always changing. One way it changes is by erosion. Some erosion is caused by the weather. For example, the wind causes erosion. In a desert, the wind blows the sand around. Rain also causes erosion. It washes away earth and even changes the shape of some rocks. Another kind of erosion is caused by rivers. When a river goes through a mountain, it cuts into the mountain. After a long time, the mountain is lower and the land is flatter.

a. Rain causes erosion.

b. Mountains change after a long time.

c. Erosion changes the earth.

2

Mt. Vesuvius in Italy and Mt. St. Helens in the United States are both famous mountains. They are both volcanoes. A volcano is a mountain that is open at the top. Smoke and hot air come out of the hole. Sometimes very hot rock also comes out of the mountain. That can mean trouble for people nearby. This is what happened with Mt. Vesuvius and Mt. St. Helens. Hot rock poured out of Mt. Vesuvius and covered the town of Pompeii in 79 A.D. Everyone in the town was killed. The Mt. St. Helens volcano did not kill many people. There were no cities close to the mountain. But the hot rock killed a large part of the forest. And a lot of dirt fell on cities many miles away.

a. Volcanoes can be dangerous.

b. The Mt. St. Helens and Mt. Vesuvius volcanoes both caused trouble.

c. A volcano is a mountain with a hole at the top.

3

Scientists know a lot about the earth. For example, they understand how mountains are made and what a volcano is. But they do not know when a volcano will send hot rock into the air. They may know about the outside of the earth. But they still are not sure about the inside. And scientists are not sure about how the earth was made. They have many different ideas about this. There are still many difficult questions for scientists who study the earth.

a. Scientists have different ideas about how the earth was made.

b. Scientists now know a lot about the earth.

c. Scientists still have many questions about the earth.

Exercise 5

Read each paragraph. Ask yourself, "What is the topic? What is the writer's idea about the topic?" Then write the main idea sentence.

1

Not all newspaper ads are for selling things. Some ads are about people. The "Help Wanted" ads give information about jobs. All kinds of jobs are found in this part of the newspaper. There are ads for secretaries and electricians, doctors and professors. Another kind of ad about people is the "Personal" ad. These ads are not about work. They are written by people who are looking for friends. Sometimes these people are even looking for husbands and wives. Newspaper ads are a very good way to get people together.

Main idea _____

_____

2

We can learn a lot about a country from the "Personal" ads. These ads tell us about people and their problems. One example of this is from Spain. In a small town in Spain there were forty-two men. But there were not many women there. The men wanted to find wives. So they put a personal ad in a city newspaper. Some women in the city were not happy living alone. So they answered the ad by telephone. They wanted to find out more about the town and the men. But the women did not go to live in the town. They did not really want to work on farms. They did not really want to marry small-town men. So the men did not find wives. And the women are still alone. Not all men and women in Spain are like these people. But this ad may tell us something about larger problems in Spain.

Main idea _____

_____

3

Personal ads are usually written for good reasons. Most of the people who write them really do want a friend. But sometimes people write personal ads for other reasons. They may write the ad as a joke. This is not a nice thing to do. The people who answer the ads may be unhappy. They may need a friend very much. Some of the people who write the ads can cause worse problems. They may want to hurt someone. So, if you answer a personal ad, you should be careful. The ad may not mean what it says.

Main idea _____

_____

Exercise 6

Read each paragraph. Ask yourself, "What is the topic? What is the writer's idea about the topic?" Then write the main idea sentence.

1

"Black Thursday" is a day many Americans will never forget. It was October 24, 1929, the beginning of the Great Depression. Before that day, business in America was growing fast. Between 1914 and 1929, it grew about 62%. But on "Black Thursday" everything changed. On that day, American business suddenly stopped growing. In fact, many businesses stopped completely. The next few years of American history are called the Great Depression. These were terrible years for business and for the people. Five thousand banks and 85,000 businesses failed. Many people lost all their money. About 12 million Americans lost their jobs.

Main idea _____

_____

2

The Great Depression of the early 1930s surprised many people. They did not think American business could have such terrible problems. For a long time, they did not believe the problems were serious. Many businessmen hoped for better times soon. Even President Hoover did not think the Depression was serious. He told Americans in 1930 that the problems were already going away. But this was not true. Millions of Americans did not have jobs. Many of these people did not have homes or food. Life was hard for many Americans. And it did not get easier for many years.

Main idea _____

_____

3

The Great Depression finally ended for several reasons. One reason was a new government with new ideas. In 1932, Franklin D. Roosevelt became President of the United States. He made many changes in the laws to help people. New laws helped American banks and businesses. Other laws gave people jobs and housing. But Roosevelt's government was only one reason for the end of the Depression. The other reason was World War II. In the late 1930s, the United States began to get ready for the war. New factories were built for war planes and ships. That meant more jobs. These jobs gave many people a chance to change their lives.

Main idea _____

_____

Exercise 7

A. Read each paragraph. Ask yourself, "What is the topic? What is the writer's idea about the topic?" Then write the main idea sentence.

1

Population growth is a serious problem around the world. At the beginning of the 20th century there were about 1.5 billion people in the world. In 1984 the world population was 4.8 billion people. By the year 2000, it will be about 6.1 billion.

Main idea _____

2

This growth in population is not happening everywhere. For example, in Europe the population is not growing at all. Families in these countries are smaller now. Only about 2.1 children are born for every woman. The United States also has smaller families. Its population is only growing a little every year.

Main idea _____

3

But in other areas of the world, the population is growing very fast. This is true in parts of Africa, South America, and Asia. Countries in these areas have a difficult future ahead. Already, these countries have serious problems. First of all, food is a problem in many countries. Many people do not get enough to eat every day. There is not enough housing or work for everyone. Also, many people do not get education or medical care. A larger population will make all these problems worse.

Main idea _____

4

But there is some hope for change. It may be possible to slow down population growth. It happened in China, for example. In 1974, China's population was growing very fast. Then the people learned how to have smaller families. By 1984, the population was not growing fast anymore. This is an important change. China is the largest country in the world, with over one billion people. If China can make this change, maybe other countries can, too.

Main idea _____

B. 1. What is the topic of this page? _____

2. What is the main idea? _____

_____

Exercise 8

A. Read each paragraph. Ask yourself, "What is the topic? What is the writer's idea about the topic?" Then write the main idea sentence.

1

American cities changed in many ways after World War II. Many people moved out of the city. They moved to the suburbs, the areas around a city. Most of the people who moved were rich. Poor people usually did not have enough money to move. They stayed in the cities.

Main idea _____

2

During the 1950s and 60s there was another important change in American cities. Businesses began to leave the city, too. They left because the people in the city were poorer. Poor people do not have much money to buy things. So, many shops and restaurants moved out to the suburbs. People in the suburbs had more money to spend.

Main idea _____

3

Cities began to have many serious problems. The rich people and the businesses did not pay city taxes anymore. The poor people could not pay much money in taxes. So cities had less money for schools and housing. Sometimes they could not pay their police officers or firefighters. And they could not take good care of their streets and parks.

Main idea _____

4

But money was only part of the problem. Many people believed that American cities were dying. They had good reason to believe this. City streets were sadly empty. Many neighborhoods and parks were dirty and dangerous. In some places buildings were even falling down. And nobody seemed to care. This was the real problem. Most of the people and businesses with money were in the suburbs. They did not care what happened to the cities.

Main idea _____

B. 1. What is the topic of this page? _____

    2. What is the main idea? _____

    _____

Finding the Pattern of Organization

Study these pictures for 60 seconds. Your teacher will time you.

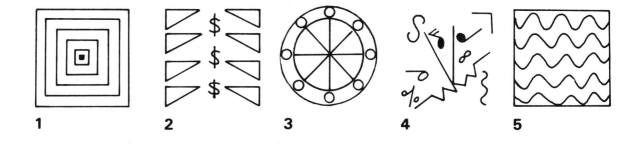

1 2 3 4 5

After 60 seconds, turn the page. Try to draw the pictures. Do not look back.

Try to remember the pictures. Draw them here.

Now look back and check your drawings.

Which picture was the most difficult to remember? _____

Why? _____

Pictures 1, 2, 3 and 5 were easy because they have a pattern. Picture 4 does not have a pattern, so it is more difficult to remember. In English, there are patterns, too. When you read, look for the patterns. They will help you understand and remember what you read.

There are many patterns in English. Writers often use these four patterns. Here are some examples:

1. Listing — Ways to travel:
    - plane
    - train
    - bus
    - ship

2. Time order — Wars in American history:
    - 1776 — American Revolution
    - 1812 — War of 1812
    - 1860 — Civil War
    - 1914 — World War I
    - 1940 — World War II

3. Cause-effect — Cause: heavy rain
    Effect: car accidents on the highway

4. Comparison — Comparing Paris and New York:
    How are they alike?
    - expensive
    - beautiful buildings
    - many art museums
    How are they different?
    - Paris is a capital city; New York is not a capital city
    - Paris is safer; New York is larger

LISTING

EXAMPLE A

Diamonds are very expensive for several reasons. First, they are difficult to find. They are only found in a few places in the world. Second, they are useful. People use diamonds to cut other stones. Third, diamonds do not change. They stay the same for millions of years. And finally, they are very beautiful.

What is the topic of this paragraph? _____

What is the main idea? _____

_____

The underlined words are signal words. They tell us about the author's pattern of organization. The signal word for this pattern is several. It tells us to look for a list.

This list tells us several reasons why diamonds are expensive. Write the reasons here:

_____

_____

_____

_____

It was easy to find the reasons. There is a signal word for each reason:

Signals	Reasons
first	difficult to find
second	useful
third	they do not change
finally	beautiful

What is the topic of this paragraph? _____

What is the main idea? _____

_____

What is the signal for this list? _____

Write the other signals. _____

Signals	Kinds of pollution
_____	air pollution
_____	water pollution
_____	pollution of the earth
_____	noise pollution

Here are some signal words for the listing pattern:

first   second   one   and   for example   or   some   many

third   other   another   also   finally   even   several

Exercise 1

Read each paragraph. Underline the signal words. Write the topic, the main idea and the pattern signal. Then list the other signal words and the details. The Answer Key is on page 264.

1

Computers are helpful in many ways. First, they are fast. They can work with information much more quickly than a person. Second, computers can work with lots of information at the same time. Third, they can keep information for a long time. They do not forget things the way people do. Also, computers are almost always correct. They are not perfect, of course, but they usually do not make mistakes.

a. Topic _____

b. Main idea _____

c. Pattern signal _____

Signals　　　　　　　　　　　　　**Details**

_____　　　_____

_____　　　_____

_____　　　_____

_____　　　_____

_____　　　_____

2

These days, it is important to know something about computers. There are a number of ways to learn. Some companies have computer classes at work. Also, most universities offer day and night courses in computer science. Another way to learn is from a book. There are many books about computers in book stores and libraries. Or, you can learn from a friend. After a few hours of practice, you too can work with computers. You may not be an expert, but you can have fun!

a. Topic _____

b. Main idea _____

c. Pattern signal _____

Signals　　　　　　　　　　　　　**Details**

_____　　　_____

_____　　　_____

_____　　　_____

_____　　　_____

_____　　　_____

Exercise 2

1

Today, computer companies sell many different programs for computers. First, there are programs for doing math problems. Second, there are programs for scientific studies. Third, some programs are like fancy typewriters. They are often used by writers and business people. Other programs are made for courses in schools and universities. And finally, there are programs for fun. There include word games and puzzles for children and adults.

a. Topic _____

b. Main idea _____

c. Pattern signal _____

Signals	Details
_____	_____
_____	_____
_____	_____
_____	_____
_____	_____

2

Computer language can be funny at times. For example, we say computers have a "memory." We know they do not really remember or think. But we still say "memory." Also, on many computer programs there is a "menu." Of course, we are not talking about restaurants or food. This is a different kind of menu. Another funny example is the "mouse" in some computers. It is hard not to think about a real mouse when you hear the word. But do not worry: there are no little gray animals in the machine.

a. Topic _____

b. Main idea _____

c. Pattern signal _____

Signals	Details
_____	_____
_____	_____
_____	_____
_____	_____
_____	_____

Exercise 3

1

The first computers were very large machines. Now computers come in all shapes and sizes. There are still big computers for companies or universities. There are other special computers for factories. These large computers tell the factory machines what to do. But there are also small personal computers to use at home or in an office. There are even computers in telephones, television sets, and cars. These computers have to be very small. They are so small you cannot even see all their parts.

a. Topic _____

b. Main idea _____

c. Pattern signal _____

Signals	Details
_____	_____
_____	_____
_____	_____
_____	_____
_____	_____

2

Computers are very useful, but they also can cause problems. One kind of problem is with the computer's memory. It is not perfect, so sometimes computers lose important information. Another problem is with the machinery. Computers are machines, and machines can break down. When computers break down, they may erase information, like chalk on a blackboard. Or they may stop doing anything at all. And there is another, different kind of problem with computers. Some doctors say they may be bad for your health. They say you should not work with computers all day.

a. Topic _____

b. Main idea _____

c. Pattern signal _____

Signals	Details
_____	_____
_____	_____
_____	_____
_____	_____
_____	_____

Exercise 4

1

Almost every profession now uses computers. They are used for all kinds of work. For example, scientists use them. So do mathematicians and economists. Business people use them to make business decisions. Doctors also use computers to help their patients. Computers make work easier for writers, too. And even students now use computers to help in their studies. Finally, some people use computers at home to help them make plans and pay bills.

a. Topic _____

b. Main idea _____

c. Pattern signal _____

Signals	Details
_____	_____
_____	_____
_____	_____
_____	_____
_____	_____
_____	_____

2

Everyone knows that computers are useful. And there are many wonderful new computer programs. But there are other reasons to like computers. Some people like the way computers hum and sing when they are working. It is a happy sound, like the sounds of toys and childhood. Computers also have lights and pretty pictures. With a computer anyone can feel like an artist. And computers even seem to have personalities. That may sound strange, but computers seem to have feelings. Sometimes they seem happy, sometimes they seem angry. It is easy to think they are like people.

a. Topic _____

b. Main idea _____

c. Pattern signal _____

Signals	Details
_____	_____
_____	_____
_____	_____
_____	_____
_____	_____

TIME ORDER

EXAMPLE A

Albert Einstein was born in 1879 in Ulm, Germany. He graduated from the University of Zurich in Switzerland in 1905. In 1905 he also did some of his most famous work in physics. In 1919 he won the Nobel Prize for Physics. Between 1919 and 1933 he lived in Germany and traveled a lot to talk to other scientists. Then in 1933 he had to leave Germany because of Hitler and the Nazi party. He moved to the United States. From 1933 until his death he lived in Princeton, New Jersey. He died on April 18, 1955.

What is the topic of this paragraph? _____

How can you tell this is a time order pattern? _____

You can tell because the signals in this paragraph are all dates. Each date points to an event in the life of Albert Einstein. Here are all the signals. Write the events:

Signals	Events
1879	_____
1905	_____
1905	_____
1919	_____
1919-1929	_____
1933	_____
1933-1955	_____
April 19, 1955	_____

EXAMPLE B

EXAMPLE B

This paragraph is about the same events as Example A. But the signal words are different.

Albert Einstein was born near the end of the 1800s, in Ulm, Germany. He graduated from the University of Zurich in Switzerland at age 26. That was also when he did his famous work in physics. Fourteen years later he won the Nobel Prize for Physics. For the next ten years he lived in Germany. He also traveled a lot to talk with other scientists. Then in the early 1930s he had to leave Germany because of Hitler and the Nazi Party. He moved to the United States. From that time until his death he lived in Princeton, New Jersey. He died at the age of 74.

Here are the signals. Write the events:

Signals	Events
near the end of the 19th century	_____
at the age of 26	_____
That was also when	_____
Fourteen years later	_____
For the next ten years	_____
In the early 1930s	_____
From that time until his death	_____
at the age of 74	_____

Dates are often signals for the time order pattern. Here are some other time order signal words:

first	next	soon	after	at last	finally	dates
last	later	before	while	then	times

Exercise 1

Read each passage. Write the topic and underline the signals. Then write the signals and the events on the lines. The Answer Key is on page 265.

1

The Vietnam War began soon after World War II. At first, in 1946, the war was between the Vietnamese and the French. The government was French, but many Vietnamese people did not want a French government. They wanted the French to leave so they could have their own government. The Vietnamese fought hard, and slowly they won more and more land. By 1953, the French army was in trouble. They were not winning the war. French soldiers were dying and the war was costing a lot of money. So, in 1954, the French army stopped fighting and left Vietnam. That was the end of the first part of the Vietnam War.

Topic _____

Signal	Events
_____	_____
_____	_____
_____	_____

2

The second part of the Vietnam War began in 1954. After the French army left, there were two Vietnams: North Vietnam and South Vietnam. There were also two governments. But both governments wanted to be the only government for all of Vietnam. So from 1954 until 1960, the North and the South were fighting all the time. The North Vietnamese grew slowly stronger. By the beginning of 1965, the North Vietnamese were winning the war. But the United States government did not want the North Vietnamese to win. So in March 1965, the United States began to help South Vietnam. They sent guns and airplanes to help the South. At first, the United States sent only a few soldiers. But by July 1965, there were about 75,000 American soldiers in Vietnam.

Topic _____

Signals	Events
_____	_____
_____	_____
_____	_____
_____	_____
_____	_____

Exercise 2

1

In 1965 the Vietnam War became an American war. That year, the United States sent airplanes with bombs over North Vietnam. The North Vietnamese were moving into South Vietnam and the United States government wanted to stop them. More and more bombs were used each year. The bombs killed thousands of North Vietnamese men, women, and children. Thousands more lost their homes and their land. The United States also sent more soldiers every year. By the end of 1967, there were almost 510,000 Americans in Vietnam. And still, the North Vietnamese were winning the war.

Topic _____

Signal	**Events**
_____	_____
_____	_____
_____	_____
_____	_____

2

In the United States, some people did not want the war. In the early 1960s only a few people felt this way. But by the late 1960s many people believed Americans should not be fighting in Vietnam. Finally, the American government had to listen to these people. In May 1968, the Americans began to talk to North Vietnam about stopping the war. For the next few months, fewer bombs were used against the North. By the end of the year, the bombing stopped. It still took a long time to end the war. American soldiers started to go home in 1970. The last Americans left three years later.

Topic _____

Signal	**Events**
_____	_____
_____	_____
_____	_____
_____	_____
_____	_____
_____	_____
_____	_____

Exercise 3

1

Anh Nguyen is Vietnamese. She was born in 1960 in Hue, a large city in South Vietnam. When she was four years old her family moved to Saigon. She finished grammar school in 1972, and then she went to high school. The first year of high school was a happy year for Anh. She liked her classes, especially French and English. In the fall, she won a prize for a French paper. That winter she decided she wanted to go to study in France. Anh dreamed about France all year. She studied very hard for her French class, and in the spring she did very well on her examinations.

Topic _____

Signal	**Events**
_____	_____
_____	_____
_____	_____
_____	_____
_____	_____
_____	_____

2

But Anh had to change all her plans because of the war. In 1973, life in Saigon was changing. The American soldiers were leaving. The war did not stop after the American soldiers left. But the South Vietnamese did not have a strong army anymore. They could not stop the North Vietnamese. In 1974, the North Vietnamese army moved into Saigon. That was the end of South Vietnam. It was also the end of the old life for Anh. For Anh and for others, there were new troubles that year. Food, clothing, and other things became more expensive. Sometimes the shops were empty. But there were worse troubles. Anh's father was taken away from his family because he once worked for the Americans. She never saw him again.

Topic _____

Signal	**Events**
_____	_____
_____	_____
_____	_____

Exercise 4

The next few years were unhappy and difficult for Anh. At first she continued to go to school. But she did not enjoy it anymore. She could not study English or French. After a while she stopped going to school and started working in a factory. Her family needed money and there were no other jobs. But she did not like factory work.

At last she decided she had to do something. She did not want to work in a factory all her life. She wanted an education. She wanted a more interesting job. So she decided to leave Vietnam and go to the United States. Other Vietnamese people had the same idea. In fact, from 1974 to 1976, hundreds of thousands of Vietnamese left their country.

The day came for Anh to say goodbye to her family. She did not know if she was going to see them again. She walked many miles to a small town by the ocean. She and about 40 other people got into a small boat. They left Vietnam at night.

For several days they sailed with no trouble. But the wind stopped and the boat stopped moving. They did not have enough food or water. Some people began to get sick. A boat came near them but it did not stop to help them.

Finally a large Japanese ship came near. It stopped and picked up all the Vietnamese. They were almost all very sick, including Anh. The ship took them to a camp in the Philippine Islands. This was a special camp for Vietnamese people. It was crowded in the camp, but Anh felt safe.

Anh had a cousin who lived in the United States. She wrote to him right away, and she asked if she could stay with him and his family in Boston. He wrote back and said yes. She showed his letter to the United States immigration office. She was ready to apply for an American visa. But she still had to wait many months for the visa. While she was waiting, she took English classes and studied hard.

Finally, almost one year later, she got her visa. A refugee group gave her a plane ticket and some money. She was ready at last to start her new life.

Topic _____

Signal	Events
_____	_____
_____	_____
_____	_____
_____	_____
_____	_____
_____	_____
_____	_____
_____	_____
_____	_____
_____	_____
_____	_____

Exercise 5

Anh arrived in Boston in December, 1979. She had only her suit-case and her English dictionary. The only person she knew in the United States was her cousin Pho. He and his wife To-van were there to meet her at the airport. She was very happy to see them!

That evening Anh asked Pho and To-Van many questions. She wanted to know about Boston and about Americans. She was surprised that To-van often could not answer her questions. To-van's friends were all Vietnamese people. She shopped only at the Vietnamese stores in their neighborhood. She worked at Pho's Vietnamese restaurant nearby. So To-van did not know much about Boston, and she did not speak English very well.

That night Anh made a decision before she went to sleep. She decided that she did not want to be like To-van. She wanted to speak English well. She wanted to go to school with Americans and she wanted to work with them. Of course she did not want to forget about Vietnam. But she wanted to be part of her new country.

It was not easy. There were many new things in her life. The first winter in Boston seemed very cold to Anh. In January, she started studying at the high school. English was a serious problem. She could not understand her teachers and they could not understand her. Anh often felt very unhappy and alone. Her old home in Saigon seemed very far away and she missed her family terribly.

But by summer the worst times were over for Anh. Her English was much better, and she began to make some friends at school. For the next two years she studied very hard. In math, science, and French she was the best student in her class. She won a prize for a chemistry experiment.

But, best of all, at the end of her last year of high school, she won a scholarship to college. The scholarship was very important to Anh. She needed the money to go to college. Going to college was the key to success, she knew. Finally Anh had a plan. She planned to study science and computers in college. After college she could get a good job. She could earn money and send it to her mother. Then her mother could come to the United States, too. It seemed a long time to wait. But Anh knew she could do it! And she did.

Topic _____

Signal	Events
_____	_____
_____	_____
_____	_____
_____	_____
_____	_____
_____	_____
_____	_____
_____	_____
_____	_____

CAUSE AND EFFECT

This pattern is not always easy to understand. These sentences show examples of causes and effects.

> **EXAMPLE**
>
> Shoes with high heels <u>can cause</u> foot problems.
>
> What is the <u>cause</u> of foot problems? *Shoes with high heels.*
> What is the effect of shoes with high heels? *Foot problems.*
> What are the signal words? *can cause*

Exercise 1

Find the cause and the effect in each sentence. Underline the signal words. The Answer Key is on page 266.

1. Exercise can make you hungry and thirsty.
   Cause _____ Effect _____

2. Many car accidents happen because of ice and snow on the road.
   Cause _____ Effect _____

3. Bad food and not enough sleep are two reasons for bad health.
   Cause _____ Effect _____

4. Many doctors today believe that smoking cigarettes may lead to cancer.
   Cause _____ Effect _____

5. Some people become nervous because of drinking coffee.
   Cause _____ Effect _____

6. Many fires in homes are due to careless smokers.
   Cause _____ Effect _____

7. Heart disease is sometimes the result of eating too much.
   Cause _____ Effect _____

8. Very bright sunlight can cause your eyes to hurt.
   Cause _____ Effect _____

9. High insurance costs are one result of car accidents.
   Cause _____ Effect _____

10. Serious family problems can cause illness.
    Cause _____ Effect _____

EXAMPLE A

In this paragraph look for one cause and several effects. The signals are underlined.

A cold winter causes serious problems in Florida. It has a bad effect on farming. The farmers there grow a lot of oranges. Very cold weather can cause orange trees to die. Cold weather also results in fewer tourists. There are many hotels and vacation places in Florida. These places are in trouble if there are fewer tourists. And finally, very cold weather can cause health problems. Many people do not have heating in their homes. So they can become ill from the cold.

Topic: the effects of cold weather in Florida

Cause	Signals	Effects
cold weather	causes	problems
	can cause	orange trees to die
	results in	fewer tourists
	can cause	health problems

EXAMPLE B

In this paragraph look for many causes and one effect. The signal words are underlined.

There are many different causes of car accidents in the United States. Sometimes accidents are caused by bad weather. Ice or snow can make roads very dangerous. Accidents also can result from problems with the car. Even a small problem like a flat tire can be serious. Bad roads are another cause of accidents. Some accidents happen because the driver falls asleep. And finally, some accidents are caused by drinking too much alcohol. In fact, this is one of the most important causes of accidents.

Topic: the cause of car accidents in the United States

Causes	Signals	Effects
bad weather	are caused by	car accidents
car problems	result from	
bad roads	cause of	
driver falls asleep	because	
drinking alcohol	are caused by	

Some cause and effect signal words:

because	results in	is a cause of	is the result of
because of	can make	had an effect on	is the reason for
lead to	causes	effects	
can help	can stop	due to	

Exercise 2

Write the topic for each paragraph. Underline the signal words. Write the causes and effects on the lines.

1

Most people do not think of coffee as a drug. But, in fact, it is a drug and it has important effects on your body. Some of the effects are good and some are not. Coffee can help you stay awake when you are driving or working. But it can also keep you awake at night when you want to sleep. Coffee makes some people feel more alive so they can work better. Other people feel too nervous when they drink coffee. After a large meal, coffee can help your stomach. But too much coffee can cause a stomachache.

Topic: _____

Causes	Signals	Effects
_____	_____	_____
_____	_____	_____
_____	_____	_____
_____	_____	_____
_____	_____	_____
_____	_____	_____

2

Aspirin is a simple drug. It has many useful effects. It can stop a headache or an earache. It helps take away pain in the fingers or knees. Aspirin can stop a fever if you have the flu. Or it can make you feel better if you have a cold. Some doctors believe that aspirin also can result in a healthy heart. They say that some people should take an aspirin every day. For those people, aspirin may stop heart disease.

Topic: _____

Causes	Signals	Effects
_____	_____	_____
_____	_____	_____
_____	_____	_____
_____	_____	_____
_____	_____	_____
_____	_____	_____

Exercise 3

Write the topic for each paragraph. Underline the signal words. Write the causes and the effects on the lines.

1

Scientists and doctors say that about 34 million Americans are too fat. Why is this? One cause is the kind of food Americans eat. Many Americans like "fast foods." These foods (such as hamburgers and ice cream) often have fattening things in them. Another cause is the way Americans eat. They often eat little snacks between regular meals. These extra foods add extra fat on the body. A third cause is not enough exercise. Americans like driving everywhere, instead of walking. They often have machines to do a lot of the work. Some Americans are also too heavy because of health problems. But for most of those 34 million Americans, the problem is the American lifestyle.

Topic: _____

Causes	Signals	Effects
_____	_____	_____
_____	_____	_____
_____	_____	_____
_____	_____	_____

2

If you are too fat, you may have serious problems with your health. A group of doctors wrote a report about some of the effects of too much fat. One important effect is on the heart. If you are fat, your heart has to work harder. This may lead to a heart attack. Or it may lead to other heart problems. Extra fat can also change the amount of sugar in your blood. This can cause serious diseases such as diabetes. High blood pressure is another possible result of being fat. Even cancer can sometimes be a result. More studies are needed about all these problems. But one thing is clear: extra fat may make your life shorter.

Topic: _____

Causes	Signals	Effects
_____	_____	_____
_____	_____	_____
_____	_____	_____
_____	_____	_____
_____	_____	_____

Exercise 4

Write the topic for each paragraph. Underline the signal words. Write the causes and the effects on the lines.

1

Some people become very unhappy and ill every winter. Doctors used to think this problem was in their minds. But doctors are learning some new facts about this. Now they think that winter really does cause problems for some people. In the wintertime the days are short and often cloudy. People do not get enough light in the winter. This may cause illness and unhappiness.

Topic: _____

Causes	Signals	Effects
_____	_____	_____
_____	_____	_____

2

In the United States, poor city children are often ill because of their diet. Some children do not get enough food. Sometimes they do not get healthy food. Poor health is also caused by bad housing. The apartments may not have heat in the winter or fresh air in the summer. Poor health may also be the result of dirty water. Or it may be caused by crowded apartments and crowded schools.

Topic: _____

Causes	Signals	Effects
_____	_____	_____
_____	_____	_____
_____	_____	_____
_____	_____	_____
_____	_____	_____

COMPARISON

Compare an apple and an orange:

How are they alike?
>   *Both* are kinds of fruit.
>   *Both* are round.
>   *Both* have skins.
>   *Both* taste good.

How are they different?
>   They are *different* colors.
>   They taste *different.*
>   Oranges grow in *warm* places. Apples grow in *cool* places.
>   Sometimes oranges *do not have seeds.* Apples always *have seeds.*

Compare the United States and Canada:

How are they both alike?
>   *Both* are in North America.
>   *Both* have many people from around the world.
>   *Both* are very large countries.
>   *Both* have land on the Atlantic and the Pacific oceans
>   *Both* countries were once part of the British Empire.

How are they different?
>   Canada has two official languages, *but* the United States has only one.
>   The United States has *more* people *than* Canada.
>   Canada has *more* land in the north *than* the United States
>   Canada is a *younger* country *than* the United States.

Compare your country and the United States:

How are they alike?

How are they different?

Some comparison signal words:

Words to show likenesses; alike, similar, same, also

Words to show difference: different, unlike, more than, less than, but, however

---

EXAMPLE A

This paragraph tells only how two fruits are alike. Underline the signal words.

Lemons and limes are very similar kinds of fruit. They are both grown in warm places. They both have hard skins and soft insides. People do not usually eat whole lemons and limes. That is because both of these fruits have a very sour taste. They are often used in cooking desserts and main dishes. People make juice from lemons and also from limes. Finally, both fruits have a lot of vitamin C in them.

What is this paragraph comparing? _____

Likenesses	Signals
grown in warm countries	both
hard skins and soft insides	both
have a sour taste	both of
used in cooking	They are used
people make juice from them	and also
they have a lot of vitamin C	both

EXAMPLE B

This paragraph tells some ways lemons and limes are different. Underline the signal words.

Lemons and limes are both citrus fruits, but they are quite different. First of all, the color is different. Lemons are yellow. Limes are green. The taste is different, too. Also, lemons are grown all over the world. But limes are grown in only a few places. This is because lemons are an old kind of fruit. But limes are new. They are really a special kind of lemon. Scientists made them from lemons only about 50 years ago.

What is this paragraph comparing? _____

Differences	Signals
color	different
taste	different
where they are grown	But
lemons are old; limes are new	But

Exercise 1

Underline the signals in each paragraph. Write the likenesses and differences on the lines. The answer key is on page 268.

1

Peter and Joe are roommates in Chicago. They both like to cook good meals and have dinner parties. But they have very different ideas about what to cook. Peter likes to cook lots of simple food. His favorite foods are steak, potatoes, and apple pie. But Joe prefers special dishes from far-away places. He likes to cook curries from India and sushi from Japan. Dinner at Peter and Joe's apartment is always delicious.

What is the paragraph comparing? _____

Differences   **Likenesses**

_____   _____

_____   _____

2

Poland and Italy may seem like very different countries. And of course, they are different in some ways. Poland is in the north of Europe, but Italy is in the south. Poland has a communist government, but Italy has a democratic government. However, there are also similarities. In both countries, the most important religion is Catholicism. In both Italy and Poland, history is very important to the people. And finally, both the Italians and the Polish are famous for their friendliness and good spirit.

What is this paragraph comparing? _____

Differences   **Likenesses**

_____   _____

_____   _____

_____   _____

_____   _____

Exercise 2

Underline the signal words in each paragraph. Write the likenesses and differences on the lines.

1

The food in India is similar to the food in China. First of all, in both countries, rice is a very important food. It is served at almost every meal in India and China. Indian and Chinese cooking can be very spicy. And they are also alike because they both use many different vegetables. In both countries, the meat dish is not always the most important dish. Finally, these are both very large countries with long histories. So both include many different kinds of cooking. In India and China, each part of the country has its own favorite kinds of food and way of cooking.

What is this paragraph comparing? _____

Likenesses

_____

_____

_____

_____

_____

2

People used to have very different ways of eating in Europe. Now everyone uses forks, knives, and spoons. But a thousand years ago, no one used forks at the table. They used only spoons and knives. Today most Europeans do not eat with their fingers. But back then many people picked up their food in their hands. In those days most people did not use glasses for drinking. Instead they drank from bowls or large wooden cups.

What is this paragraph comparing? _____

Differences

_____

_____ _____

_____

_____

_____

Exercise 3

Underline the signal words in each paragraph. Write the likenesses and differences on the lines.

1

In some ways English breakfasts are very similar to American breakfasts. In both countries people usually eat large breakfasts. English and American breakfasts both include several dishes. They may include some fruit juice, cereal, and then eggs and toast. In both places, there may also be some meat with the breakfast. However, there are also some differences between American and English breakfasts. In England, people usually drink tea in the morning. However, most Americans prefer coffee. The English usually do not eat sweet things for breakfast, but many Americans like sweet bread or coffee cake.

What is this paragraph comparing? _____

Likenesses	**Differences**
_____	_____
_____	_____
_____	_____
_____	_____

2

American breakfasts are very different from breakfasts in Italy. In general, American breakfasts are much larger than Italian breakfasts. Americans may eat several different foods for breakfast. They may eat cereal and eggs and toast. But Italians usually just have bread and coffee. Many Americans also like to eat some kind of meat. Italians almost never eat meat early in the morning. Finally, American coffee is different from Italian coffee. Americans do not drink strong coffee in the morning. Italians always like their coffee strong and dark.

What is the paragraph comparing? _____

Differences

_____

_____

_____

_____

_____

Exercise 4

Underline the signals in each paragraph. Write the likenesses and differences on the lines.

1

Shopping for food in the United States today is not the same as it used to be. Fifty years ago every neighborhood had a little food market. Now every neighborhood has a big supermarket. These are very different places. The old markets were usually small and friendly. People from the neighborhood often stopped there to hear the news or to talk. However, this is not true in supermarkets. Supermarkets are very large and not very friendly. They are not good places for meeting friends or talking. People in supermarkets always seem to be tired and in a hurry. Often they are not very polite.

What is this paragraph comparing? _____

Differences

_____

_____

_____

_____

_____

_____

2

Medical care is very different in England and in the United States. In England medical care is national. That means the government pays for all medical care. But in the United States it is private. That means each person pays for their own medical care. English doctors, dentists and hospitals are free. But in the United States they are all very expensive. Everyone in England gets medical care, even the poor people. It is not like this in the United States. Only Americans with a lot of money can pay for good medical care. Poor Americans sometimes get help from the government and sometimes they do not.

What is this paragraph comparing? _____

Differences

_____

_____

_____

_____

_____

_____

Exercise 1   USING ALL FOUR PATTERNS

For each paragraph, decide what the pattern is (listing, time order, comparison, or cause-effect). Write the name of that pattern. Then read the extra sentences at the bottom of the page. Find the sentence that fits the pattern best. Write the letter of that sentence beside the paragraph.

1. ____   The kitchen in Linda's new house had many problems. The first problem was the sink. The water did not go down the drain. And finally, there was also a problem with the refrigerator. Water came pouring out and it made a terrible mess.

Pattern _____

2. ____   Linda had a terrible time in her new house last week. On Monday, the sink was not draining well. She had to call the repair company. Next, on Wednesday, the stove broke. The repair person had to come back to her house. The repair person spent many hours working in Linda's house that week.

Pattern _____

3. ____   Linda thought the problem with the stove was serious. But then she found out that the refrigerator problem was worse. The stove was not easy to fix. But the refrigerator was much more difficult. It was also much more expensive to fix the refrigerator.

Pattern _____

4. ____   Linda had a difficult week because of all the problems in her house. She couldn't cook any food because the stove did not work. And then, all her food was ruined because her refrigerator broke. She had to throw it all away. Linda was very upset. She almost decided to sell her new house.

Pattern _____

Sentences:

a. The refrigerator problem was also much messier than the sink problem.

b. And then, on Friday, the refrigerator made a terrible mess.

c. Linda decided to buy a new stove and a new refrigerator.

d. Another problem was with the stove. It did not get very hot.

e. She could not wash her dishes because of the broken sink.

Exercise 2

For each paragraph, decide what the pattern is. Write the name of that pattern. Then read the extra sentences at the bottom of the page. Find the sentence that fits the pattern best. Write the letter of that sentence beside the paragraph.

1. _____   Shakespeare was born in Stratford-on-Avon on April 16, 1564. For a few years he studied at a school near home. He moved to London when he was still young. By the age of 35, he was already a well-known writer.

Pattern _____

2. _____   Two great writers were born in England in 1564. One was William Shakespeare. The other was Christopher Marlowe. Shakespeare lived until the age of 52. But Marlowe died suddenly when he was only 29. Both were famous in their time and both are still loved today.

Pattern _____

3. _____   Many people ask why Shakespeare was so great. He was a genius, of course. He had many ideas about life and he had a wonderful way with words. But Shakespeare was also great because he lived at the right time. The English, in those days, were interested in new ideas. They loved plays and poetry.

Pattern _____

4. _____   Shakespeare wrote three kinds of plays. One kind of play was the history play. Another kind was the tragedy, such as "Macbeth."

Pattern _____

Sentences:

a. At the age of 18, he married Ann Hathaway.

b. He also wrote many comedies, such as "A Midsummer Night's Dream."

c. Shakespeare wrote many plays and some poetry. But Marlowe only finished four plays.

d. A genius like Shakespeare had a chance to use his great mind.

e. Some people think Shakespeare's plays were written by someone else.

Using Reference Words _____

Writers do not like to use the same word many times. They often use other words which mean almost the same thing.

PRONOUNS

Sometimes pronouns are used instead of nouns. They are small words, but they are very important when you are reading. You will understand more if you pay attention to pronouns.

he	she	it	they	we	you
I	them	him	her	these	those

In these Examples, the pronouns are underlined:

EXAMPLE A

Mary Simms lives in New York City. <u>She</u> has an apartment near Central Park. Mary jogs in the park. <u>She</u> thinks that jogging is good for <u>her</u>. So <u>she</u> jogs three times a week.

All the underlined pronouns take the place of the noun, Mary Simms. "Mary Simms" is called the referent.

EXAMPLE B

Jogging is good for your health for a few reasons. <u>It</u> is especially good for your heart. If you do <u>it</u> a few days a week, your heart will be stronger. <u>It</u> is also good for your legs. And many people believe <u>it</u> is good for your mind.

All of the underlined pronouns take the place of the noun _____ .

_____ is the referent.

Exercise 1

In these sentences, the pronouns are underlined. Circle the referent. The Answer Key is on page 269.

1. Running is not a new sport. People were doing <u>it</u> hundreds of years ago.
2. Runners know that a good diet is important. <u>They</u> eat very healthy foods, especially before a race.
3. Every year, there are many long races in many parts of the world. Sports fans watch <u>them</u> on television.
4. The Boston race is called the Boston Marathon. <u>This</u> is one of the oldest races in the United States.
5. In some races, the winners get large amounts of money. But for almost 100 years, <u>they</u> got no money at all in the Boston race.
6. In 1985, more than 6,000 people ran in the Boston Marathon. <u>They</u> came from all over the world.

Exercise 2

In this passage, the pronouns are underlined. Write the pronouns and their referents on the lines below.

The Boston Marathon

Every year, in the middle of April, thousands of people go to Boston. <u>They</u> go to run the Boston Marathon. <u>This</u> is one of the oldest road races in the United States. <u>It</u> began in 1897.

Each year, more runners join the Boston Marathon. <u>They</u> come from every part of the world. In 1984, 6,164 runners from 34 different countries ran in the Marathon. About 5,290 of <u>them</u> finished <u>it</u>.

The Boston race is 26.2 miles, or 42 kilometers. The runners go through thirteen towns during the race. <u>It</u> ends in the center of Boston. Crowds of people watch <u>them</u> as <u>they</u> go through the towns. <u>They</u> clap <u>their</u> hands and cheer for <u>them</u>.

Pronouns	Referents
_____	_____
_____	_____
_____	_____
_____	_____
_____	_____
_____	_____
_____	_____
_____	_____
_____	_____
_____	_____

Exercise 3

In this passage, the pronouns are underlined. Write the pronouns and their referents on the lines below.

Jogging is a very popular activity in New York City. In the winter, the weather is too cold for <u>it</u>. But in the spring, <u>it</u> is warmer, and many New Yorkers go out to jog in Central Park. <u>This</u> is a very good place to run.

Other New Yorkers also like to go to Central Park. Many of <u>them</u> go there with their dogs. Dogs can run in the park. Sometimes the dogs run after the joggers. <u>They</u> may try to bite <u>them</u>. So the joggers sometimes kick the dogs or throw stones at <u>them</u>. The dog owners do not understand. <u>They</u> wonder why the joggers do not like dogs. The park police are trying to solve this problem. <u>They</u> want all of the people to use the park in peace.

Pronouns   **Referents**

_____   _____

_____   _____

_____   _____

_____   _____

_____   _____

_____   _____

_____   _____

_____   _____

Exercise 4

There are 17 pronouns in this passage. Write the pronouns and their referents below.

Mary Simms and Jim Fuller went jogging in Central Park last Saturday. They ran into a problem: a large white dog. It ran after them and tried to bite their legs.

They were scared and did not know what to do. Mary took a big stick and tried to hit the dog. She wanted to scare it away. But the dog just barked at her.

Then Jim threw a large rock at the animal. It hit the dog on the head.

The dog's owner was very angry.

"Stop hurting my dog!" she shouted. "It will not hurt you. It is just a puppy."

Then she took a large stick and tried to hit Mary and Jim.

Just then, a park police officer came along the path. He saw them fighting.

"This is terrible!" he said. "Stop fighting!"

Pronouns	Referents
_____	_____
_____	_____
_____	_____
_____	_____
_____	_____
_____	_____
_____	_____
_____	_____
_____	_____
_____	_____
_____	_____
_____	_____
_____	_____
_____	_____
_____	_____
_____	_____
_____	_____

Sometimes pronouns can take the place of a group of words.

EXAMPLE A

The Central Park police officer often meets dangerous people. Some people go to the park to steal. Other people are there to sell drugs. And sometimes serious gun fights start in the park. The park police officer may meet any of these in the park.

Pronouns   **Referents**

these   people who steal
                                      people who sell drugs
                                      peope who start gunfights

---

EXAMPLE B

It is not easy to be the mayor of a large American city. Many people need homes and jobs. The buildings and streets need to be fixed. The schools are old, and the students are not learning enough. The streets are dangerous at night because of crime. These are big problems, and the mayor must work on all of them.

Pronouns   **Referents**

These

them

Exercise 5

In these passages, the pronouns are underlined. Circle the referents.

1. Running on a very hot day can be dangerous. It can cause serious illness.

2. Runners often wear special shoes, socks, shorts, and shirts. These are all important. But runners agree that shoes are the most important.

3. If you go to Central Park, you will see joggers, dogs, and bicyclists. They are all part of life in the park.

Exercise 6

The pronouns in these passages are underlined. Circle the referents.

1. Two Frenchmen went up in a basket under a balloon. They built a fire to make the air hot. This made the balloon stay up in the air.

2. The pilot of a balloon can control its altitude. He can raise and lower the balloon to find a good wind direction. That is how a good pilot can control where the balloon goes.

3. Early photographers had to carry film and heavy equipment everywhere they went. But this did not stop them.

4. Hellen Keller was deaf and blind. She could not speak until she was seven year old. But these problems did not stop her. She became a famous writer and teacher.

5. A tornado is a very dangerous storm. It brings strong winds and it travels very fast. The strong winds can blow over cars, destroy houses, and kill people. And this happens in just a few minutes.

6. Tornadoes blow dust and dirt into the air. They make a cone shape in the sky. When people see this, they get ready for the storm.

7. When tornadoes touch the ground, they move along at about 35 to 45 kilometers per hour. No one knows which way they will go.

8. In a small town, a tornado can destroy a street full of homes and stores. Many people can be killed. The government tries to help when this happens.

9. Tornadoes are common in the middle part of the United States. Kansas, Arkansas, Nebraska, Iowa, and Missouri are states with many tornadoes every year. People in those states worry when they see a cone-shaped cloud in the sky.

10. The wind of a tornado is strong. No one knows exactly how fast the wind is in the center. The wind always breaks the machines used for measuring it!

RELATED WORDS: SPECIFIC TO GENERAL

Related words are words which refer to the same idea.

EXAMPLE A

David had a wonderful trip to Paris this spring. He loved the beautiful buildings in the <u>French capital</u>. To him, it was a <u>city</u> full of magic and beauty.

What does "French capital" refer to? _____

What does "city" refer to? _____

"French capital," "city," and "Paris" are related words.

EXAMPLE B

The Pope visited Colombia, Peru, and Mexico last year. Crowds of Catholics greeted him in <u>these countries</u>. It was his first visit to <u>that part of the world</u>.

What does "these countries" refer to? _____

_____

What does "that part of the world" refer to? _____

_____

Both phrases are related to _____

_____

When writers use related words, the second word is usually less specific, and the next is even more general.

EXAMPLE C

French capital, Paris, city

1. Specific: Paris
2. Less specific: French capital
3. General: city

EXAMPLE D

Colombia, Peru, and Mexico; that part of the world; these countries

1. Specific: Colombia, Peru, and Mexico
2. Less specific: these countries
3. General: that part of the world.

Exercise 1

Put these related words in order from specific to general. Put number 1 above the most specific word. Put number 2 above the less specific word. And put number 3 above the most general word. The first one is done for you. The Answer Key is on page 270.

           3   1   2

1. Music, rock music, twentieth-century music

2. Japanese mountain, Mount Fuji, mountain

3. problems, water pollution problems, pollution problems

4. pine tree, evergreen tree, tree

5. musicians, Michael Jackson, popular musicians

6. Nicaragua, country, central American country

7. man, Dr. Diamond, dentist

8. place, Boston, city

9. *The New York Times*, newspaper, reading material

10. group, Diamond family, people

11. storm, tornado, wind storm

12. president, person, political leader

13. shirt, white shirt, clothing

14. flute, musical instrument, wind instrument

15. company, IBM corporation, organization

Exercise 2

In each passage, there is a word underlined. Find and circle the related words in the passage. The first one is done for you.

1. Liz and Val moved to (Paris) last month. They like the city very much.

2. Hiroko plays the violin in the Boston Symphony Orchestra. The sound of this stringed instrument is very special.

3. The president of the city council gave a long speech. As the leader, she has to plan many new projects.

4. The tornado hit a small town in Kansas. The storm swept down the main street. The terrible winds caused five stores to fall down.

5. Lemons, limes, and oranges are all very good to eat. These citrus fruits are also very healthy for you. They are a good source of vitamin C.

6. Many Americans skip breakfast. They say they do not have time for food in the morning. But this is a mistake. The human body needs that meal.

7. Joanne's big car uses a lot of gasoline. She has to stop often to fill the tank with fuel.

8. We saw a lion with three little cubs at the wild animal park. The cats were lying on the rocks in the warm afternoon sun. We were happy to see such wonderful animals in such a nice place.

9. In some countries, the winter is long and cold. It is not a very popular season. Some people are so unhappy at that time of the year, that they get sick.

10. Astronauts from the United States and the Soviet Union all have one problem: they get motion sickness. This illness makes it difficult to do their work. Doctors and scientists are working on this problem.

Exercise 3

Look back at Exercise 2B. Write the related words from each passage in order, from specific to general. The first one is done for you.

1. Paris

   city

2.

3.

4.

5.

6.

7.

8.

9.

10.

Skimming _____

Speed is often very important when you are reading. You may have a lot to read, but not much time. For this kind of reading you usually do not want to know and remember everything. You only want to find out something about it. You can do this by skimming.

You may want to skim:

- newspaper or magazine articles.
- book covers in a book store (so you can find out if you want to buy the book).
- library books (so you can find out if they have the information you need).
- mystery, detective or other novels.

SKIMMING FOR POINT OF VIEW

Skimming is helpful when you want to find out quickly about the writer. You may want to find out what the writer thinks about some idea. This is the writer's *point of view*.

When you want to know the point of view you do not need to read everything. You only need to read a few important words.

EXAMPLE A

Dogs are often a <u>problem</u> at home. Many dogs are <u>noisy</u> and <u>dirty</u>. They may even be <u>dangerous</u> for small children.

Does this writer like dogs at home? <u>no</u>

You do not need to read all the sentences to learn this. You only have to read the words "problem," "noisy," "dirty" and "dangerous." From those words you can tell the writer's point of view. This writer is <u>against</u> dogs at home.

EXAMPLE B

An apartment looks much nicer with some plants. The green leaves make it seem cooler in summer. The flowers give it a happy feeling.

Does this writer like plants in an apartment? _____

How do you know this? List the important words: _____

_____

Exercise 1

Read these sentences very quickly. Ask yourself, "Is the writer for or against the idea?" Then make a check beside the answer. You should finish the page in less than 60 seconds. Time yourself. The Answer Key is on page 270.

Starting Time _____

1. Candy is not good for your teeth. It is especially bad for children's teeth. If children eat a lot of candy, they will have problems later.

   For _____ Against _____

2. Large cars can cause problems. They are more difficult to park than small cars. They also use more gas.

   For _____ Against _____

3. In San Francisco, the air is always a comfortable temperature. It is never too hot or too cold. It is perfect weather all year.

   For _____ Against _____

4. Some people take many vitamin pills every day. These people believe lots of vitamin pills are good for their health. But they are wrong. Too many vitamin pills can hurt you health.

   For _____ Against _____

5. There is something sad about animals in the zoos. They never really look happy. Maybe they are thinking about their real home. Maybe they do not like people looking at them all the time.

   For _____ Against _____

6. Computers are very helpful for all kinds of work. They are usually quicker and more correct than people.

   For _____ Against _____

7. Computers may cause serious problems in our world. Now it is possible to keep a lot of information on a computer. The people who have that information may be dangerous.

   For _____ Against _____

8. "A spoonful of sugar helps the medicine go down." This is from a popular song, but it is often true. Sometimes there are good reasons to give children sugar or candy.

   For _____ Against _____

Finishing Time _____

Exercise 2

Read these sentences very quickly. Ask yourself, "Is the writer for or against the idea?" Then make a check beside the answer. You should finish the page in less than 60 seconds. Time yourself.

Starting Time _____

1. Many people believe that meat is an important food to eat. It is not true. You do not need to eat meat at all. In fact, you may be more healthy if you do not eat meat.

   For _____ Against _____

2. Travel is not always fun. Often there are problems with transportation, language or hotels. It is also very tiring to travel, and you can easily get sick.

   For _____ Against _____

3. Today it is better not to have a camera when you travel. A camera is heavy and difficult to carry. It is also not necessary. You can buy good picture postcards almost everywhere.

   For _____ Against _____

4. A bicycle is the best way to see a country. It does not need gas. It is not expensive. And you also get some exercise at the same time you are traveling.

   For _____ Against _____

5. Bicycles can be very dangerous. You can hurt yourself by falling off the bicycle. You can also get seriously hurt if you are hit by a car.

   For _____ Against _____

6. Everyone should learn another language. A second language is very useful these days. It also may teach you something about other people and places.

   For _____ Against _____

7. It is not easy to move to another country. There may be problems with language or culture. It may be difficult to find a job or a place to live. And in another country, you do not have family or friends to help.

   For _____ Against _____

8. Music often makes you feel better about life. It can make you happy if you are sad. It can make you relax when you are nervous.

   For _____ Against _____

Finishing Time _____

SKIMMING FOR PATTERN OF ORGANIZATION

Sometimes you need to find out quickly how a book or article is organized. You want to know its pattern. You do not need to know the details for this. You do not need to read all the words. You only have to read the signal words and they will tell you about the pattern.

EXAMPLE A.

A whale eats a lot of ocean food every day. That is <u>because</u> it is a very large animal.

What is the pattern of organization for this passage? Make a check beside the best answer.

____ listing   ____ time-order
____ comparison-contrast   ____ cause-effect

The pattern is <u>cause-effect</u>.

What is (are) the signal word(s)? <u>because</u>

EXAMPLE B.

The book has a lot of information about Poland. First it tells about the history. It also explains how to travel around the country. And finally, it lists some interesting places to visit.

What is the pattern of organization for this passage? Make a check beside the best answer.

____ listing   ____ time-order
____ comparison   ____ cause-effect

The pattern is <u>cause-effect</u>.

What is (are) the signal word(s)? <u>First, also, And finally</u>

Exercise 1

Read these sentences quickly. Read only to find the pattern of organization. Make a check beside the best answer. Try to finish the page in less than 60 seconds. Time yourself.

Starting Time_____

1. A parakeet is a small bird that lives in southern forests. The parrot is similar to a parakeet, but it is larger. Both birds sometimes can learn how to say words.

   ____ listing   ____ time-order
   ____ comparison   ____ cause-effect

2. Some kinds of birds cannot fly. The penguin is one of these birds. It lives mostly in the very cold Antarctic climate. Another kind of bird that cannot fly is the ostrich. It lives in Africa.

   _____ listing   _____ time-order
   _____ comparison   _____ cause-effect

3. Lisa plans to travel in Europe this summer. In June she will visit Sicily. Then in July, she will bicycle in northern Italy. In August she will travel through France. By September, she hopes to be in Paris.

   _____ listing   _____ time-order
   _____ comparison   _____ cause-effect

4. Headaches are often the result of psychological causes. For example, worrying about something can cause a headache.

   _____ listing   _____ time-order
   _____ comparison   _____ cause-effect

5. The clambake is a popular New England dinner. It usually includes many different kinds of seafood. Clams are the most common kind of seafood at a clambake. There may also be lobster and mussels.

   _____ listing   _____ time-order
   _____ comparison   _____ cause-effect

6. Many people do not like to use computers for writing. They prefer to use typewriters. They know computers are faster and more accurate. But they are more comfortable with typewriters.

   _____ listing   _____ time-order
   _____ comparison   _____ cause-effect

7. Gold was first found in California in about 1840. The next ten years in American history are called the California Gold Rush. Many people moved to the west during those years to look for gold. By 1850, there were many new "Gold Rush" towns in California.

   _____ listing   _____ time-order
   _____ comparison   _____ cause-effect

8. Cola and ginger ale are both kinds of soft drinks. Both these drinks have a lot of sugar in them. But Cola has caffeine in it, and ginger ale does not.

   _____ listing   _____ time-order
   _____ comparison   _____ cause-effect

   Finishing Time _____

Exercise 2

Read these sentences very quickly. Read only to find the pattern of organization. Make a check beside the best answer. Try to finish the page in less than 60 seconds. Time yourself.

Starting Time _____

1. Leif Ericson was probably the first European to see America. He visited some of the northern areas in about 1000. The next European visitor to America was Christopher Columbus in 1492.

    ____ listing   ____ time-order
    ____ comparison   ____ cause-effect

2. The Spanish kings and queens sent many people to find out about America. Christopher Columbus was one of these people. Ponce de Leon was another. And Vasco da Gama was yet a third.

    ____ listing   ____ time-order
    ____ comparison   ____ cause-effect

3. Leif Ericson probably had a more difficult trip across the Atlantic Ocean than Christopher Columbus. Ericson sailed across the cold northern part of the Atlantic. But Columbus sailed across the south where it was warmer.

    ____ listing   ____ time-order
    ____ comparison   ____ cause-effect

4. Many American Indians died soon after the Europeans arrived. There was one important reason for this. The Europeans brought new kinds of diseases with them. These diseases caused thousands of deaths in a short time.

    ____ listing   ____ time-order
    ____ comparison   ____ cause-effect

5. Some of the early Americans did not want to come to this country. For example, there were many Africans who had come as slaves. Some Europeans had to come for religious reasons.

    ____ listing   ____ time-order
    ____ comparison   ____ cause-effect

6. When you study for an exam, you should follow these three steps. First, you should make sure you have all the information you need. Next you should put that information in order. Then you should make a list of the most important things.

    ____ listing   ____ time-order
    ____ comparison   ____ cause-effect

7. Some people believe that changes in the weather cause changes in their health. This may be the reason why many people get the "flu" in New England. In New England, the weather can change very suddenly.

    ____ listing   ____ time-order
    ____ comparison   ____ cause-effect

8. Many American history books leave out some important information. For example, they often do not tell much about the American Indians. They also leave out some history about women.

____ listing   ____ time-order
____ comparison   ____ cause-effect

Finishing Time _____

SKIMMING FOR IDEAS

You can also skim when you want to find out the general idea quickly. Speed is important for this kind of skimming, too. You should skim at least two times faster than you usually read.

But you can only do this if you change the way you read. You cannot read every word or even every sentence. You have to leave out a lot. In fact, you should leave out everything except a few important words. These are the words that tell you the general idea.

Here are the steps for skimming a chapter from a book or an article from a magazine or newspaper:

1. Read the first few sentences at your usual speed. Ask yourself, "What is this about?"

2. Go to the next paragraph as soon as you can guess the general idea. Remember, you do not need to know the details. You only want to learn something very general about the chapter or article.

3. Read only a few words in each paragraph after that. You should look for the words that tell you more about the general idea. Often they are at the beginning of the paragraph. But they may also be at the end.

4. Always work quickly. Remember that details are not important.

1. McDonald's is a
   a. kind of Mexican food.
   b. Mexican company.
   c. restaurant company.
   d. kind of hamburger.

2. There were no McDonald's in Mexico because
   a. Mexicans do not like hamburgers.
   b. Mexicans only eat Mexican food.
   c. there were McDonald's in other countries.
   d. the Mexican government did not want them.

3. The "Big Mac" is a
   a. restaurant.
   b. kind of hamburger.
   c. kind of Mexican food.
   d. person who works for McDonald's.

Exercise 1

Skim this book review as quickly as possible. Remember, you only want to find out the general ideas about the book. You should only read the underlined sentences. Then try to answer the questions. You may check your answers by reading the rest of the review. The Answer Key is on page 270.

Murder in the Language Lab
by M.L. Allen

This book is an unusual detective story. It begins with a crime, a murder. A scientist is killed in a laboratory. But no one knows who killed the scientist. Inspector Barker is the detective. He must find the killer, but he needs help.

He gets help from Sally, a chimpanzee. She lives in the laboratory. In this laboratory, scientists are studying language. They are interested in how animals like Sally can learn some language. Sally is a very smart chimpanzee. She cannot talk, but she can understand many words. She can answer questions by using a computer. Sally saw the murder. She is afraid of Inspector Barker at first. But she wants to help. So, she tells Inspector Barker who the murderer is.

If you like detective stories, you will enjoy this one. But you probably will not be able to guess who the murderer is!

1. This story is
    a. full of information.
    b. sad.
    c. fun to read.
    d. difficult to read.

2. Inspector Barker
    a. finds the murderer himself.
    b. never finds the murderer.
    c. is studying language.
    d. gets help from a chimpanzee.

3. Sally is
    a. a scientist.
    b. a very smart animal.
    c. not a very smart animal.
    d. a murderer.

Exercise 2

Skim this review as quickly as possible for the general ideas about the book. Remember you only need to read a *few* sentences and words. Then try to answer the questions. You should finish in less than 60 seconds.

Mother Teresa
by Catherine Podijil

(Scott, Foresman and Company)

In 1979, Mother Teresa won the Nobel Prize for Peace. This book tells about her life-long work with poor people and how she finally became famous.

The story begins with her childhood in Yugoslavia. She was born in 1910. At the age of 18, she decided to become a nun. The Catholic religion was very important to her. But for her, the most important part of the religion was helping other people. She especially wanted to help the poor people in India.

She first worked as a schoolteacher in India. But her students were not poor people. So, finally, she left the school. That was when she began her real life's work. She walked the streets in Indian cities looking for people who needed help. She gave them food, clothing or medicine.

After a while, other nuns began to help her. She built hospitals and schools for the poor. She also started a special group of nuns called the Order of the Missionaries of Charity. They began to work with the poor people in many countries around the world.

Important people sometimes gave Mother Teresa money or cars for her work. But the money and cars always went to the poor people. She lived very simply and worked very hard. The Nobel Prize gave her $100,000. She will use this money to continue her work.

This book gives many interesting details about her life and work. We may not be able to give our lives to the poor like Mother Teresa. But we can learn a lot from her.

1. This book probably
   a. is fun to read.
   b. is good for children.
   c. has a lot of useful information.
   d. tells about the problems of poor people.

2. Mother Teresa is famous because she
   a. is an Indian.
   b. helps poor people.
   c. has a lot of money.
   d. is a schoolteacher.

3. People gave Mother Teresa money
   a. because she was poor.
   b. so she could win the Nobel Prize.
   c. so she could travel.
   d. so she could help poor people.

Exercise 3

Skim this newspaper article. You should finish in less than 60 seconds. Then answer the questions.

A New Drug for Heart Attacks

Doctors may now be able to stop many heart attacks. An important new study reports that doctors have a new drug. This drug is called TPA. It may be better than any other heart drug.

Many doctors now use a drug called Streptokinase. But this drug sometimes causes problems for patients. It can even cause bleeding in the brain. Some doctors do not use streptokinase. Streptokinase can save about ⅓ of the people with heart attacks. But TPA will save about ⅔. This means many people. About 1.5 million Americans have heart attacks every year.

One reason TPA can help more people is because of time. This new drug is easier and faster to use. It will give doctors more time in hospitals. Then they can study the problem well. People with heart problems can also keep some TPA at home. When a heart attack starts, they can take some TPA right away. Then they will have time to get to the hospital. This is important because about 860,000 people in the United States die before they get to the hospital.

There is another reason why TPA is good news for people with heart attacks. According to the study, it is much safer. It does not cause other problems like streptokinase. TPA works only on the heart. It does not have an effect on the blood or cause bleeding, like streptokinase.

Doctors plan to do more studies about TPA. They need to test this new drug on many more people with heart attacks. But in a few years, many doctors and hospitals will probably start using this exciting new drug.

1. The new drug is
   a. the same as streptokinase.
   b. better than streptokinase.
   c. called streptokinase.
   d. bad for people wtih heart attacks.

2. The study says that TPA
   a. is safer and faster than the old drug.
   b. is very dangerous.
   c. slower and harder to use than the old drug.
   d. causes many problems.

3. This new drug may mean
   a. more people will die from heart attacks.
   b. the same number of people will die from heart attacks.
   c. fewer people will die from heart attacks.
   d. no one will die from heart attacks.

Exercise 4

Skim this magazine article. You should finish in less than 60 seconds. Then answer the questions.

Sports in the German Democratic Republic

(adapted from the *World Press Review*, October 1984)

Many East Germans are already thinking about the year 2000. That is an Olympics year. The East Germans are very serious about the Olympic Games. They want to do well in 2000, so they are getting ready now.

Teachers, sports coaches, and parents are watching children at play. They are looking for children who will be good at sports. They say they can tell a lot about a very young child. They can already tell if the child will be good at sports.

These children will have special training. The Germans believe it is important to start at a very young age. The children may be only six or seven years old. For two hours, three times a week, they will train at a sport.

When they are a little older, they may go to the children's Olympic Games. These are specially for East Germans. The children come from all over East Germany for these games. In 1983, for example, there were 665,000 younger children and 332,000 teenagers at the children's Olympics. The children who win are the best in the country.

The winners at the children's Olympics continue to work hard. Rene Holitz, 13, is one of these teenagers. She won a prize in judo. Now she goes to a special sports school. Every morning she gets up at 6:30. She goes first to her regular classes. Then she spends six or seven hours a day training with her judo coach. She hopes to win the gold medal at the 2000 Olympics.

This is not an impossible dream. The East Germans often win many medals at the Olympics. Their planning seems to work well. Probably they will continue to win medals at future Olympics. And Rene Holitz may be one of the winners.

1. Many East Germans
   a. have children.
   b. are sports coaches.
   c. care a lot about sports.
   d. like to go running.

2. Rene Holitz probably
   a. is a very unusual child in East Germany.
   b. is not very good at sports.
   c. is not very unusual in East Germany.
   d. wants to study at the university.

3. The Germans believe you should learn a sport
   a. when you are a teenager.
   b. when you are very young.
   c. when you are in college.
   d. early in the morning.

Exercise 5

Skim this magazine article. You should finish in less than 60 seconds. Then answer the questions.

Women in China Today

(adapted from the *World Press Review*, March 1985)

What kind of jobs do women have in China today? Well, here are a few examples: Zhao Changbai is a manager of one of China's largest companies. Zou Hon is the manager of a large restaurant company. Wan Shiren is an important scientist who works in China's space program.

The list could go on. According to Zhang Guoying of the All-China Women's Federation, women are now important to the country. She says the government believes this too. China needs educated women to help make the country more modern.

This was not true 50 years ago. Then, there were few women in important jobs. Women worked mostly at home or in factories. But now there are more than 40 million women working in China. That is 40% of all the people who work. These working women include many women who work in factories. But now there are also many women scientific and technical workers—almost two million. And about 7,000 of these women are professors, engineers, chemists, and biologists. Some women are also working in important government positions, as governors or ministers.

It was not easy for these women, says Zhang Guoying. She believes that Chinese women have more difficulties than Chinese men. Women still have to take care of their families. That means they really have two jobs. One is at their office or factory and the other is at home. This is the same problem women have in many other parts of the world.

The government in China is trying to make life better for women. It is building more day-care centers for the children of working mothers. It is helping women get a better education and find better jobs. According to Zhang Guoying, the future for women in China should even be better.

1. In China today,
   a. more women are working.
   b. most women do not work.
   c. fewer women are working.
   d. women do not like to work.

2. Chinese women now
   a. have jobs only in factories.
   b. have few important jobs.
   c. have important jobs.
   d. do not work for the government.

3. For a Chinese women
   a. life is now very easy.
   b. work is now very easy.
   c. life is still not easy.
   d. families are not important.

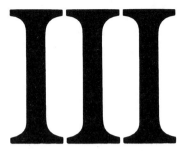

Passages for Reading Faster

When you read these passages:

- Always preview before you start reading. (See Unit 1 in Part II.)
- Time yourself (minutes and seconds).
- Do not use a dictionary. Guess the meanings of new words.
- Do not try to read every word. Read for ideas.
- Ask questions while you read.
- Keep a record of your Reading Rate on the Progress Chart on page 276.

1

Dr. Sam Diamond and his wife Susan are very different. Mrs. Diamond is tall and thin. Dr. Diamond is short and fat. Mrs. Diamond has blond hair and blue eyes. Dr. Diamond has dark hair and brown eyes. Mrs. Diamond is a quiet person. She can work for hours alone in her laboratory. Dr. Diamond loves to talk and meet people. He can talk for hours with his patients. It is hard to believe the Diamonds are married.

In fact, they were married thirty years ago. They have two children, Ted and Jane. Ted and Jane now have their own homes. The Diamonds share their home with several pets: a cat, a dog, and a bird.

Most of the time, Dr. and Mrs. Diamond are happy in Rosebud. But often they think about other parts of the world. Ted and his wife Maria live in Italy. Their daughter Jane lives in California. So sometimes the Diamonds dream about travel. They want to see their children, of course. They also want to see new places and have new experiences.

"We're not getting any younger!" Dr. Diamond often says to his wife.

"Maybe next year we'll go somewhere," she usually answers. "Now we're just too busy."

Starting time _____

Finishing time _____

Reading time _____

Turn the page and answer the questions.
Don't look back at the passage.

Circle the best answer.

1. This passage is about
   a. Ted and Jane Diamond.
   b. Mrs. Diamond.
   c. Dr. and Mrs. Diamond.
   d. Dr. Diamond.

   1. [　]

2. Dr. Diamond and Mrs. Diamond look
   a. different.
   b. the same.
   c. old.
   d. nice.

   2. [　]

3. Ted and Jane live
   a. in their own homes.
   b. with their parents.
   c. in New Jersey.
   d. in New York.

   3. [　]

4. The Diamonds
   a. like animals.
   b. are afraid of animals.
   c. do not have any animals.
   d. do not like animals.

   4. [　]

5. Most of the time the Diamonds
   a. want to move.
   b. are happy in Rosebud.
   c. want to travel.
   d. are happy in New York.

   5. [　]

6. Dr. and Mrs. Diamond want to
   a. work hard.
   b. live in New York City.
   c. have children.
   d. see their children.

   6. [　]

7. The Diamonds do not travel because they
   a. are happy.
   b. are too busy.
   c. want to see new places.
   d. are not getting any younger.

   7. [　]

8. Mrs. Diamond thinks
   a. her husband does not want to travel.
   b. her husband is too old.
   c. they will never travel.
   d. they may travel next year.

   8. [　]

Go back and answer the questions a second time. You may look back at the passage. Write the answers in the boxes on the right.

Check your answers in the Answer Key on page 271.
Number correct _____
Find your Reading Rate. Fill in the Progress Chart.

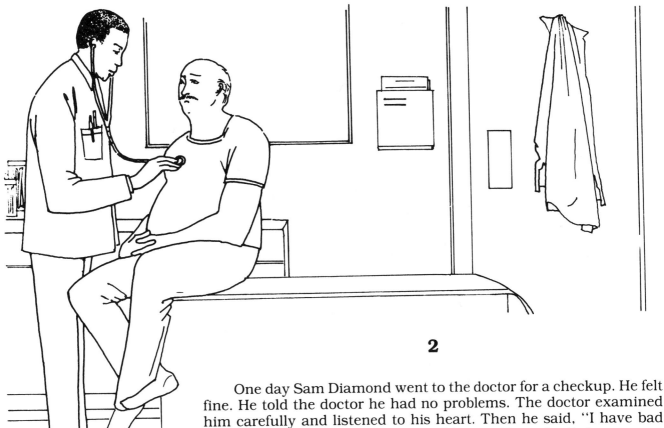

2

One day Sam Diamond went to the doctor for a checkup. He felt fine. He told the doctor he had no problems. The doctor examined him carefully and listened to his heart. Then he said, "I have bad news for you. You'll have heart trouble soon if you don't change your life. You must lose weight. You must exercise more and you must get more rest."

Sam was unhappy. He liked to eat good food. He usually did not exercise. And he liked to work hard at his job. But he was worried about his heart.

Sam told Susan the bad news. She was worried, too. Then she said, "Maybe the doctor is right. Maybe we do need to make some big changes in our lives."

"This WILL be a big change. I'll have to eat less and start to exercise!" said Sam.

"I'll help you," said Susan. "I'll exercise with you. But I was thinking of some other changes too. I was thinking about taking a real vacation. Let's take a trip somewhere. Let's go some place where you can really relax."

"We can go visit Ted in Italy!" said Sam.

"Or Jane in California!" said Susan.

Starting time _____

Finishing time _____

Reading time _____

Turn the page and answer the questions.
Don't look back at the passage.

Circle the best answer.

1. This passage is about
   a. exercise and dieting.
   b. how the doctor examined Sam.
   c. how Sam's heart trouble may change his life.
   d. how Sam feels about exercise and dieting.

   1. ☐

2. When Sam went to the doctor, he did not
   a. feel well.
   b. feel sick.
   c. know what to say.
   d. have trouble.

   2. ☐

3. After he saw the doctor, Sam did not
   a. worry.
   b. go home.
   c. have any problems.
   d. feel happy.

   3. ☐

4. The doctor told Sam he must
   a. change his life.
   b. work harder.
   c. feel sick.
   d. feel happy.

   4. ☐

5. Sam worried because
   a. he wanted to exercise.
   b. he had heart trouble.
   c. he didn't have heart trouble.
   d. he didn't want to eat good food.

   5. ☐

6. When she heard the bad news, Susan was
   a. sad.
   b. happy.
   c. sick.
   d. worried.

   6. ☐

7. Susan told Sam she
   a. did not want to exercise.
   b. did not want to go to California.
   c. wanted to go to Italy.
   d. wanted to help him get exercise.

   7. ☐

8. Susan wanted to go to California because
   a. it is not far away.
   b. it is far away.
   c. Jane lives there.
   d. it is different.

   8. ☐

Go back and answer the questions a second time. You may look back at the passage. Write the answers in the boxes on the right.

Check your answers in the Answer Key. Number correct _____
Find your Reading Rate. Fill in the Progress Chart.

3

The next day, Sam began to make some changes in his life. No more cookies at lunch, no more cake for dessert, and no sweets in the afternoon. It was hard. All day his stomach made funny noises. At night he dreamed about big and delicious meals. He also began to exercise with Susan. They jogged every morning before work. This was even harder than the diet.

"We're crazy," Sam told his wife one morning. It was raining. "My legs hurt and I'm cold."

"Think about Italy or California," Susan said.

Sam really just wanted a warm bath and breakfast, but he thought about sunny beaches. He thought about a picnic with bread and cheese and Italian wine.

"Let's go to Italy," he said to Susan when they got home. "Everyone says the food is wonderful and the people are very friendly."

"Jane says the same thing about California," Susan said. "She says San Francisco is the most beautiful city."

They decided to get more information from a travel agent. She told them a trip to California was cheaper and easier to plan. But she said Italy was more unusual and exciting. "You have to decide what you want for your vacation," she explained. "They're both beautiful places."

Starting time _____

Finishing time _____

Reading time _____

Turn the page and answer the questions.
Don't look back at the passage.

Circle the best answer.

1. This passage is about   1. ☐
   a. new problems and questions in the Diamonds' life.
   b. how crazy Susan and Sam are every morning.
   c. taking a vacation.
   d. what their children and friends tell them.

2. Sam dreamed about   2. ☐
   a. jogging.
   b. food.
   c. Italy.
   d. a vacation.

3. Sam did not enjoy   3. ☐
   a. jogging.
   b. eating.
   c. traveling.
   d. dreaming.

4. Susan told Sam to think about Italy or California   4. ☐
   a. because she wanted to go there.
   b. to help him.
   c. to make him tired.
   d. because she was cold.

5. Everyone says the people in Italy are   5. ☐
   a. beautiful.
   b. friendly.
   c. rich.
   d. unfriendly.

6. According to Jane, the most beautiful city is   6. ☐
   a. New York.
   b. San Francisco.
   c. Rome.
   d. California.

7. Susan and Sam went to a travel agent   7. ☐
   a. in New York.
   b. to buy plane tickets.
   c. on their way home.
   d. to find out more about Italy and California.

8. The travel agent told the Diamonds that   8. ☐
   a. Italy and California are both beautiful places.
   b. California is the best place for a vacation.
   c. Italy is the best place for a vacation.
   d. California and Italy are terrible places.

Go back and answer the questions a second time. You may look back at the passage. Write the answers in the boxes on the right.

Check your answers in the Answer Key. Number correct _____
Find your Reading Rate. Fill in the Progress Chart.

4

This was the beginning of an unhappy time for the Diamonds. After they went to the travel agent, Susan wanted to go to California. But Sam wanted to go to Italy.

"We want to change our lives, don't we?" he asked Susan. "Then we should go someplace really different!"

"But Italy's so expensive," Susan answered. "We're not millionaires!"

"We waited for many years, our whole lives, for this vacation!" said Sam. "We may not get another chance. You know, we're not getting any younger!"

"You just want to go to Italy because of the food!" said Susan. "That's not true!"

"You'll eat too much and get sick," said Susan. "I know you. You'll never be able to diet in Italy!"

And so, they began to argue. They argued while they were jogging. They argued at breakfast. They argued at dinner. And all the time they were in a terrible mood. They didn't enjoy the things they used to enjoy. They stopped going to parties and they didn't invite friends over for dinner. Sam didn't talk much to his patients. Susan didn't want to work in her garden. Even the pets were unhappy. The cat ran away and the dog hid under the bed.

Starting time _____

Finishing time _____

Reading time _____

Turn the page and answer the questions.
Don't look back at the passage.

Circle the best answer.

1. This passage is about   1. ☐
   a. how Sam wants to go to Italy.
   b. why Susan doesn't want to go to Italy.
   c. an unhappy time for Susan and Sam.
   d. a terrible mood.

2. Sam wanted to go to Italy because   2. ☐
   a. it's very different.
   b. it's not very different.
   c. it's expensive.
   d. he's not a millionaire.

3. Susan thought Sam wanted to go to Italy because of 3. ☐
   a. his heart.
   b. his diet.
   c. the Italian food.
   d. her diet.

4. Sam thought they probably were   4. ☐
   a. going to take another vacation.
   b. not going to get another chance to travel.
   c. going to travel often after this.
   d. not going to go to Italy.

5. Susan and Sam were arguing about   5. ☐
   a. where to take their vacation.
   b. Sam's diet.
   c. their friends.
   c. about food.

6. They did not visit their friends because they   6. ☐
   a. were not getting any younger.
   b. were not millionaires.
   c. were not home.
   d. were in a terrible mood.

7. Susan thought Italian food was   7. ☐
   a. healthy for Sam.
   b. unhealthy for Sam.
   c. too expensive.
   d. good for a diet.

8. The dog hid under the bed because   8. ☐
   a. it liked arguing.
   b. it was not getting any younger.
   c. it did not like Susan.
   d. it did not like arguing.

Go back and answer the questions a second time. You may look back at the passage. Write the answers in the boxes on the right.

Check your answers in the Answer Key. Number correct _____
Find your Reading Rate. Fill in the Progress Chart.

5

Then one evening in the middle of an argument, the telephone rang. Susan answered it. Jane was calling from California and she was very excited.

"Guess what?" she said. "I have a new job! My company is sending me to New York."

"That's wonderful!" said Susan. "What kind of job? When are you coming?"

"The job starts in six weeks. I'll be the manager of the New York office. I'll help them sell more computers in New York."

"Six weeks! What will you do about your apartment there in San Francisco? Where will you live in New York?"

"I'll have to give up this apartment. In New York I'll look for a new place. I'm excited about the job and I'm excited about New York. But they say it's really hard to find a nice apartment there."

"You can stay here, of course, until you find something," said Susan.

"Thank you," said Jane. "What about your vacation? Are you still going?"

"We couldn't decide where to go," said Susan. "I wanted to go to California. Your father wanted to go to Italy. California's not the same without you. So I guess it'll be Italy after all. But not right away. We want to see you first."

Starting time _____

Finishing time _____

Reading time _____

Reading time _____

Turn the page and answer the questions.
Don't look back at the passage.

Circle the best answer.

1. This passage is about
   a. moving to New York.
   b. a telephone call from Jane.
   c. apartments in New York.
   d. a new job.

1. ☐

2. Jane was very excited about
   a. San Francisco.
   b. moving to New York.
   c. her parents.
   d. a vacation.

2. ☐

3. Jane's company
   a. sells computers.
   b. sells apartments.
   c. makes telephones.
   d. is a travel agency.

3. ☐

4. Jane's new job starts
   a. next year.
   b. next week.
   c. in three years.
   d. in six weeks.

4. ☐

5. Jane was worried about
   a. living with her parents
   b. finding an apartment in New York.
   c. finding an apartment in San Francisco.
   d. leaving San Francisco.

5. ☐

6. Jane thought that apartments in New York
   a. were expensive.
   b. were exciting.
   c. were hard to find.
   d. were nice.

6. ☐

7. Jane will
   a. probably stay with her parents.
   b. stay in a hotel.
   c. stay with friends.
   d. find an apartment right away.

7. ☐

8. Now Susan and Sam will probably
   a. go to California.
   b. never go on vacation.
   c. go to New York.
   d. go to Italy.

8. ☐

Go back and answer the questions a second time. You may look back at the passage. Write the answers in the boxes on the right.

Check your answers in the Answer Key. Number correct _____
Find your Reading Rate. Fill in the Progress Chart.

6

So the Diamonds decided to go to Italy. Sam bought an Italian dictionary and an Italian cookbook. He invited all their friends for dinner. They enjoyed his favorite Italian dish, spaghetti with meat sauce. Everyone laughed when he tried to speak Italian.

Susan didn't eat much spaghetti. "It's very heavy," she told Sam. "You shouldn't eat so much of it. It's not good for you."

"This is a special day," he said. "Can't we forget about my heart for one day?"

But Susan couldn't stop worrying about everything. She was very worried about this trip.

"Rome is a big city," she said to Sam. "People say it's dangerous, too. We might get lost and then what will we do?"

"No problem," said Sam. "I'll speak Italian. We'll be fine. Stop worrying! We'll have a great time!"

Susan was not so sure. But she tried to forget her worries. She asked Jane to stay in their house with the pets. Sam asked his friend Dr. Hamilton to take care of his patients. They bought the plane tickets and made all their plans. Then they wrote a letter to Ted and Maria. "Guess what!" it said. "We're coming to Italy. We'll arrive in Rome on the 10th of May. We can't wait to see you!"

Starting time _____	
Finishing time _____	
Reading time _____	

Turn the page and answer the questions.
Don't look back at the passage.

Circle the best answer.

1. This passage is about   1. ☐
    a. how Sam learns Italian.
    b. how the Diamonds get ready for their trip.
    c. why Susan worries about Italy.
    d. the Diamond's vacation.

2. Everyone laughed because   2. ☐
    a. Sam spoke excellent Italian.
    b. Sam didn't speak any Italian.
    c. Sam didn't like to speak Italian.
    d. Sam's Italian sounded funny.

3. Susan didn't want Sam to   3. ☐
    a. speak Italian.
    b. eat too much spaghetti.
    c. have a special occasion.
    d. invite their friends for dinner.

4. Susan was afraid of Rome because   4. ☐
    a. it is far away.
    b. it is Italian.
    c. it is large and dangerous.
    d. it is expensive.

5. Susan was worried about   5. ☐
    a. buying plane tickets.
    b. the trip.
    c. Ted and Maria.
    d. their pets.

6. Sam thought   6. ☐
    a. he spoke good Italian.
    b. he couldn't speak any Italian.
    c. Susan could speak Italian.
    d. he could speak English in Rome.

7. Susan   7. ☐
    a. didn't want to go to Italy.
    b. thought they would have a great time.
    c. wanted to stay home.
    d. wanted to go to Italy.

8. Susan and Sam wrote to Ted   8. ☐
    a. to tell him about Rosebud.
    b. to tell him their plans.
    c. about Italy.
    d. for more information.

Go back and answer the questions a second time. You may look back
at the passage. Write the answers in the boxes on the right.

Check your answers in the Answer Key. Number correct _____
Find your Reading Rate. Fill in the Progress Chart.

7

Dear Mom and Dad,

We have some exciting news for you. Maria is going to have a baby! We didn't tell you right away. At first the doctor said she might have some trouble with the baby. Now he says she is just fine. She's very healthy and happy — and large! She still works on her paintings every day. But she stopped teaching art classes. She gets tired more quickly now.

There is going to be another big change in our lives. We're moving back to New York! We wanted to be closer to you and to Jane. It's much nicer to be near the family for something important like a baby. Maria grew up in Mexico, and she doesn't have a family. So that makes you even more important to us.

Maria is a little worried about working in New York. She will have to start again there. In Italy her paintings are already popular. But I'm sure people will like them in New York, too. My job won't be any problem. I'm still going to work for *The New York Times*. I'll be writing about the United Nations in New York.

We're planning to move next month. See you then!

Love,
Ted

Starting time _____

Finishing time _____

Reading time _____

Turn the page and answer the questions.
Don't look back at the passage.

Circle the best answer.

1. This passage is about
   a. New York.
   b. changes in Susan and Sam's life.
   c. changes in Ted and Maria's life.
   d. having a baby.

2. Maria
   a. is going to get married.
   b. is not going to have any children.
   c. is going to have a child.
   d. has a child.

3. Maria
   a. works at the United Nations
   b. is an artist.
   c. is a doctor.
   d. is a writer.

4. Maria and Ted are
   a. planning to stay in Italy.
   b. moving to California.
   c. planning to move to New York.
   d. not sure about their plans.

5. Ted wants to live
   a. closer to Maria's family.
   b. closer to his family.
   c. far away from his family.
   d. in Italy.

6. Maria
   a. doesn't have a large family.
   b. has a large family.
   c. doesn't like families.
   d. never had a family.

7. Maria is worried about
   a. her family.
   b. working in New York.
   c. Ted's job.
   d. teaching art.

8. Ted
   a. works for the United Nations.
   b. is an artist.
   c. works for *The New York Times*.
   d. doesn't work.

1. ☐
2. ☐
3. ☐
4. ☐
5. ☐
6. ☐
7. ☐
8. ☐

Go back and answer the questions a second time. You may look back at the passage. Write the answers in the boxes on the right.

Check your answers in the Answer Key. Number correct _____
Find your Reading Rate. Fill in the Progress Chart.

8

Susan and Sam were very excited about the news from Ted and Maria. Soon they were going to be grandparents! And soon their children were all going to be home again.

But they didn't know what to do now about their vacation.

"Maybe we should forget about a vacation," said Susan.

"We could still go somewhere later," said Sam.

"Where? That's always the problem."

"How about England?" asked Sam. "I hear they have great breakfasts."

"Well, language is not a problem in England," said Susan.

"And you could visit the famous English gardens," said Sam.

"True," said Susan. "There's Kew Gardens and Kensington Gardens and all those big houses."

"So it's England?" asked Sam.

"Oh, why not? But only if you don't eat too many of those breakfasts!" said Susan.

"I won't eat anything until teatime," said Sam.

"But they have cakes and cookies at teatime!"

"I'm only joking!" Sam laughed. "I'll just drink tea all day, if you want."

"Okay, okay," said Susan, and she laughed too.

Finally, Susan and Sam could stop arguing. Sometimes in the evenings they talked about their children. Sometimes they talked about their travel plans. While they were talking, the cat sat in Susan's lap. The dog lay down beside Sam's chair. The house was quiet again.

Starting time _____

Finishing time _____

Reading time _____

Turn the page and answer the questions.
Don't look back at the passage.

Circle the best answer.

1. This passage is about
   a. traveling in England.
   b. the Diamond's children.
   c. how the Diamonds decide to go to England.
   d. the Diamonds on vacation.

   1. ☐

2. Susan thought they
   a. should forget the vacation.
   b. should not argue.
   c. should go on vacation right away.
   d. should never go on vacation.

   2. ☐

3. Sam wanted to go to England because
   a. the children were coming home soon.
   b. he wanted to learn a new language.
   c. the English have great breakfasts.
   d. he likes gardens.

   3. ☐

4. Sam likes to
   a. be serious with Susan all the time.
   b. get angry at Susan.
   c. joke with Susan.
   d. laugh at Susan.

   4. ☐

5. Susan wanted to go to England because of
   a. the tea.
   b. the gardens
   c. the breakfasts.
   d. Sam.

   5. ☐

6. Sam said he was going to
   a. eat lots of cakes.
   b. drink only water.
   c. eat big breakfasts.
   d. drink only tea.

   6. ☐

7. Susan and Sam decided to go to
   a. Italy.
   b. Rosebud.
   c. New York.
   d. England.

   7. ☐

8. The cat came home because
   a. now the house was quiet again.
   b. it wanted to go to England.
   c. Susan and Sam were still arguing.
   d. the children were coming.

   8. ☐

Go back and answer the questions a second time. You may look back at the passage. Write the answers in the boxes on the right.

Check your answers in the Answer Key. Number correct _____
Find your Reading Rate. Fill in the Progress Chart.

The next month passed very quickly. Susan and Sam were very busy. They cleaned out Ted and Jane's old bedrooms. They called many of their old friends and their aunts, uncles and cousins. They wanted everyone to know all the good news.

At last, the big day came. Susan and Sam drove to the airport to meet Ted and Maria. They found out that the flight from Rome was late. So they sat down in the coffee shop and ordered tea. But they did not have time to drink it. They heard someone say:

"The flight from Rome is arriving now at Gate 12."

So they left their tea and rushed over to Gate 12. Ted and Maria were getting off the plane. Susan and Sam watched them go through the long line for customs. Finally, they were all together. There was a lot of hugging and kissing. Everyone was talking at once. Susan was even crying a little.

"It's too much!" she said. "I'm too happy! You're here and Jane will be here next week..."

Sam put his arm around her shoulder. "This isn't a time for crying," he said. "This is a time to celebrate. Let's go home to Rosebud. I'll cook up a nice big spaghetti dinner for us all."

Starting time _____

Finishing time _____

Reading time _____

Turn the page and answer the questions.
Don't look back at the passage.

Circle the best answer.

1. This passage is about   1. ☐
   a. Susan and Sam.
   b. when Ted and Maria came home.
   c. when Jane came home.
   d. airports.

2. Susan and Sam wanted to tell everyone   2. ☐
   a. about Jane.
   b. about their vacation.
   c. all the good news.
   d. about their jobs.

3. At the airport, they found out that   3. ☐
   a. the flight was early.
   b. Ted and Maria weren't coming.
   c. the airport was closed.
   d. the flight was late.

4. While they were waiting, Susan and Sam   4. ☐
   a. went home.
   b. went to a coffee shop.
   c. read the newspaper.
   d. fell asleep.

5. Susan and Sam ordered   5. ☐
   a. tea.
   b. a taxi.
   c. dinner.
   d. spaghetti.

6. Ted and Maria had to   6. ☐
   a. go through customs.
   b. stay on the plane.
   c. go back to Rome.
   d. go to the airport coffee shop.

7. When they were together, Susan felt   7. ☐
   a. sad.
   b. worried.
   c. happy.
   d. nervous.

8. Sam said   8. ☐
   a. they should all go to New York.
   b. they should all go home and have dinner.
   c. he was not hungry.
   d. Jane is not coming.

Go back and answer the questions a second time. You may look back at the passage. Write the answers in the boxes on the right.

Check your answers in the Answer Key. Number correct _____
Find your Reading Rate. Fill in the Progress Chart.

10

The next week, Jane arrived in New York. Susan and Sam went to the airport to meet her. They were very surprised when they saw her. She looked very different. Jane used to be a student. Before she went to California she always dressed like a student. She had long hair and she wore blue jeans. Now she was wearing a fancy suit and she had a new haircut. She didn't look like their daughter at all. She looked like a New York business woman.

Jane was full of ideas for her new life in New York. She wanted to find an apartment in the city. She wanted to do well at her job. She wanted to visit all her friends in New York.

"But don't you want to get married some day?" asked Susan when she heard all these plans.

"I'm in no hurry!" said Jane. "Right now there are so many other things I want to do."

"I was married when I was 25," said Susan. "When I was your age, I already had a child."

"Things are different now," said Jane. "Maybe I'll get married some day. Maybe not. I have to meet the right man, you know!"

Starting time _____

Finishing time _____

Reading time _____

Turn the page and answer the questions.
Don't look back at the passage.

Circle the best answer.

1. This passage is about   1. ☐
   a. Jane's clothes.
   b. Jane's new job.
   c. Jane's ideas about her life.
   d. Jane's plans to get married.

2. Susan and Sam were surprised because   2. ☐
   a. Jane was moving to New York.
   b. Jane looked very different.
   c. Jane looked like their daughter.
   d. Jane looked younger.

3. Before she went to California, Jane dressed like   3. ☐
   a. a business woman.
   b. her mother.
   c. a student.
   d. someone else.

4. Jane wanted to live   4. ☐
   a. in New York City.
   b. with her parents.
   c. in California.
   d. with her friends.

5. Jane planned to visit   5. ☐
   a. her company.
   b. her parents.
   c. her friends.
   d. an art museum.

6. Susan thought Jane   6. ☐
   a. wanted to get married.
   b. should get married.
   c. was married.
   d. didn't want to get married.

7. Jane   7. ☐
   a. had many married friends.
   b. was in a hurry to get married.
   c. was too old to get married.
   d. wanted to do many other things.

8. Jane says she may get married when   8. ☐
   a. she is 25.
   b. she meets the right man.
   c. she finds an apartment.
   d. she has a child.

Go back and answer the questions a second time. You may look back at the passage. Write the answers in the boxes on the right.

Check your answers in the Answer Key. Number correct _____
Find your Reading Rate. Fill in the Progress Chart.

11

Soon Jane was very busy. She went in to the city early every morning and came home very late. She was working hard, but she was also enjoying herself very much.

"So, how do you like New York?" asked Sam one day. It was the end of Jane's first week.

"Well, in some ways San Francisco is a nicer city," said Jane. "It's cleaner, first of all. The air is cleaner and so are the streets. People in California don't leave their garbage on the sidewalks. But they do in New York."

"Also, San Francisco has less crime. I was never afraid there. But here people are always afraid. My friends in New York have strong locks on their doors. They worry at night. They're always telling me to be careful on the streets."

"And there's another nice thing about San Francisco. The people there are much friendlier. If you're lost you can ask anyone for information. They're always glad to help you. Not here in New York! Everyone here is always in a hurry. They don't have time to be friendly. They walk faster and they drive faster. I think they even talk faster!"

Starting time _____

Finishing time _____

Reading time _____

Turn the page and answer the questions.
Don't look back at the passage.

Circle the best answer.

1. This passage is about   1. ☐
   a. Jane's first week at work.
   b. why Jane thinks San Francisco is nicer than
      New York.
   c. why Jane thinks New York is nicer than
      San Francisco.
   d. how people in New York are always in a hurry.

2. Every day Jane comes home   2. ☐
   a. often.
   b. early.
   c. late.
   d. at 5:00.

3. In New York the streets are   3. ☐
   a. long.
   b. clean.
   c. nice.
   d. dirty.

4. People in California don't   4. ☐
   a. put their garbage away.
   b. put their garbage on the sidewalks.
   c. clean their sidewalks.
   d. have garbage.

5. Jane's friends are afraid of   5. ☐
   a. the subway.
   b. the garbage.
   c. crime.
   d. locks.

6. Jane thinks San Francisco   6. ☐
   a. is not a nice place to live.
   b. is safer than New York.
   c. has a lot of crime.
   d. is not a safe place to live.

7. Jane says that people in San Francisco are   7. ☐
   a. not very helpful.
   b. very helpful.
   c. in need of information.
   d. always asking questions.

8. People in New York are not friendly because   8. ☐
   a. they are often lost.
   b. they are always in a hurry.
   c. New York is larger.
   d. they are glad to help you.

Go back and answer the questions a second time. You may look back
at the passage. Write the answers in the boxes on the right.

Check your answers in the Answer Key. Number correct _____
Find your Reading Rate. Fill in the Progress Chart.

12

"We like New York City," said Sam Diamond to Jane. "But we don't go there very often together.

"Let's all go!" said Jane. "I'll show you some nice places."

A week later, they all took the train to New York City. First they went to some stores. Susan needed a new raincoat for their trip. She tried on many coats. Sam liked all of them. But Susan thought they were too fancy, and too expensive. So she did not buy anything.

Then they visited the Museum of Modern Art. They looked at pictures made with newspapers, wood and metal.

"Is this art?" asked Sam. "I don't think I understand it."

"This is Picasso!" said Jane. "He's the most famous modern artist in the world!"

"Then I guess I don't like modern art," said Sam.

Next they walked around Greenwich Village. Susan liked the old style of the houses and the funny old kind of street lights. Sam did too, but he was more interested in all the restaurants. On every street there were wonderful smells. Finally, he said, "How about dinner? I'm hungry!"

Jane and Susan were hungry, too. They stopped at a Japanese restaurant and had a delicious meal.

Starting time _____

Finishing time _____

Reading time _____

Turn the page and answer the questions.
Don't look back at the passage.

Circle the best answer.

1. This passage is about
   a. modern art.
   b. Greenwich Village.
   c. Jane's trip to New York.
   d. the Diamonds in New York.

   1. ☐

2. Susan and Sam
   a. never go to New York.
   b. don't go to New York together very often.
   c. don't ever go to New York.
   d. often go to New York.

   2. ☐

3. Susan didn't buy a raincoat because
   a. they were too expensive and fancy.
   b. there were too many.
   c. Sam didn't like them.
   d. they weren't nice.

   3. ☐

4. Picasso sometimes made pictures
   a. with nothing in them.
   b. in an old style.
   c. with newspapers, wood and metal.
   d. of museums.

   4. ☐

5. Sam didn't like
   a. raincoats.
   b. old-style houses.
   c. modern art.
   d. old-style art.

   5. ☐

6. Greenwich Village is probably
   a. modern.
   b. fancy.
   c. dark.
   d. old.

   6. ☐

7. Sam often thinks about
   a. art.
   b. history.
   c. food.
   d. clothes.

   7. ☐

8. In Greenwich Village Susan liked
   a. only the modern things.
   b. the art.
   c. the old style things.
   d. the new houses.

   8. ☐

Go back and answer the questions a second time. You may look back at the passage. Write the answers in the boxes on the right.

Check your answers in the Answer Key. Number correct _____
Find your Reading Rate. Fill in the Progress Chart.

13

The big day came for Susan and Sam. They were finally ready to leave on their trip to England. Ted, Maria and Jane drove with them to the airport.

"I'm sure we forgot something," Susan said to Sam. "Do you have the plane tickets?"

"Oh yes. They're in my pocket."

"What about our passports?" Susan asked.

"They're in my pocket, too," Sam said and he looked in his pocket to make sure. There were the tickets, but no passports! "I was sure I put them in this pocket," he said. "Maybe they're in my coat pocket."

He looked in his coat pocket, in his travel bag and in his suitcase. "They must be on the table at home!" he said.

"How could you!" said Susan.

"But they were with the travel information. I thought you had all that."

"Wait a minute. Maybe I do," said Susan. She looked in her bag. There were the passports.

"Let's go have a cup of coffee," said Ted. "You have lots of time and I think you need to relax."

But Sam and Susan were feeling nervous. They didn't want to miss their flight. So they all said goodbye, and Susan and Sam got on the plane.

Starting time _____

Finishing time _____

Reading time _____

Turn the page and answer the questions.
Don't look back at the passage.

Circle the best answer.

1. This passage is about   1. ☐
   a. Susan and Sam's passports.
   b. the airport.
   c. travel information.
   d. how Susan and Sam left for their trip.

2. At first, Susan was worried about   2. ☐
   a. the plane tickets.
   b. forgetting something.
   c. leaving soon.
   d. going to the airport.

3. Sam thought the passports were   3. ☐
   a. on the plane.
   b. at the airport.
   c. in his pocket.
   d. in the car.

4. After Sam looked for the passports   4. ☐
   a. he decided they were at home.
   b. he found them.
   c. he went back home.
   d. they all went back home.

5. Susan and Sam's passports were   5. ☐
   a. in Susan's bag.
   b. in Sam's pocket.
   c. lost.
   d. at the airport.

6. Susan and Sam were feeling   6. ☐
   a. happy.
   b. nervous.
   c. unhappy.
   d. relaxed.

7. Ted thought a cup of coffee was going to   7. ☐
   a. give them more time.
   b. make them late.
   c. help them relax.
   d. make them more worried.

8. Susan and Sam were worried about   8. ☐
   a. saying goodbye.
   b. the tickets.
   c. flying to England.
   d. missing their flight.

Go back and answer the questions a second time. You may look back
at the passage. Write the answers in the boxes on the right.

Check your answers in the Answer Key. Number correct _____
Find your Reading Rate. Fill in the Progress Chart.

14

Dear Ted, Maria and Jane,

London is wonderful! We walked all around the city yesterday and today. We're both so glad we decided to come here. It's a very large city, with almost 10 million people. But it doesn't feel large the way New York does. First of all, there are no skyscrapers. Many of the buildings are small because they are very old. Also, a lot of people live in houses. There aren't many large apartment buildings.

Londoners are proud of their city and they want it to look nice. You don't see as much garbage as in New York. You also don't see a lot of poor people. The English government takes good care of its people. There is usually food and housing for everyone. Even the poor neighborhoods are not run down and ugly. They're not like the Bronx in New York, for example. The poor people in London usually have homes and food.

Another nice thing about London is the parks. You see them everywhere. These English parks are not like American parks. These are clean and full of flowers. No one here picks the flowers or throws paper on the grass.

I wonder about Americans — why can't we take better care of our cities, our people and our parks?

We'll write again soon and tell you more.

Love,
Mom

| Starting time _____ |
| Finishing time _____ |
| Reading time _____ |

Turn the page and answer the questions.
Don't look back at the passage.

Circle the best answer.

1. This passage is about
   a. the size of London.
   b. the city of London.
   c. how Susan and Sam visited English parks.
   d. why Susan and Sam liked London.

   1. ☐

2. Compared with New York, London
   a. seemed larger.
   b. seemed smaller.
   c. looked newer.
   d. was more crowded.

   2. ☐

3. The sidewalks in London were
   a. covered with garbage.
   b. smaller than New York.
   c. clean.
   d. dirty.

   3. ☐

4. Londoners
   a. are more careful than New Yorkers about public places.
   b. are less careful than New Yorkers about public places.
   c. care very little about public places.
   d. don't care much about public places.

   4. ☐

5. The Bronx in New York is
   a. a rich neighborhood.
   b. an old neighborhood.
   c. a nice neighborhood.
   d. a poor neighborhood.

   5. ☐

6. The poor people in England
   a. don't live in London.
   b. don't have homes and food.
   c. go to the Bronx in New York.
   d. usually have homes and food.

   6. ☐

7. Susan and Sam saw
   a. more parks in America.
   b. more people in English parks.
   c. a few parks in London.
   d. many parks in London.

   7. ☐

8. American parks are
   a. clean and beautiful.
   b. larger than English parks.
   c. often not very clean.
   d. like English parks.

   8. ☐

Go back and answer the questions a second time. You may look back at the passage. Write the answers in the boxes on the right.

Check your answers in the Answer Key. Number correct _____
Find your Reading Rate. Fill in the Progress Chart.

15

Dear Mom and Dad,

A terrible thing happened yesterday. But let me tell you first that everything is all right. Jane was mugged. But don't worry. She's okay now.

This is what happened.

Yesterday Jane had to stay late at work. When she finished everything at the office, it was dark. Jane knows New York City very well, so she was not afraid. She walked to the apartment of her friends Janet and Bill and rang their doorbell. They didn't hear the bell, so she rang it again.

While she was standing there, a man and woman walked by. They saw her and stopped. Jane didn't see them. Suddenly they grabbed her from behind. She tried to scream and fight. But they covered up her mouth and hit her. Just then, Jane's friends came to the door. The robbers took Jane's handbag and ran away.

Poor Jane! She was not badly hurt. She only has a black eye. But she is very upset. Today she stayed home from work. Maria is with her. She is trying to help her relax and forget what happened.

I'm glad to hear you like London. It's one of my favorite cities — and it's very safe! Write again soon.

Love,
Ted

Starting time _____
Finishing time _____
Reading time _____

Turn the page and answer the questions.
Don't look back at the passage.

Circle the best answer.

1. This passage is about   1. ☐
   a. how Jane walks alone in new York.
   b. how Jane was mugged.
   c. thieves in New York.
   d. night life in New York.

2. Jane was walking in the dark because   2. ☐
   a. she knows New York well.
   b. she wanted to visit her friends.
   c. she had to stay late at work.
   d. she was not afraid.

3. Jane probably   3. ☐
   a. is often afraid of things.
   b. isn't usually afraid of things.
   c. thinks a lot about crime.
   d. often has bad experiences.

4. Jane's friends   4. ☐
   a. didn't want to open the door.
   b. didn't know it was Jane.
   c. were afraid of crime.
   d. didn't hear the bell at first.

5. The robbers   5. ☐
   a. grabbed Jane from behind.
   b. pulled Jane inside.
   c. walked quietly away from her.
   d. screamed and fought.

6. The robbers hit Jane when she   6. ☐
   a. called the police.
   b. tried to scream and fight.
   c. opened the apartment door.
   d. grabbed them.

7. Now Jane is upset   7. ☐
   a. and also badly hurt.
   b. but not badly hurt.
   c. and very relaxed.
   d. and she doesn't remember what happened.

8. After this Jane will probably   8. ☐
   a. not go visit her friends again.
   b. relax and forget what happened.
   c. be more afraid in New York.
   d. never go to New York again.

Go back and answer the questions a second time. You may look back at the passage. Write the answers in the boxes on the right.

Check your answers in the Answer Key. Number correct _____
Find your Reading Rate. Fill in the Progress Chart.

16

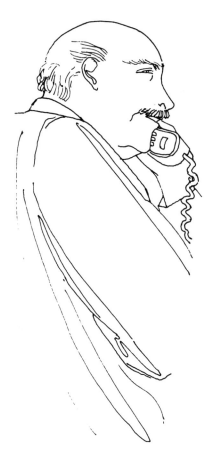

"Hello, Maria?"

"No, this is Jane."

"Jane! How are you?!?"

"Dad? Is that you? I can't hear you very well."

"We were worried about you. Are you really all right?"

"What? You have to talk louder. Are you in London?"

"No, we're in Salisbury now. Tomorrow we're going to look at the famous church here. But tell me, how are you now?"

"What?"

"HOW ARE YOU?"

"I'm okay. Really. I'm fine now. But I still have a black eye."

"Are you back at work?"

"Well, I have to walk to get to the subway. Taxis are too expensive."

"No, I said, are you back at WORK?"

"Work? Yes, yes. Everything's fine at work. I'm still a little nervous on the streets. That's all."

"You're WHAT on the streets?!?"

"NERVOUS!"

"Nervous?"

"Yes, a little nervous, because of what happened."

"This is terrible. There are all kinds of funny noises every time you say something! Is Ted there?"

"No, he and Maria went out to dinner."

"Well, give them our love. We shouldn't talk any more. I guess this call is expensive. Your mother's here. She sends you a hug and a kiss."

"Give her my love too."

"Okay. Bye."

"Bye."

Starting time _____

Finishing time _____

Reading time _____

Turn the page and answer the questions.
Don't look back at the passage.

Circle the best answer.

1. This passage is about   1. ☐
   a. a phone call from Jane to her parents.
   b. telephones.
   c. Jane's work.
   d. a phone conversation between Sam and Jane.

2. Sam was calling because   2. ☐
   a. he thought Jane was Maria.
   b. he wasn't in London.
   c. he was worried about Jane.
   d. he wanted to talk to Maria.

3. Jane   3. ☐
   a. couldn't hear anything her father said.
   b. had trouble hearing her father.
   c. could hear her father very well.
   d. wasn't listening to her father.

4. When Jane heard "work" the first time, she   4. ☐
   a. thought her father said "walk."
   b. decided to take a taxi.
   c. got nervous.
   d. asked Sam about London.

5. Jane still felt   5. ☐
   a. happy to be in New York.
   b. a little nervous on the streets.
   c. afraid to go to work.
   d. worried about the funny noises.

6. Sam heard funny noises   6. ☐
   a. on the street.
   b. at home.
   c. on the telephone.
   d. in New York.

7. The phone call was expensive because   7. ☐
   a. there were funny noises.
   b. Jane was at work.
   c. English phones don't work very well.
   d. Sam was calling from England.

8. Ted and Maria   8. ☐
   a. went to New York.
   b. were at home eating dinner.
   c. were not at home.
   d. did not want to talk to Sam.

Go back and answer the questions a second time. You may look back at the passage. Write the answers in the boxes on the right.

Check your answers in the Answer Key. Number correct _____
Find your Reading Rate. Fill in the Progress Chart.

17

Dear Ted, Maria and Jane,

We made a great discovery yesterday. We went into our first English pub. What is a pub? First of all, it's a place to go for some great cider. Cider is made from apples, like our apple juice. But English cider has much more flavor than American apple juice!

Many pubs also serve good cheap food. Some Americans think the meat pies and sausages are a bit heavy. But I think they are delicious. I guess Londoners think so, too. The pubs are often crowded at mealtimes.

There is still another reason why the English go to pubs. It seems to be a meeting place too. People meet their friends and talk until late at night. They talk to foreigners too. Some of my friends at home said the English were not friendly. But it's not true at all, not in the pubs anyway. Last night we didn't get home until almost midnight! We were in a pub all evening talking to people. A young doctor from Manchester was nice and interesting.

You'll have to come here sometime. I know you'd all like the pubs too. How about it, Jane? You might meet a nice young man too!

Hope you're all well.

Much love,
Dad

Starting time _____

Finishing time _____

Reading time _____

Turn the page and answer the questions.
Don't look back at the passage.

Circle the best answer.

1. This passage is about
   a. the English countryside.
   b. how friendly the English are.
   c. why people like English pubs.
   d. how Sam likes English people.

1. ☐

2. Sam thinks American apple juice
   a. is better than English cider.
   b. has more flavor than English cider.
   c. is not as good as English cider.
   d. costs more than English cider.

2. ☐

3. Londoners think that pub food is
   a. very expensive.
   b. very heavy.
   c. too rich.
   d. very good.

3. ☐

4. Sam probably likes
   a. weak tea.
   b. political meetings.
   c. only light foods.
   d. most foods.

4. ☐

5. The pubs are popular places for
   a. business meetings.
   b. learning English.
   c. meeting friends.
   d. people from Manchester.

5. ☐

6. Everyone told Sam that the English
   a. liked to talk with foreigners.
   b. liked to talk about business.
   c. were not very interested in America.
   d. were not very friendly to foreigners.

6. ☐

7. In the pub, Susan and Sam
   a. didn't talk much.
   b. met some Americans.
   c. talked until late.
   d. didn't meet anyone.

7. ☐

8. Sam thinks Jane might meet
   a. a nice, young man.
   b. Ted and Maria.
   c. the young doctor from Manchester.
   d. foreigners.

8. ☐

Go back and answer the questions a second time. You may look back at the passage. Write the answers in the boxes on the right.

Check your answers in the Answer Key. Number correct _____
Find your Reading Rate. Fill in the Progress Chart.

18

All around the world, people drink tea. But tea does not mean the same thing to everyone. In different countries people have very different ideas about drinking tea.

In China, for example, tea is always served when people get together. The Chinese drink it at any time of day, at home or in teahouses. They prefer their tea plain, with nothing else in it.

Tea is also important in Japan. The Japanese have a special way of serving tea called a tea ceremony. It is very old and full of meaning. Everything must be done a special way in the ceremony. There is even a special room for it in Japanese homes.

Another tea-drinking country is England. In England the late afternoon is "teatime." Almost everyone has a cup of tea then. The English usually make tea in a teapot and drink it with cream and sugar. They also eat cakes, cookies and little sandwiches at teatime.

In the United States people drink tea mostly for breakfast or after meals. Americans usually use tea bags to make their tea. Tea bags are faster and easier than making tea in teapots. In the summer, many Americans drink cold tea — "iced tea." They sometimes drink iced tea from cans, like soda.

Starting time	_____
Finishing time	_____
Reading time	_____

Turn the page and answer the questions.
Don't look back at the passage.

Circle the best answer.

1. This passage is about   1. ☐
   a. Chinese tea.
   b. how tea is important.
   c. English teatime.
   d. different ways of drinking tea in different
      countries.

2. Tea is popular   2. ☐
   a. all around the world.
   b. only in the United States.
   c. only in English-speaking countries.
   d. in Asian countries.

3. The Chinese drink tea   3. ☐
   a. for breakfast.
   b. in a special ceremony.
   c. when they get together.
   d. only in teahouses.

4. The tea ceremony is a   4. ☐
   a. kind of Japanese tea.
   b. special way of serving tea in Japan.
   c. kind of restaurant.
   d. special time of the afternoon.

5. Teatime in England is   5. ☐
   a. in the evening.
   b. in the morning.
   c. after dinner.
   d. in the afternoon.

6. The English like to   6. ☐
   a. eat cakes and cookies with their tea.
   b. drink their tea plain.
   c. have tea with dinner.
   d. drink their tea in a special room.

7. Americans usually   7. ☐
   a. make tea in teapots.
   b. drink tea in restaurants.
   c. make tea from tea bags.
   d. do not drink tea.

8. Iced tea is popular   8. ☐
   a. in the winter.
   b. in England.
   c. for breakfast.
   d. in the United States.

Go back and answer the questions a second time. You may look back at the passage. Write the answers in the boxes on the right.

Check your answers in the Answer Key. Number correct _____
Find your Reading Rate. Fill in the Progress Chart.

19

Dear Mom and Dad,

So many things are happening here! But don't worry, they are all very good things. Here's the first big news: Maria and I found a nice little house in Hartwell. It's only six miles from Rosebud. We will move there next week. Then we will be all ready for the baby. Only one month before the baby arrives!

We also both have good news about our jobs. Maria showed some of her paintings in a gallery here in New York. She was nervous about this because she is new to the city. No one knows her here. In Italy, she was popular, but people here are much harder to please. The opening of the show went very well. Everyone liked the paintings. There were even some newspaper reporters. They said they were going to write a story about Maria's artwork. They talked with Maria and asked lots of questions.

My good news is about my book. I had a meeting with an editor at a big publishing company. She said they were interested in my ideas about Italy. Now I have to write down those ideas. Then I'll show them to the editor. It's all very exciting for me.

Much love,
Ted

| Starting time _____ |
| Finishing time _____ |
| Reading time _____ |

Turn the page and answer the questions.
Don't look back at the passage.

Circle the best answer.

1. This passage is about
   a. Ted's new book about Italy.
   b. Maria's paintings.
   c. Ted and Maria.
   d. the good things happening to Ted and Maria.

1. ☐

2. Ted and Maria's new home is
   a. in New York.
   b. near Susan and Sam's house.
   c. far from Susan and Sam's house.
   d. in an apartment building.

2. ☐

3. Maria will have her baby
   a. in New York.
   b. in a week.
   c. in a month.
   d. next year.

3. ☐

4. Maria was nervous about her art show because
   a. she isn't very good.
   b. she doesn't like reporters.
   c. everyone knows her in New York.
   d. no one knows her.

4. ☐

5. Ted thinks people in Italy are
   a. easier to please than New Yorkers.
   b. harder to please than New Yorkers.
   c. going to write articles about her paintings.
   d. going to make her popular.

5. ☐

6. At the opening to Maria's show
   a. the reporters talked with everyone.
   b. the reporters talked with Maria.
   c. everyone talked with Maria.
   d. Ted talked with everyone.

6. ☐

7. Ted has good news about
   a. a new job as an editor.
   b. writing an article.
   c. the book he wants to write.
   d. living in Italy.

7. ☐

8. An editor at a big publishing company
   a. met with Maria and asked questions.
   b. is interested in Ted's book.
   c. wants to live in Italy.
   d. wants Ted to live in Italy.

8. ☐

Go back and answer the questions a second time. You may look back at the passage. Write the answers in the boxes on the right.

Check your answers in the Answer Key. Number correct _____
Find your Reading Rate. Fill in the Progress Chart.

20

THE NEW YORK CITY GAZETTE   May 16, 1986

A New Artist in New York

by Sandra Shaw

A wonderful new show of paintings opened in New York last week. Maria Arroyo-Diamond, the artist, is new to New York. She is not new to art. She grew up in Mexico. She studied with several famous artists in Mexico City. Five years ago, she married Ted Diamond and they moved to Italy. While they were living in Italy, she was quite popular. She also won several important awards.

Ms. Arroyo-Diamond is a small, very quiet person. But her paintings are very large. They are full of color and excitement. She explained that the colors she uses are Mediterranean colors. In the Mediterranean area the sky and the sea are usually very bright blue. The houses are often pink, yellow or orange.

In her paintings, the excitement comes partly from these colors. It also comes from her style. She likes to paint large shapes that seem to move. Ms. Arroyo-Diamond's paintings do not show us the real world. Instead they show us her feelings about the world.

We look forward to seeing more work from this young and very fine artist.

Starting time _____

Finishing time _____

Reading time _____

Turn the page and answer the questions.
Don't look back at the passage.

Circle the best answer.

1. This passage is about   1. ☐
   a. the color and excitement in Maria's paintings.
   b. Maria's feelings about the world.
   c. Maria Arroyo-Diamond.
   d. Maria and her art.

2. This passage was   2. ☐
   a. written by Ted.
   b. from a newspaper.
   c. written by Maria.
   d. from a book.

3. When she was living in Italy, Maria   3. ☐
   a. won several awards.
   b. had no luck with her art.
   c. showed her paintings in New York.
   d. began to paint.

4. Maria's paintings are   4. ☐
   a. small and neat.
   b. larger than she is.
   c. smaller than she is.
   d. large.

5. The colors in Maria's paintings come from   5. ☐
   a. the Mediterranean area.
   b. the past.
   c. New York.
   d. Mexico.

6. This reporter says Maria's style is   6. ☐
   a. realistic
   b. unusual.
   c. exciting.
   d. moving.

7. Maria's paintings show us   7. ☐
   a. the life of the Mediterranean area.
   b. the real world.
   c. the sea, the sky and houses.
   d. large, colorful shapes.

8. This reporter thinks that Maria   8. ☐
   a. is too young.
   b. works hard.
   c. is a good artist.
   d. is not a good artist.

Go back and answer the questions a second time. You may look back at the passage. Write the answers in the boxes on the right.

Check your answers in the Answer Key. Number correct _____
Find your Reading Rate. Fill in the Progress Chart.

21

THE NEW YORK CITY GAZETTE   MAY 19. 1986

CRIME IN BIG CITIES

by Carmen Cipolla

Crime is a serious problem in big cities. And it is getting worse every year. This is what police departments around the country said in their reports last week. There were more robberies and murders this year than last year. The subways are more dangerous. The streets are more dangerous. You may not even be safe in your own home.

Why is the problem so serious now? This is not an easy question to answer. There may not be a single answer. Many problems together seem to make cities so dangerous.

One of the problems is money. To fight crime a city needs police officers, cars and guns. These cost a lot of money. But right now cities do not have much extra money. So there are not enough police officers, cars and guns for the cities.

Another problem is drugs. Crime studies show that many criminals use and sell drugs. After they start taking drugs, they want to have more. But drugs are very expensive. So these people may sell drugs to other people to make money. Or they may steal money to get more drugs.

The laws about guns are also part of the crime problem. It is very easy to buy a gun in the United States. Anyone can have a gun. That means robbers carry guns. Many people are killed during robberies. Anyone can have a gun at home. So an angry husband may shoot his wife or children. A crazy person is more dangerous with a gun. In general, crimes are more serious because everyone has guns.

But there is an even more important cause of crime. Cities have rich and poor neighborhoods. In the poor neighborhoods, the schools are often very bad. Jobs are hard to find. Many young people don't have much hope for a better life. They only know one way to make a better living for themselves. That way is to sell drugs or steal. So, some of these young people become criminals.

It is not going to be easy to change these crime problems. We must first change many of the laws about drugs and guns. We much change the way cities spend their money. We must also begin to make changes in the neighborhoods. Until then, the crime problem will not go away. And we will live our lives in fear.

Starting time _____

Finishing time _____

Reading time _____

Turn the page and answer the questions.
Don't look back at the passage.

Circle the best answer.

1. This passage is about
   a. police department reports.
   b. the drug problem in big cities.
   c. problems of city life.
   d. the crime problem in big cities.

   1. ☐

2. People in big cities are
   a. usually safe on the streets.
   b. safer this year than last year.
   c. not very worried about crime.
   d. afraid of crime.

   2. ☐

3. Money is part of the crime problem because
   a. it costs a lot to fight crime.
   b. the city needs extra money.
   c. drugs are expensive.
   d. criminals steal money.

   3. ☐

4. Many criminals
   a. have extra money.
   b. use or sell drugs.
   c. stop taking drugs.
   d. are afraid of drugs.

   4. ☐

5. In the United States
   a. only police officers have guns.
   b. children have guns.
   c. many people have guns.
   d. only robbers have guns.

   5. ☐

6. Many young people in poor neighborhoods
   a. work hard for a better life.
   b. move to richer neighborhoods.
   c. don't have much hope for a better life.
   d. don't want a better life.

   6. ☐

7. These young people can only make a better living
   a. through hard work.
   b. through education.
   c. by stealing or selling drugs.
   d. by changing the laws.

   7. ☐

8. The crime problem will not go away
   a. until there are no drugs.
   b. in big cities.
   c. until there are many changes.
   d. if there are changes.

   8. ☐

Go back and answer the questions a second time. You may look back at the passage. Write the answers in the boxes on the right.

Check your answers in the Answer Key. Number correct _____
Find your Reading Rate. Fill in the Progress Chart.

22

Tourists in New York may think it is one big city. But the neighborhoods really are very different. There are rich neighborhoods and poor neighborhoods. And there are some neighborhoods full of people from the same country. These neighborhoods don't really look like they are part of the same city. The people are different and so are the buildings.

For example, in the southern part of the city is New York's Chinatown. New Yorkers from all parts of the city like to go there. They enjoy shopping at the Chinese stores and eating at the Chinese restaurants. But most of the people who live in Chinatown are Chinese. The shop signs are all written in Chinese. Everyone in the shops speaks Chinese. This is one of the most crowded and colorful neighborhoods in the city. It is also growing fast. More Chinese people are arriving every day.

Not far from Chinatown is Little Italy. Many Italians moved there from Italy in the early 1900s. Some of them stayed in the neighborhood. There are still good Italian shops, restaurants and cafes in Little Italy. You can hear Italian spoken on the streets. Every year there is a big Italian festival.

Greenwich Village is another kind of neighborhood. There the buildings are small, old and comfortable. Twenty-five years ago the rent for apartments in Greenwich Village was cheap. Young people with little money often lived there. For many years this was also where writers, artists and students lived. Famous books were written in the neighborhood. Famous artists painted their first pictures there.

Greenwich Village became more expensive in the 1960s. So, some artists and writers moved down the street to a neighborhood called Soho. There were many old factories in this area. Now most of the old factory buildings are studios for artists. There are many new art galleries, restaurants and shops. Soon this neighborhood may also be too expensive for artists!

The most beautiful and expensive neighborhood in New York is the Upper East Side. That is where many of the richest people live. The apartment buildings are large and very fancy. The streets are always clean. The shops sell all kinds of special foods and clothing. People from all over the world come to shop on the Upper East Side. Or they just look in the shop windows and dream.

Starting time _____
Finishing time _____
Reading time _____

Turn the page and answer the questions.
Don't look back at the passage.

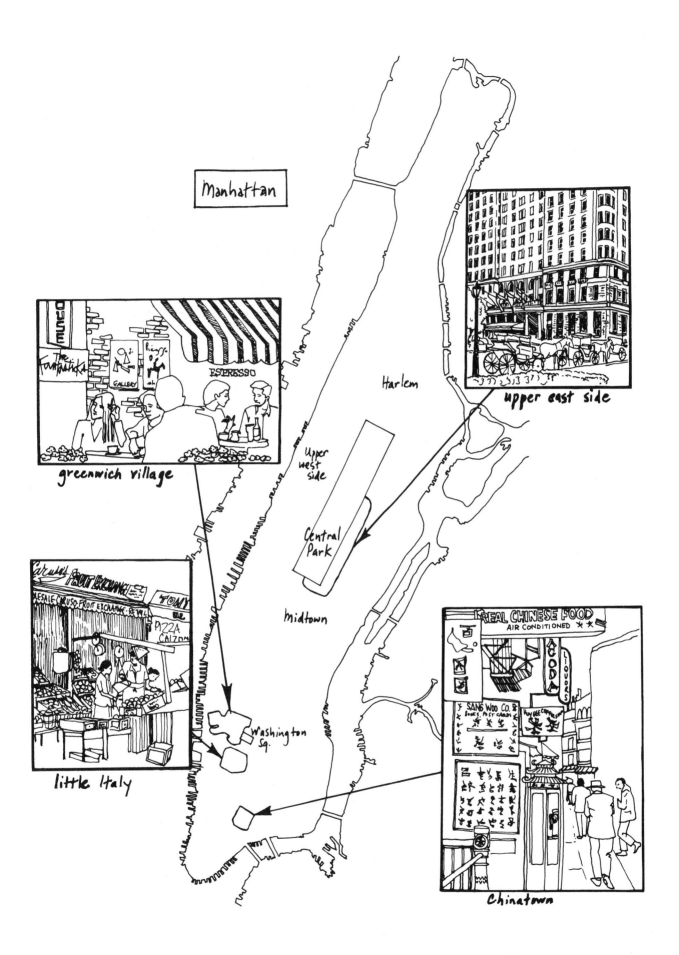

Manhattan

greenwich village

upper east side

Harlem

Upper west side

Central Park

midtown

little Italy

Washington Sq.

Chinatown

Circle the best answer.

1. This passage is about
   a. Greenwich Village.
   b. people who live in New York.
   c. New York.
   d. the neighborhoods of New York.

   1. ☐

2. People like to visit Chinatown
   a. because they are Chinese.
   b. because they speak Chinese.
   c. to go shopping or have dinner.
   d. because Chinatown is growing fast.

   2. ☐

3. Little Italy is probably
   a. a lively neighborhood.
   b. far away from Chinatown.
   c. growing faster than Chinatown.
   d. further south than Chinatown.

   3. ☐

4. Greenwich Village used to be popular with
   a. Italians.
   b. New Yorkers.
   c. students and artists.
   d. rich people.

   4. ☐

5. Apartments in Greenwich Village were usually
   a. expensive.
   b. large.
   c. lively.
   d. inexpensive.

   5. ☐

6. Now the most popular area for artists is
   a. Greenwich Village.
   b. Soho.
   c. the Upper East Side.
   d. the southern part of the city.

   6. ☐

7. In general, the neighborhoods in New York
   a. often change.
   b. always stay the same.
   c. aren't as nice as they used to be.
   d. are all the same.

   7. ☐

8. The Upper East Side is for people
   a. with only a little money.
   b. in fancy clothing.
   c. with a lot of money.
   d. from around the world.

   8. ☐

Go back and answer the questions a second time. You may look back at the passage. Write the answers in the boxes on the right.

Check your answers in the Answer Key. Number correct _____
Find your Reading Rate. Fill in the Progress Chart.

23

Michael Greenberg is a very popular New Yorker. He is not in the government, and he is not famous in sports or the arts. But people in the streets know about him, especially poor people.

For these poor people, he is not Michael or even Mr. Greenberg. For them his name is "Gloves" Greenberg. "Here comes Gloves," they say when they see him walking down the street. How did he get that name? He looks like any other businessman. He wears a suit and he carries a briefcase. But he's different. His briefcase doesn't just have papers and books. It also has several pairs of gloves.

On cold winter days, Mr. Greenberg does not act like other New Yorkers. He does not look at the sidewalk and hurry down the street. He looks around at people. He is looking for poor people with cold hands. That is why he carries gloves in his briefcase. He stops when he sees someone with no gloves. If they look poor he gives them a pair of gloves. "Merry Christmas!" he says. He shakes their hand. Then he moves on, looking for more people with cold hands.

Every day during the winter Mr. Greenberg gives away gloves. During the rest of the year, he buys gloves. People who know about him send him gloves. He has a mountain of gloves in his apartment. There are gloves of all colors and sizes: children's gloves, work gloves and evening gloves for ladies.

Mr. Greenberg began giving away gloves 21 years ago. Now, many of the poor people in New York know him. They know why he gives away gloves. But some people don't know him. They are sometimes surprised by him. They think he wants money for the gloves. They don't understand that he just wants to make them happy.

The Greenberg family was poor. But Michael's father always gave things away. He believed it made everyone happier. Michael Greenberg feels the same way. He wants to do something for the poor people in New York. He feels that winter is a hard time for them. Many of these poor people have no warm place to go and no warm clothing. A pair of gloves may be a small thing. But he feels it can make a big difference in the winter. No wonder he is popular among the street people of New York.

Starting time _____

Finishing time _____

Reading time _____

Turn the page and answer the questions.
Don't look back at the passage.

Circle the best answer.

1. This passage is about
   a. gloves.
   b. winter in New York.
   c. Michael Greenberg.
   d. poor people in New York.

1. ☐

2. The people who like Michael Greenberg most are
   a. famous.
   b. poor.
   c. businessmen.
   d. rich.

2. ☐

3. Mr. Greenberg is called ''Gloves'' because he
   a. looks like any other businessman.
   b. always wears gloves.
   c. makes gloves.
   d. gives away gloves.

3. ☐

4. In the winter, Mr. Greenberg looks for
   a. his briefcase.
   b. clothing.
   c. friends.
   d. people with cold hands.

4. ☐

5. Mr. Greenberg gives the gloves to
   a. his family.
   b. poor people.
   c. businessmen.
   d. anyone.

5. ☐

6. In his apartment, Mr. Greenberg has
   a. many gloves.
   b. only gloves for children.
   c. a few pairs of gloves.
   d. lots of briefcases.

6. ☐

7. People are sometimes surprised because
   a. Mr. Greenberg wants money.
   b. they want money.
   c. gloves usually aren't free.
   d. they have gloves already.

7. ☐

8. Greenberg wants to
   a. be famous.
   b. keep warm.
   c. make people happier.
   d. make a lot of money.

8. ☐

Go back and answer the questions a second time. You may look back at the passage. Write the answers in the boxes on the right.

Check your answers in the Answer Key. Number correct _____
Find your Reading Rate. Fill in the Progress Chart.

24

Susan and Sam Diamond were enjoying themselves very much in London. They were lucky with the weather. No rain for ten days! They couldn't believe it. England is famous for bad weather. Londoners couldn't believe it either. Everyone was smiling all the time. At lunch time the parks were full of people sitting in the sun.

With the good weather, Susan and Sam spent many hours outside. They visited Kew Gardens and Kensington Gardens several times. The flowers there seemed bigger and more beautiful than the flowers at home. Susan especially loved the roses. She wished she could take some home with her.

The Diamonds visited many of the historical places around the city. They went to the Tower of London. It is one of the oldest buildings in the city. King William built it in about 1080 to keep his family safe. Later it became a prison. Many famous kings and queens were prisoners in the Tower. Now it is a place for tourists to visit.

Susan and Sam also went to Westminster Abbey, the most famous old church in London. Many people are buried there. Susan and Sam looked at all the names. They found the names of kings, queens, poets and scientists. For example, Queen Elizabeth I is buried there. So are Charles Darwin and Robert Browning. Susan and Sam were learning a lot of history. There was so much more history in England than in America!

And of course, the Diamonds went to many museums. In the British Museum they found very interesting and very old art from Greece and Egypt. They were surprised to see all these things in England. In the National Gallery and the Tate Gallery they saw fine examples of English art. Susan decided her favorite painter was John Constable. She liked his pictures of English farms, hills and rivers.

But the museum they both preferred was the Victoria and Albert Museum. There they saw very interesting old clothing from different times and places. They also saw old musical instruments from Italy. Sam's favorite was a beautiful old violin made by Antonio Stradivari in 1690.

Susan and Sam were very happy at the end of every day in London. But they also were very, very tired. One evening, they went to the opera at Covent Garden. They both fell asleep in the middle of a song!

Starting time _____

Finishing time _____

Reading time _____

Turn the page and answer the questions.
Don't look back at the passage.

Circle the best answer.

1. This passage is about   1. ☐
   a. English museums.
   b. how Susan and Sam enjoyed London.
   c. how tired Susan and Sam were at the end of every day.
   d. historical places in London.

2. In London ten days of good weather is   2. ☐
   a. not surprising.
   b. not lucky.
   c. unusual.
   d. famous.

3. Susan thought that English roses were   3. ☐
   a. not as beautiful as American roses.
   b. difficult to grow.
   c. more beautiful than American roses.
   d. not as big as American roses.

4. The Tower of London is   4. ☐
   a. full of prisoners.
   b. a famous church.
   c. one of the oldest buildings in the city.
   d. where the king lives.

5. The Diamonds think England   5. ☐
   a. has a longer history than the U.S.
   b. has less history than the U.S.
   c. has few museums.
   d. isn't interesting.

6. Many famous people   6. ☐
   a. lived in Westminster Abbey.
   b. were prisoners in Westminster Abbey.
   c. are in the British Museum.
   d. are buried in Westminster Abbey.

7. Susan and Sam are especially interested in   7. ☐
   a. science.
   b. history and art.
   c. opera.
   d. English farms.

8. At the end of every day, Susan and Sam were   8. ☐
   a. at the opera.
   b. thinking about New York.
   c. happy and tired.
   d. unhappy.

Go back and answer the questions a second time. You may look back at the passage. Write the answers in the boxes on the right.

Check your answers in the Answer Key. Number correct _____
Find your Reading Rate. Fill in the Progress Chart.

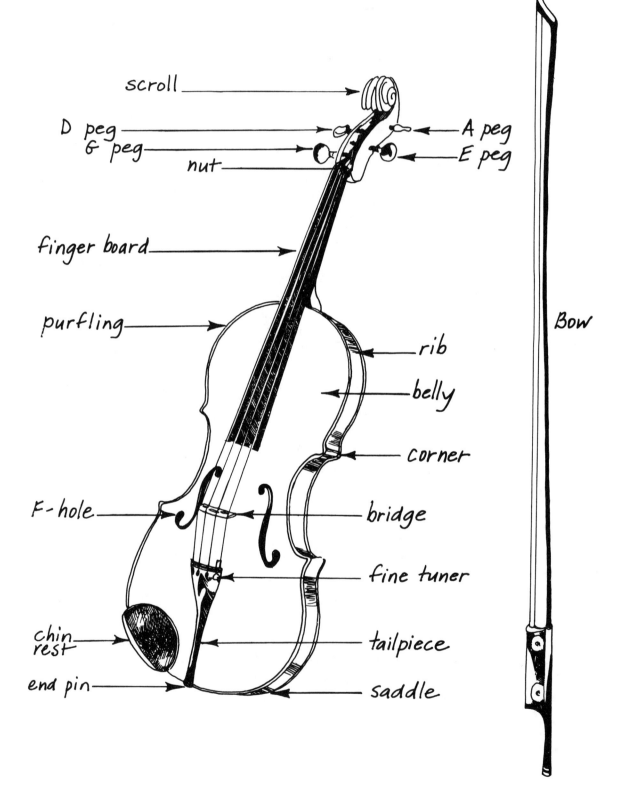

scroll

D peg

G peg

nut

A peg

E peg

finger board

purfling

rib

belly

corner

F-hole

bridge

fine tuner

chin rest

tailpiece

end pin

saddle

Bow

25

Most musicians agree that the best violins were first made in Italy. They were made in Cremona, Italy, about 200 years ago. These violins sound better than any others. They even sound better than violins made today. Violin makers and scientists try to make instruments like the Italian violins. But they aren't the same. Musicians still prefer the old ones. Why are these old Italian violins so special? No one really knows. But many people think they have an answer.

Some people think it is the age of the violins. They say that today's violins will also sound wonderful someday. But there is a problem here. Not all old violins sound wonderful. Only the old violins from Cremona are special. So age cannot be the answer. There must be something different about Cremona or those Italian violin makers.

Other people think the secret to those violins is the wood. The wood of the violin is very important. It must be from certain kinds of trees. It must not be too young or too old. Perhaps the violin makers of Cremona knew something special about wood for violins.

But the kind of wood may not be so important. It may be more important to cut the wood a special way. Wood for a violin must be cut very carefully. It has to be the right size and shape. The smallest difference will change the sound of the violin. Musicians sometimes think that this was the secret of the Italians. Maybe they understood more than we do about how to cut the wood.

Size and shape may not be the answer either. Scientists measured these old violins very carefully. They can make new ones that are exactly the same size and shape. But the new violins still do not sound as good as the old ones. Some scientists think the secret may be the varnish. Varnish is what covers the wood of the violin. It makes the wood look shiny. It also helps the sound of the instrument. No one knows what the Italian violin makers used in their varnish. So no one can make the same varnish today.

There may never be other violins like the violins of Cremona. Their secret may be lost forever. Young musicians today hope this is not true. They need fine violins. But there aren't very many of the old violins left. Also, the old violins are very expensive. Recently, a famous old Italian violin was sold for about $300,000!

Starting time	_____
Finishing time	_____
Reading time	_____

Turn the page and answer the questions.
Don't look back at the passage.

Circle the best answer.

1. This passage is about
   a. making violins.
   b. musical instruments.
   c. scientific ideas.
   d. the old Italian violins.

1. ☐

2. The best violins
   a. are modern.
   b. were lost many years ago.
   c. were made in Italy 200 years ago.
   d. were made by scientists.

2. ☐

3. Some people think that modern violins
   a. will sound better in the future.
   b. will sound worse in the future.
   c. sound wonderful.
   d. are too old.

3. ☐

4. Other people think the Italian violin makers
   a. did not know much about violins.
   b. were lucky.
   c. used many kinds of wood.
   d. knew something special.

4. ☐

5. The size and shape of the violin
   a. do not matter.
   b. are a secret.
   c. can make a difference.
   d. are different today.

5. ☐

6. Violins made today
   a. have the same size and shape as the old ones.
   b. sound the same as the old ones.
   c. are better than the old ones.
   d. have the same varnish as the old ones.

6. ☐

7. Some scientists believe the secret of the old violins was
   a. their sound.
   b. their color.
   c. their varnish.
   d. the music.

7. ☐

8. The old violins are
   a. lost forever.
   b. inexpensive.
   c. expensive.
   d. easy to get.

8. ☐

Go back and answer the questions a second time. You may look back at the passage. Write the answers in the boxes on the right.

Check your answers in the Answer Key. Number correct _____
Find your Reading Rate. Fill in the Progress Chart.

26

American and British people both speak English of course. But sometimes it does not seem like the same language. In fact, there are some important differences between British and American English.

First of all, they sound very different. Often, Americans don't say each word separately. They say several words together. Americans may say "I dunno" instead of "I don't know." Or they may say "Whaddya say?" instead of "What did you say?" However, the British are more careful in their speech. They usually say all the words and keep them separate.

British	American
I don't know.	I dunno.
What did you say?	Whaddya say?

Also, some letters have different sounds. For example, the Americans say the "a" in half like the "a" in cat. But the British say the "a" in half like the "o" in soft.

British "a"	American "a"
half = soft	half = cat

Sound is not the only difference between British English and American English. Words sometimes have different meanings too. Some American words are never used in England. The same thing is true of some British words in America. For example, the vocabulary for cars and driving is very different. Americans use the word *highway*, but the British say *motorway*. Americans drive *trucks*, but in England they drive *lorries*. The back of a car is called a *trunk* in America. In England it is a *boot*. The American word for the front of the car is *hood*, but the British say *bonnet*.

British	American
motorway	highway
lorry	truck
boot	trunk
bonnet	hood

Many expressions are also different in the two countries. In England, if you are going to telephone friends, you "ring them up." In America you "give them a call." When you are saying goodbye in England you might say "Cheerio!" In America you might say, "See you later."

British	American
I'll ring you up.	I'll give you a call.
Cheerio.	See you later.

There are also sometimes differences in grammar. For example, Americans usually use the helping verb *do* when they ask a question. They say "Do you have class today?" But the British often leave out the helping verb. They say "Have you class today?"

All these differences can be confusing if you are learning English. But most languages are like this. Languages change over time. When people live in separate places, the languages change in different ways. This is what happened to English. It also can happen to other languages, such as French. Many people in Canada speak French. But their French is very different from the French of France.

Starting time _____

Finishing time _____

Reading time _____

Turn the page and answer the questions.
Don't look back at the passage.

Circle the best answer.

1. This passage is about   1. ☐
   a. English vocabulary.
   b. the way the British say words.
   c. how American sounds are different from British sounds.
   d. differences between American and British sounds.

2. Compared to the British, Americans are usually   2. ☐
   a. more careful about saying words.
   b. less careful about saying words.
   c. easier to understand.
   d. slower speakers.

3. Some letters in English   3. ☐
   a. always sound the same.
   b. have different sounds in the U.S. and England.
   c. don't change.
   d. have an unusual sound.

4. The vocabulary for cars and driving is   4. ☐
   a. an example of British English.
   b. different in the U.S. and England.
   c. an example of modern technology.
   d. the same in the U.S. and England.

5. People in the U.S. and in England   5. ☐
   a. always use the same expressions.
   b. often say goodbye.
   c. don't use expressions often.
   d. sometimes use different expressions.

6. When Americans ask questions they usually   6. ☐
   a. use the helping verb "do."
   b. don't use the helping verb.
   c. don't use any grammar.
   d. cause confusion.

7. English can be confusing   7. ☐
   a. because it never changes.
   b. because it is different in different places.
   c. when you ask questions.
   d. because British English is the only kind of English.

8. Languages   8. ☐
   a. change over time.
   b. are difficult to say.
   c. don't change much.
   d. are the same in all places.

Go back and answer the questions a second time. You may look back at the passage. Write the answers in the boxes on the right.

Check your answers in the Answer Key. Number correct _____
Find your Reading Rate. Fill in the Progress Chart.

27

If you like unusual places, you should go sometime to the
Hebrides Islands. Not many people live on these islands in the northwest of Scotland. The land is not good for farming. The winters are
long, cold and wet. It is hard to make a living in the Hebrides. But
for a visitor, these islands can be very special.

They're not for everyone, however. Even summer days are cool
and often windy. The water is too cold for swimming. There are only
a few trees, no forests and few green fields. Instead of fields there are
just rocks and bushes. The hills, too, are just piles of rocks. Sometimes
the scenery looks like pictures of the moon.

But there is beauty in this wild place. It's in the wide, unforgettable views. From the beach you can often see all the way to the rocky
hills. From the hills you can see far out to other islands and the open
ocean. The colors, too, are unforgettable. Blue is everywhere. It's
in the sky and in the ocean. It is in the tiny flowers that grow on
the hills. In the spring there is also green in the hills. In the summer and fall they are more purple. And often the air is soft and gray
with clouds and rain.

In these islands you can forget about the rest of the world. You can forget about city problems of noise, dirt and crime. The nights are quiet. The restaurants close early and there isn't much nightlife. There aren't even many hotels. Most visitors stay in guesthouses or "Bed and Breakfasts" as they are called in Scotland. These are really people's homes. They rent out rooms for the night and serve breakfast to their guests. These homes may be simple, but guests are usually comfortable and well fed. You can meet some friendly people this way. It's also a way to learn more about life on the islands.

You do not feel much like a tourist in the Hebrides. There are only a few historic places, no museums and a few shops. The shops are small. The only interesting thing to buy is the "tweed" from the island of Harris. This is a kind of wool cloth that is famous around the world.

But people do not come to the Hebrides to go sightseeing or shopping. They come to walk in the clean, cool air. They come for the quiet beauty and for the views.

Starting time _____

Finishing time _____

Reading time _____

Turn the page and answer the questions.
Don't look back at the passage.

Circle the best answer.

1. This passage is about
   a. islands.
   b. Scotland.
   c. the Hebrides Islands.
   d. vacations.

   1. ☐

2. Not many people live in the Hebrides because
   a. the water is too cold.
   b. it is hard to make a living there.
   c. it is in the northwest of Scotland.
   d. the summers can be cool.

   2. ☐

3. The weather in the Hebrides is
   a. usually warm and sunny.
   b. never warm and sunny.
   c. usually cold and wet.
   d. nice in the summer.

   3. ☐

4. Some of the scenery looks like the moon because
   a. it is so green.
   b. it is so rocky.
   c. the colors are so beautiful.
   d. there is no sun.

   4. ☐

5. The colors on the islands
   a. are unforgettable.
   b. are always the same.
   c. are like the colors everywhere else.
   d. make it look like the moon.

   5. ☐

6. In the Hebrides you can forget about
   a. yourself.
   b. your vacation.
   c. noise, dirt and crime.
   d. life.

   6. ☐

7. Visitors usually
   a. stay in hotels.
   b. stay out late at night.
   c. stay at "Bed and Breakfasts."
   d. buy a lot of gifts.

   7. ☐

8. People usually come to the Hebrides to
   a. shop
   b. go sightseeing.
   c. paint pictures.
   d. look at the views.

   8. ☐

Go back and answer the questions a second time. You may look back at the passage. Write the answers in the boxes on the right.

Check your answers in the Answer Key. Number correct _____
Find your Reading Rate. Fill in the Progress Chart.

28

TRAVEL TODAY MAGAZINE   May 19, 1986

Health Tips for Travelers

Tom O'Neal

Travel is fun. Travel is exciting. But it's not fun or exciting if you get sick. You may think, "Not me. I won't get sick on my vacation!" But, for many people, that is what happens.

Of course you do not want to spend your vacation sick in bed. If you have heart trouble, you don't want to make it worse. So what can you do to stay in good health? There are three things you should remember when you travel: relax, sleep and eat well.

A vacation is supposed to be a time for relaxing. But very often it is not. Think about what you do when you are a tourist. There are so many places to visit: museums, shops, parks and churches. You may spend most days walking around these places. This can be very tiring. Your feet may hurt. You may have a terrible headache after a few hours. If this is the way you feel, you should take a rest. Do not ask your body to do too much. A tired body means a weak body. And a weak body gets sick easily. So sit down for a few hours in a nice spot. In good weather, look for a quiet park bench. Or you can stop at a cafe. You can learn a lot by watching people while you rest.

Sleep is also important. If you want to stay healthy you need to get enough sleep. You may have trouble sleeping at night when you travel. Your hotel room may be noisy or the bed may be uncomfortable. If this is true, don't be afraid to change rooms or hotels. Or, you may not get enough sleep for another reason.

You may want to stay out late at night. In many cities the night life can be very exciting. Then you should plan to sleep for an hour during the day. That extra hour can make a big difference.

Finally, if you want to stay healthy, you must eat well. That means eating the right kinds of foods. Your body needs fresh fruits and vegetables, and some meat, milk or cheese. When you are in a new country, you may want to try new foods. But you need to be careful about how much you eat. Lots of rich food is not good for you.

So, remember this: if you want to enjoy your vacation, take good care of yourself. Give your body some rest. Get enough sleep and eat good, healthy food.

Starting time _____

Finishing time _____

Reading time _____

Turn the page and answer the questions.
Don't look back at the passage.

Circle the best answer.

1. This passage is about   1. ☐
   a. what to eat when you travel.
   b. how exciting travel is.
   c. relaxing when you travel.
   d. how to stay healthy when you travel.

2. A vacation is not fun if   2. ☐
   a. you don't want to go.
   b. you go sightseeing.
   c. you get sick.
   d. you are in a new place.

3. Sightseeing is   3. ☐
   a. the best way to relax.
   b. very tiring.
   c. never any fun.
   d. unhealthy.

4. It's a good idea to   4. ☐
   a. spend every day in bed.
   b. take short vacations.
   c. get some rest every day.
   d. take lots of medicines.

5. You can get sick more easily if you are   5. ☐
   a. tired.
   b. sleepy.
   c. in a hotel.
   d. strong and healthy.

6. Your body needs sleep to   6. ☐
   a. enjoy the nightlife.
   b. change hotels.
   c. stay strong and healthy.
   d. learn a lot about a new place.

7. When you travel your body needs   7. ☐
   a. new foods.
   b. fresh fruits and vegetables.
   c. lots of rich foods.
   d. more food.

8. For good health you need   8. ☐
   a. to travel.
   b. to get enough sleep and good food.
   c. to enjoy the nightlife.
   d. to eat new foods.

Go back and answer the questions a second time. You may look back
at the passage. Write the answers in the boxes on the right.

Check your answers in the Answer Key. Number correct _____
Find your Reading Rate. Fill in the Progress Chart.

29

Dear Mom and Dad,

Guess what! You are now grandparents! And I'm a very happy father. Yesterday Maria had a little girl. We named her Elena. That was the name of Maria's mother. Everybody says Elena looks like me already. She does have blue eyes like me. But I think she looks more like Maria. They both have round faces and dark hair.

The doctors were worried about the baby. She arrived a little early, after only eight months. When she first came out she wasn't breathing. She didn't make any noise. I thought maybe she wasn't alive. But after a moment she began to move. Then she began to cry very loudly. It was a good sound. Elena is small, only six pounds, but very healthy.

The doctors were also worried about Maria. For a while they were afraid for her life, too. She went into the hospital at 2:00 p.m. on Monday. The baby was born at 8:00 p.m. on Tuesday. That's 30 hours! Poor Maria. She had a very difficult time for those 30 hours. In fact, the doctors say she shouldn't have another child. It might be dangerous for her. We were a little sad when we heard the doctor. We wanted to have two children and now maybe we can't.

But we do have Elena. That is the important thing. I'm in love with her already. She's such a pretty little girl. Not all babies are pretty, you know. Some of the other babies at the hospital are almost ugly. But our Elena has a perfect nose and perfect little ears. And she has the biggest, most beautiful blue eyes. All the nurses love her because she doesn't cry very often. She also smiles a lot. She's really a very happy baby.

For the next few months I'm planning to work less. My boss says I can work part-time, only 25 hours per week. Then I will have more time to be with Maria and Elena. I don't know much about babies, but I guess I'll learn! I'm just afraid I'll hurt this little daughter. She's so very, very small!

Jane is at the hospital now with Maria. I'm at home and I couldn't sleep because I was too excited. I wanted to call you but I didn't know your telephone number. Maybe you could call us when you get this letter. I hope you are enjoying Scotland.

Much love,
Ted

Starting time _____

Finishing time _____

Reading time _____

Turn the page and answer the questions.
Don't look back at the passage.

Circle the best answer.

1. This passage is about
   a. how Ted feels about babies.
   b. Maria's health.
   c. having children.
   d. Ted and Maria's new baby.

1 ▢

2. The baby was named
   a. Maria.
   b. Elena.
   c. Susan.
   d. Margaret.

2. ▢

3. Maria and the baby both have
   a. the same name.
   b. blue eyes.
   c. little ears.
   d. round faces and dark hair.

3. ▢

4. When the baby first came out it
   a. wasn't alive.
   b. wasn't breathing.
   c. made a lot of noise.
   d. was very large.

4. ▢

5. The doctors say Maria
   a. shouldn't have another child.
   b. should stay in the hospital for 30 hours.
   c. can have many children.
   d. is going to have another baby.

5. ▢

6. Ted thinks Elena is
   a. like all other babies.
   b. prettier than other babies.
   c. not as pretty as other babies.
   d. an ugly baby.

6. ▢

7. Elena
   a. is popular in the hospital.
   b. is a difficult baby.
   c. cries a lot.
   d. never smiles.

7. ▢

8. Ted will have more time now
   a. to work for *The New York Times*.
   b. to relax.
   c. to be with Maria and Elena.
   d. to be at the hospital.

8. ▢

Go back and answer the questions a second time. You may look back at the passage. Write the answers in the boxes on the right.

Check your answers in the Answer Key. Number correct _____
Find your Reading Rate. Fill in the Progress Chart.

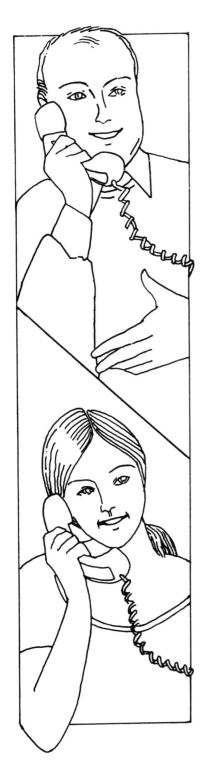

30

"Hello, Ted?"

"Hello. Mom? Is that you? I'm so glad you got my letter."

"What letter?"

"The letter about Maria and the baby."

"Baby!"

"Yes, it's a girl. She came a little early. But Maria's fine and the baby's fine. We named her Elena. Didn't you get my letter? How come you're calling?"

"Because of your father. I have some bad news."

"What happened?!?!?"

"It's his heart. He had a small heart attack. Just a small one. The doctor says he has to stay in the hospital for a few weeks. But it's not too serious."

"Is he there? Can I speak with him?"

"No. I'm not at the hospital now. But you can call him at the hospital. He will be glad to hear from you."

"How did it happen?"

"Well, we were in the Hebrides Islands for a few days. Maybe it was the cold weather there. Maybe he was drinking too much tea and eating too many tea cakes. I don't know and the doctors don't know either. Anyway, we arrived in Edinburgh last night. After dinner he suddenly didn't feel well. Then he fell down in the middle of the street! It was terrible! But the people here were very helpful. Someone called the police. Someone called the hospital.

"You're sure Dad is okay?"

"Yes. Dr. Campbell is taking care of him. They say he's the best heart doctor in Scotland. He says Dad may feel sick for a while, but he'll be fine. He just has to rest now. Is Jane there?"

"No, she isn't home yet. I'll tell her when she gets home. Maybe she will want to go to Edinburgh. I can't leave Maria and the baby right now. Unless it is serious. Are you really sure Dad's okay?"

"Yes, he's going to be fine. And Maria... You're sure she's okay? Your father will be so happy when I tell him about the baby. He wanted so much to be a grandfather! Tell Maria I'll be glad to help her when we get home. It's too bad it happened so early. I wanted to be there with her. Can I speak with her now?"

"No, she's still in the hospital, too. She'll be home tomorrow."

"Well, give her my love. I'd love a picture of the baby."

"Okay. Tell Dad I'll call him tomorrow. Be sure you get some rest. Goodbye, Mom."

Starting time _____
Finishing time _____
Reading time _____

Turn the page and answer the questions.
Don't look back at the passage.

Circle the best answer.

1. This passage is about
     a. a heart attack.
     b. Maria and Ted's new baby.
     c. long distance telephone calls.
     d. a phone conversation.

1. [ ]

2. This conversation is between
     a. Ted and Susan.
     b. Maria and Susan.
     c. Jane and Sam.
     d. Jane and Susan.

2. [ ]

3. Susan did not know about the baby because
     a. it came early.
     b. she didn't have a telephone.
     c. she didn't get Ted's letter.
     d. she got Ted's letter early.

3. [ ]

4. Sam is
     a. in the Hebrides.
     b. in London.
     c. at the hotel.
     d. in the hospital.

4. [ ]

5. Sam
     a. had a very serious heart attack.
     b. had a small heart attack.
     c. did not have a heart attack.
     d. was afraid of a heart attack.

5. [ ]

6. The heart attack happened in
     a. London.
     b. the Hebrides.
     c. New York.
     d. Edinburgh.

6. [ ]

7. When Sam fell down, people
     a. were helpful.
     b. did not help much.
     c. walked by in a hurry.
     d. stopped to talk to him.

7. [ ]

8. Maria
     a. wants to go to Edinburgh.
     b. does not want to talk with Susan.
     c. is at home in bed.
     d. is still in the hospital.

8. [ ]

Go back and answer the questions a second time. You may look back at the passage. Write the answers in the boxes on the right.

Check your answers in the Answer Key. Number correct _____
Find your Reading Rate. Fill in the Progress Chart.

31

Dear Ted and Maria,

It's hard to believe I'm here in Scotland. This all happened so quickly! I'm so glad I came. Dad was very happy to see me. He's still very sick, but Dr. Campbell says he's all right. They want to watch him for a while and do some tests. So he'll probably stay in the hospital for a few more weeks. Then he will have to be careful in the future. Less dessert and fewer meat pies! We're very lucky this happened in Scotland. Here they have a National Health Service. The doctors and the hospitals are all paid by the government. We don't have to pay them!

Dad looks different because he's still weak and he's thinner. But he sounds fine. The nurses all love him because he tells them funny stories. He talks with Dr. Campbell a lot about fishing, too. I found a beautiful poster of a Scottish lake for his room. It's a nice, large room with big windows and a view of the city of Edinburgh.

Poor Mom is also very glad I'm here. She was staying with Dad all day every day in the hospital. Now she can go back to our room and rest sometimes. We're staying in a nice little place near the hospital. It's a "Bed and Breakfast," not a hotel. It's much more comfortable and more like home.

Mom was right about Dr. Campbell. He's really an excellent doctor. All his patients like him and I can see why. He's always kind to them and he'll answer any questions. He's very friendly to me, too. And, if you ask me, he's VERY handsome!

Andrew — that's his first name — is showing me more of Scotland. Last night he took me to a Scottish dance. The dancing was fun, but not always easy. All the men there were wearing the Scottish national costume, the kilt. These kilts are unusual and colorful. Andrew also wants me to go sailing with him next weekend. He likes dancing and sports and activities like that.

How is Elena? Give her an extra hug and kiss for me. I hope Ted is cooking some nice dinners for you! Give him my love too. Mom and Dad both send their love and many hugs and kisses. Mom says she will write again soon. I miss you all!

Love,
Jane

Starting time _____

Finishing time _____

Reading time _____

Turn the page and answer the questions.
Don't look back at the passage.

Circle the best answer.

1. This passage is about   1. ☐
   a. what Jane saw on her vacation.
   b. what Jane found out in Edinburgh.
   c. Dr. Campbell.
   d. "Bed and Breakfasts."

2. Dr. Campbell is   2. ☐
   a. Jane's doctor.
   b. Susan's doctor.
   c. Maria's doctor.
   d. Sam's doctor.

3. Sam is   3. ☐
   a. very sick.
   b. still very sick.
   c. all better.
   d. not at all sick.

4. Susan and Jane are staying at   3. ☐
   a. a hotel.
   b. the hospital.
   c. a friend's house.
   d. a "Bed and Breakfast."

5. Sam says he feels   5. ☐
   a. terrible.
   b. sick.
   c. fine.
   d. unhappy.

6. Jane said, "Dr. Campbell is   6. ☐
   a. too young."
   b. too thin."
   c. a good fisherman."
   d. an excellent doctor."

7. Jane and Andrew Campbell   7. ☐
   a. may take a tour around Edinburgh.
   b. may go sailing.
   c. will get married.
   d. don't like sports.

8. Jane thinks Dr. Campbell is   8. ☐
   a. not very friendly.
   b. too friendly.
   c. handsome and friendly.
   d. handsome, but not very friendly.

Go back and answer the questions a second time. You may look back at the passage. Write the answers in the boxes on the right.

Check your answers in the Answer Key. Number correct _____
Find your Reading Rate. Fill in the Progress Chart.

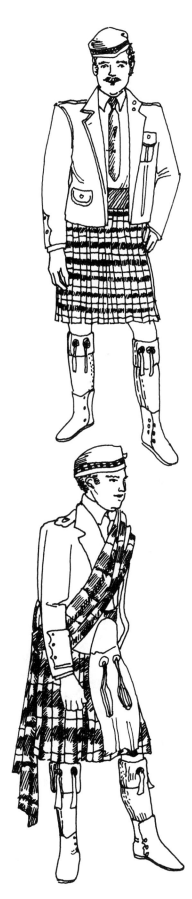

32

In Europe men don't usually wear skirts. But the Scottish national costume for men is a kind of skirt. It is called a kilt. The Scottish like to be different. They are also proud of their country and its history, and they feel that the kilt is part of that history. That's why the men still wear kilts at old-style dances and on national holidays. They believe they are wearing the same clothes that Scottish men always used to wear.

That's what they believe. However, kilts are not really so old. Before 1730, Scottish men wore a long shirt and blanket around their shoulders. These clothes got in the way when the men started to work in factories. So, in 1730 a factory owner changed the blanket into a skirt: the kilt. That's how the first kilt was made.

Then, in the late 1700s Scottish soldiers in the British Army began to wear kilts. One reason for this was national feeling: the Scottish soldiers wanted to look different from the English soldiers. The British Army probably had a different reason: a Scottish soldier in a kilt was always easy to find! The Scottish soldiers fought very hard and became famous. The kilt was part of that fame, and in the early 1800s men all around Scotland began to wear kilts.

These kilts had colorful stripes going up and down and across. In the 1700s and early 1800s, the color of the stripes had no special meaning. Men sometimes owned kilts in several different colors. But later the colors became important to the Scottish families. By about 1850, most families had special colors for their kilts. For example, men from the Campbell family had kilts with green, yellow and blue stripes. Scottish people often believe that the colors of the kilts are part of their family history. In fact, each family just chose the colors they liked best.

This is not the story you will hear today if you are in Scotland. Most Scottish people still believe that kilts are as old as Scotland and that the colors are as old as the Scottish families. Sometimes feelings are stronger than facts!

Starting time _____
Finishing time _____
Reading time _____

Turn the page and answer the questions.
Don't look back at the passage.

Circle the best answer.

1. This passage is about
   a. Scottish men.
   b. the history of Scotland.
   c. kilts.
   d. Scottish families.

1. ☐

2. A kilt is
   a. a kind of shirt.
   b. a kind of blanket.
   c. a national holiday.
   d. a kind of skirt.

2. ☐

3. The first kilt was made
   a. in Paris.
   b. in the British Army.
   c. by a factory owner.
   d. by a Scottish family.

3. ☐

4. Scottish soldiers wore kilts partly because of
   a. the colors.
   b. the weather.
   c. national feeling.
   d. the style.

4. ☐

5. Kilts are made of
   a. old cloth.
   b. striped cloth.
   c. old shirts.
   d. Army cloth.

5. ☐

6. The colors of the kilts are
   a. part of Scottish family history.
   b. older than the Scottish families.
   c. not part of Scottish family history.
   d. for the Campbell family only.

6. ☐

7. By about 1850, Scottish families
   a. all wore the same color kilts.
   b. had special colors for their kilts.
   c. wore blankets.
   d. all wore green, yellow and blue kilts.

7. ☐

8. Most people in Scotland
   a. know the true history of kilts.
   b. don't know the true history of kilts.
   c. don't have any feelings about Scotland.
   d. don't wear kilts.

8. ☐

Go back and answer the questions a second time. You may look back at the passage. Write the answers in the boxes on the right.

Check your answers in the Answer Key. Number correct _____
Find your Reading Rate. Fill in the Progress Chart.

33

Sailing may seem like a difficult sport, but it really is not hard to learn. You do not need to be strong. But you do need to be quick. And you need to understand a few basic rules about the wind.

First, you must ask yourself, "Where is the wind coming from? Is it coming from ahead or behind or from the side?" You must be thinking about this all the time on the boat. The wind direction tells you what to do with the sail.

Let's start with wind blowing from behind. This means the wind and the boat are going in the same direction. (Picture 1.) You should let the sail out all the way. It should be at a 90° angle to the boat. (Picture 2.) Then it will catch the wind best.

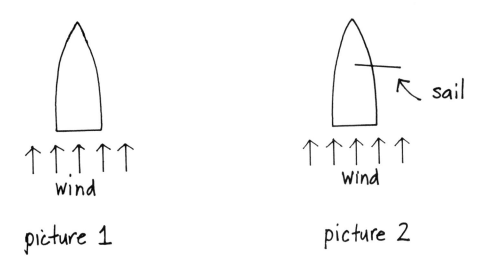

picture 1

picture 2

If the wind is blowing from the side, it is blowing across the boat. (Picture 3.) In this case, you must let the sail about half way out. (Picture 4.) It should be at about a 45° angle to the boat. It needs to be out far enough to catch the wind, but it shouldn't be flapping. It shouldn't look like a flag on a flagpole. If it is flapping, it is probably out too far, and the boat will slow down.

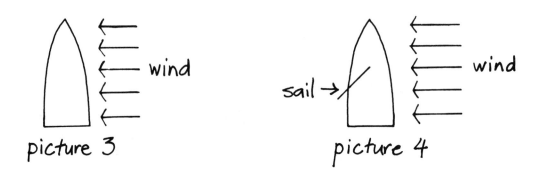

picture 3   picture 4

Sailing into the wind is not possible. (Picture 5.) If you try, the sails will flap and the boat will stop. You may want to go in that direction. It is possible, but you can't go in a straight line. You must go back and forth. (Picture 6.) This is called tacking. When you are tacking, you should bring your sail in all the way. It should be parallel to the boat. (Picture 7.) This is the most difficult kind of sailing. It is also the most exciting. You have to watch the sail all the time. The wind may change suddenly. Then you must be ready to change the sail.

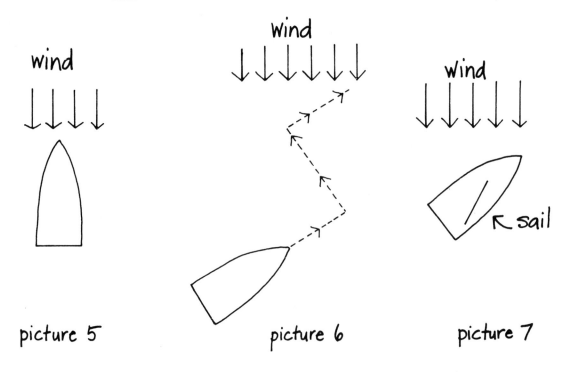

picture 5   picture 6   picture 7

These are the basic rules about wind direction. They may be difficult to follow at first. Sometimes it is difficult to know where the wind is even coming from! But soon you will learn to feel it on your face. Before long, you will also get used to the boat and the sail. But remember — do not go out alone until you really know what you are doing. Sailboats are fun, but they are not just toys!

Starting time _____

Finishing time _____

Reading time _____

**Turn the page and answer the questions.
Don't look back at the passage.**

Circle the best answer.

1. This passage is about
   a. boats.
   b. the wind.
   c. sailing.
   d. sails.

1. ☐

2. You must always think about
   a. where the wind is coming from.
   b. the water.
   c. the boat.
   d. how far you have to go.

2. ☐

3. When the wind is from behind,
   a. the boat and the wind are going the same way.
   b. the sail is flapping.
   c. the boat is going south.
   d. the wind is going a different way.

3. ☐

4. You should let the sail half way out when the
   a. wind is from behind.
   b. boat is going into the wind.
   c. wind is from the side.
   d. boat isn't going anywhere.

4. ☐

5. If the sail is too far out,
   a. the boat will tack.
   b. it will start flapping.
   c. the boat will go faster.
   d. the boat will change direction.

5. ☐

6. It's impossible to go
   a. before the wind.
   b. close to the wind.
   c. across the wind.
   d. into the wind.

6. ☐

7. The sail should be in all the way when you are
   a. sailing.
   b. going fast.
   c. flapping.
   d. tacking.

7. ☐

8. You can tell where the wind is coming from by
   a. looking at it.
   b. sailing in a straight line.
   c. feeling it on your face.
   d. going out alone.

8. ☐

Go back and answer the questions a second time. You may look back at the passage. Write the answers in the boxes on the right.

Check your answers in the Answer Key. Number correct _____
Find your Reading Rate. Fill in the Progress Chart.

34

Dear Jane,

We were so glad to get your letter. Ted wasn't sure what to do. He was so worried about your father. I told him he really didn't need to worry about me and Elena. So he was all ready to go to Scotland. But your letter made us feel better. It really doesn't sound too serious. Now maybe Ted will wait and see. If your father is still in the hospital in a few weeks, then he'll go.

You can tell your parents that the house in Rosebud is fine. We go there often to make sure everything is okay. Dr. Hamilton says your father shouldn't worry about his patients. They all ask about him. Dr. Hamilton says he will take good care of them, and I'm sure he will. Also, tell your mother that all the pets are very healthy. But the bird doesn't sing anymore. I think it misses your mother!

Our life here is very different now. It's not easy having a little baby in the house! Elena often wakes up at night, so I don't sleep much. Then, all day long it seems there is always something to do. Sometimes I get very, very tired. Then I remember my own mother, with five children. How did she do it? In those days, women didn't get much help from their husbands. My father was a wonderful person in many ways. But I don't think he ever washed a dish in his life.

Ted is a very different kind of father He's working part-time for *The New York Times* now. He also is starting to write his book about Italy. He goes to his office only twice a week, and he only writes for a few hours a day. So that means he can do a lot around the house. He does the laundry often and goes shopping. He loves to play with the baby while I sleep or paint. You should see him with Elena. He's like a little boy himself! I always thought he would be a good father. But I never knew he loved to play so much!

You must be having a good time there in Scotland. Dancing, sailing — what next? Tell me more about this Dr. Campbell. Are you serious about him? It's too bad we can't talk about all this. You must write me a long letter and tell me everything.

Give my love to your parents. Ted also sends his love, and Elena, too.

Much love,
Maria

Starting time _____

Finishing time _____

Reading time _____

Turn the page and answer the questions.
Don't look back at the passage.

Circle the best answer.

1. This passage is about
   a. having a baby.
   b. fathers.
   c. Maria's life and thoughts.
   d. Jane's life and thoughts.

1. ☐

2. Ted
   a. wanted to be with Jane.
   b. only wanted to stay with Maria.
   c. didn't want to go to Scotland.
   d. wanted to be with both Sam and Maria.

2. ☐

3. Maria thinks Jane might
   a. never get married.
   b. not like Scottish men.
   c. sound like her mother.
   d. marry Dr. Campbell someday.

3. ☐

4. Maria and Ted
   a. are taking care of the pets.
   b. don't like pets.
   c. have many pets.
   d. are worried about the pets.

4. ☐

5. Maria says her life is different because of
   a. the baby.
   b. the bird.
   c. her father.
   d. Ted.

5. ☐

6. In the past, women
   a. got a lot of help from their husbands.
   b. didn't get help from their husbands.
   c. didn't do a lot of work in the house.
   d. had fewer children.

6. ☐

7. Maria's father
   a. often helped in the house.
   b. liked to play with children.
   c. didn't go to work.
   d. never helped with the housework.

7. ☐

8. Ted works part-time, so he can
   a. make more money.
   b. read the newspaper.
   c. do some of the housework.
   d. sit in his favorite chair.

8. ☐

Go back and answer the questions a second time. You may look back at the passage. Write the answers in the boxes on the right.

Check your answers in the Answer Key. Number correct _____
Find your Reading Rate. Fill in the Progress Chart.

35

THE NEW YORK CITY GAZETTE   June 12, 1986

Family Life in the United States

William Whipple

Family life in the United States is changing. Twenty-five years ago the housewife cleaned, cooked and cared for the children. She was the most important person in the home. The father earned the money for the family. He was usually out working all day. He came home tired in the evening. So he did not see the children very much, except on weekends. His work at home was usually outside in the yard. The cooking and the cleaning were for women only.

These days, however, many women work outside the home. They can't be at home with the children all day. They, too, come home tired in the evening. They do not want to spend the evening cooking dinner. They do not have time to clean the house or wash the clothes. So who is going to take care of the children now? Who is going to do the housework?

For every family the answer to this question may be different. But usually the wife does not have to do all the work herself. Today she can get help. One kind of help is the day-care center. Mothers can leave their children at these centers during the day. Then they are free to go to work. Most children enjoy these centers. There are toys and games and other children to play with.

Another kind of help may come from the company a woman works for. The company may allow her to work part-time. That way, she can earn some money. But she can also be with her children part of every day.

But the most important help a woman can get is from her husband. Today, many men share the housework with their wives. In these families the men clean the kitchen and do the laundry. On some nights, the wife may cook dinner. On other nights it may be the husband. They may both go shopping and they may clean the house together. The husband may also spend more time at home with the children. Some men may even stop working for a while or work only part-time. For these men there is a new word: the "househusband." In the United States more and more men are becoming househusbands every year.

These changes in the home mean changes in the family. Fathers can be closer to their children because they are at home more. They can learn to understand their children better. The children can get to know their fathers better. Husbands and wives may also find changes in their marriage. They, too, may have a better understanding of each other.

```
Starting time  _____

Finishing time  _____

Reading time  _____
```

Turn the page and answer the questions.
Don't look back at the passage.

Circle the best answer.

1. This passage is about   1. ☐
   a. housewives.
   b. American men.
   c. how more American women are working.
   d. how family life in America is changing.

2. Twenty-five years ago most women   2. ☐
   a. had no children.
   b. worked.
   c. weren't housewives.
   d. were housewives.

3. In those days men   3. ☐
   a. saw their children in the evenings and on weekends.
   b. spent a lot of time with their children.
   c. worked with the children all day.
   d. never saw the children.

4. Today there are   4. ☐
   a. more housewives.
   b. more women working outside the home.
   c. not as many women working.
   d. no jobs for women.

5. Day-care centers help   5. ☐
   a. working mothers with their children.
   b. housewives.
   c. with cooking and cleaning.
   d. women with the housework.

6. Some mothers work part-time   6. ☐
   a. so they can be with their children.
   b. so they can earn more money.
   c. because they have no time.
   d. because they do not like their work.

7. Househusbands   7. ☐
   a. earn a lot of money.
   b. do not do any housework.
   c. do the housework and take care of the children.
   d. are unusual in the United States.

8. These changes in the American home may   8. ☐
   a. not change the children at all.
   b. cause problems for a marriage.
   c. not happen.
   d. be easy for the family.

Go back and answer the questions a second time. You may look back at the passage. Write the answers in the boxes on the right.

Check your answers in the Answer Key. Number correct _____
Find your Reading Rate. Fill in the Progress Chart.

36

THE NEW YORK CITY GAZETTE   June 15, 1986

Dear Editor:

I read with interest the article on American families. In general I agree with it. But there are some important things it left out. It didn't tell the reader much about the life of a househusband. It's not an easy life. I know, because I'm now a househusband myself. A househusband has to change many of his ideas and his ways.

First of all, he has to change the way he thinks about time. Before I was a househusband, I worked for *The New York Times*. I was a reporter and time was always very important. We had to finish our articles quickly and give them to the editor. Everyone was always in a hurry. This is the way many other men work, too. Businessmen, lawyers, bankers, doctors: they all have to work quickly.

At home it's very different. The househusband can't be in a hurry all the time. If you rush around, you will make everyone very unhappy! The children will be unhappy because they don't understand. For them time is not important. Your wife will be unhappy because the children are unhappy. You will be unhappy too because they are all unhappy. So you have to learn to slow down. That is the first and most important rule for a househusband.

But there is something else the househusband also has to learn. He must learn to show how he feels about things. At work, you usually don't talk about feelings. If you do, people think you are strange. They may think something is wrong with you and tell you to see a doctor! So, many men are not used to telling anyone about their feelings. They don't know how to talk about their anger, worries or love. But children need to know how you feel. They need to know if you are angry at them. They need to know how much you love them. Your wife also needs to know about your feelings. If you don't say anything, your family may get the wrong idea. Then there may be serious problems.

People talk a lot about househusbands these days. Usually they talk about the housework, about cooking, cleaning and shopping. But for me, these are the easiest things to learn. It is much harder to change the way you think about time. It is hard to change the way you act with your family. It is harder, but it is very necessary if you want to be a happy househusband!

Ted Diamond

Hartwell, New Jersey

Starting time _____

Finishing time _____

Reading time _____

Turn the page and answer the questions.
Don't look back at the passage.

Circle the best answer.

1. This passage is about   1. ☐
   a. fathers and children.
   b. life as a househusband.
   c. ideas about time.
   d. American families.

2. This letter was written by   2. ☐
   a. William Whipple to Ted.
   b. a newspaper publisher to Ted.
   c. Ted Diamond to the editor.
   d. Maria Diamond for the newspaper.

3. At work most people   3. ☐
   a. have to hurry.
   b. take their time.
   c. have lots of time.
   d. have to slow down.

4. The househusband has to learn   4. ☐
   a. to do things more slowly.
   b. how to do things more quickly.
   c. about the importance of time.
   d. how to understand his work.

5. Children   5. ☐
   a. are usually unhappy.
   b. are always in a hurry.
   c. usually don't think time is important.
   d. don't know how to show their feelings.

6. Many men   6. ☐
   a. like to talk about their worries.
   b. don't have any worries.
   c. don't often talk about their worries.
   d. have terrible problems.

7. Family problems can happen if   7. ☐
   a. men don't talk enough with their families.
   b. men talk too much with their families.
   c. men get wrong ideas.
   d. people talk about househusbands.

8. The author of this letter thinks   8. ☐
   a. learning about housework is easy.
   b. learning about housework is a problem.
   c. cooking is the easiest thing to learn.
   d. being a househusband is easy.

Go back and answer the questions a second time. You may look back at the passage. Write the answers in the boxes on the right.

Check your answers in the Answer Key. Number correct _____
Find your Reading Rate. Fill in the Progress Chart.

37

MY ITALY

by Ted Diamond

Chapter One: Pisa

Pisa was one of the first cities I visited in Italy. That is one reason why it is one of my favorite Italian cities. But I was in love with Pisa even before I saw it.

You see, I used to dream about it when I was a boy. I read about the famous building called the Leaning Tower of Pisa. But when I read the word Pisa, I was thinking of pizza. I thought this tower was a place to buy pizza. It must be the best pizza in the world, I thought. If it's so famous it must really be delicious.

Many years later I finally saw the Leaning Tower. I knew then that it was *Pisa* and not *pizza*. But there was still something special about it for me. The tower got its name because it really does lean to one side. Some people want to try to fix it. They are afraid it may fall over and they do not like the way it looks.

I do not think it's a good idea to try to fix it. The tower probably will not fall down. It is 600 years old. Why should anything happen now? And, if you ask me, I like the way it looks. I like the way it leans over the city. To me it is a very human kind of leaning. Nothing is perfect, it seems to say.

And who cares? Why do people want things to be perfect? Why should the tower stand up straight? Imperfect things may be more interesting. Let's take the tower in Pisa. Why is it so famous? There are many other older, more beautiful towers in Italy. But Pisa's tower is one of the most famous. People come from all over the world to see it.

I am one of those people. After my first visit, I returned many times. And every time, I liked it just as much. Pisa still makes me think of pizza. But that is not why I like the city and its tower. They are special for me in the same way that Italy is special.

Many Americans tell me that Italy has a lot of problems: the trains are never on time, the telephones do not always work, the streets are not always clean. Things are not perfect at all. "Why don't the Italians fix all them?" they ask. But that is what I like about Italy. It is old and imperfect and very human.

| Starting time _____ |
| Finishing time _____ |
| Reading time _____ |

Turn the page and answer the questions.
Don't look back at the passage.

Circle the best answer.

1. This passage is about   1. ☐
   a. Ted Diamond.
   b. Italy's problems.
   c. how the Leaning Tower of Pisa got its name.
   d. why Ted likes Pisa.

2. This passage was written by   2. ☐
   a. a writer.
   b. Ted Diamond.
   c. an Italian.
   d. Sam Diamond.

3. This writer used to think Pisa   3. ☐
   a. was in Spain.
   b. wasn't very famous.
   c. was not the same as pizza.
   d. was the same as pizza.

4. The famous tower in Pisa   4. ☐
   a. really does lean.
   b. really is straight.
   c. will fall down.
   d. doesn't really lean.

5. The Leaning Tower of Pisa is   5. ☐
   a. modern.
   b. falling down.
   c. 600 years old.
   d. 60 years old.

6. This writer   6. ☐
   a. doesn't like the way the tower looks.
   b. likes the way the tower looks.
   c. thinks it's the most beautiful tower in Italy.
   d. doesn't like towers.

7. This writer thinks the tower is interesting because 7. ☐
   a. it's old.
   b. it's perfect.
   c. it sells pizza.
   d. it's imperfect.

8. Many Americans say that   8. ☐
   a. Italy is perfect.
   b. Italians are good at fixing things.
   c. Italy has many problems.
   d. the trains are usually on time in Italy.

Go back and answer the questions a second time. You may look back at the passage. Write the answers in the boxes on the right.

Check your answers in the Answer Key. Number correct _____
Find your Reading Rate. Fill in the Progress Chart.

38

Dear Ted and Maria,

Dad is out of the hospital now and he's feeling much stronger. This morning we took a short walk to the park. Dad was so glad to be out in the open air. He started talking about fishing, but he's not ready for that yet! Dr. Campbell said Dad will be ready to travel next week. I made plane reservations for the 10th of July.

Now we're both beginning to think more about Rosebud. Scotland is very beautiful and the people here are friendly, but we'll be glad to be home again. We miss you all so much. And, of course, we really want to see our new little granddaughter.

Our life in Rosebud will be a bit different after all this. There will be changes for both of us at work. Your father says he may only work part-time. The doctor thinks it will be better for his heart. Your father says he just wants to have more time for fishing and relaxing. He also wants to be a good grandfather. He was always busy when you and Jane were little, Ted. So he didn't have much time to play with you. Now he wants to have time for Elena.

I may have even less time for relaxing. Our laboratory is going to be very busy soon. Yesterday I got a letter from the government with some good news. The government is going to give more money to our lab. Now we will start a big new study about acid rain.

Acid rain is part of the problem of air pollution. Right now it is killing plants and fish in lakes. This is happening in the United States and in Europe. Many fishermen — like your father! — are getting worried. There won't be any fish left, if acid rain does not stop. In the future this acid rain may also hurt people. That is why it is important to study it. We want to find out more about acid rain. Then maybe the government can stop it.

People in Scotland are also worried about acid rain. There was a long article about it in the Edinburgh Sunday newspaper. The reporter said that the fish are dying in some parts of the country. The Scots are very upset because fishing is a very popular sport here.

I can hardly wait to see both of you — and Elena. She must be a very big baby now!

With all our love,
Mom

| Starting time _____ |
| Finishing time _____ |
| Reading time _____ |

Turn the page and answer the questions.
Don't look back at the passage.

Circle the best answer.

1. This passage is about   1. ☐
   a. Susan and Sam in Scotland.
   b. acid rain.
   c. life in Rosebud.
   d. news from Susan in Scotland.

2. Dr. Campbell says Sam will   2. ☐
   a. never be ready to travel.
   b. be ready to travel in a week.
   c. never go fishing again.
   d. have to stay for a few more weeks.

3. Sam may   3. ☐
   a. change his job.
   b. become a doctor.
   c. work harder than before.
   d. work only part-time.

4. Sam wants to have more time for   4. ☐
   a. his patients.
   b. his children.
   c. playing with Elena.
   d. work.

5. Susan's laboratory   5. ☐
   a. got more money from the government.
   b. needs more money.
   c. will be open part-time.
   d. is in Scotland.

6. Susan will be studying   6. ☐
   a. the whole problem of air pollution.
   b. acid rain.
   c. lakes in Europe.
   d. the government.

7. Acid rain is   7. ☐
   a. not much of a problem.
   b. a problem only in Scotland.
   c. a serious problem.
   d. a problem only for fish.

8. In Scotland, acid rain is   8. ☐
   a. helping the fishermen.
   b. killing fish.
   c. killing fishermen.
   d. not serious.

Go back and answer the questions a second time. You may look back at the passage. Write the answers in the boxes on the right.

Check your answers in the Answer Key. Number correct _____
Find your Reading Rate. Fill in the Progress Chart.

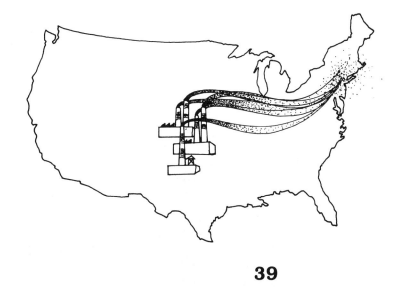

39

Acid Rain

by Sandra Atherton

The fish are dying in the Adirondack lakes in northern New York State. Fishermen are worried. This used to be a favorite spot for sport fishing. But every year there are fewer fish. Some lakes — 6% of them — now have no fish at all. Scientists are beginning to get worried too. What is killing the fish?

The problem is acid rain. Acid rain is a kind of air pollution. It is caused by factories that burn coal or oil or gas. These factories send smoke high into the air. The wind often carries the smoke far from the factories. Some of the unhealthy things in the smoke may come down with the rain hundreds of miles away. This is what is happening in the Adirondacks. There are many factories in the Midwestern states. They are sending a lot of smoke into the air. The wind blows the smoke towards the east. That means towards New York State and the Adirondack area.

The rain in the Adirondacks isn't natural and clean any more. It's full of acid chemicals. When it falls in lakes, it changes them too. The lakes become more acidic. Acid water is like vinegar or lemon juice. It hurts when it gets in your eyes. It also kills the plants and animals that usually live in lake water. That is why the fish are dying in the Adirondacks.

But dead fish may be just the beginning of the problem. Scientists are finding other effects of acid rain. In large areas of the eastern United States, trees are dying. Not just one tree here and there, but whole forests. At first scientists couldn't understand why. There were no bugs or diseases in these trees. The weather was not dry. But now they think that the rain was the cause. Acid rain is making the earth more acidic in these areas. Some kinds of trees cannot live in earth that is very acidic.

Now scientists are also beginning to study the effects of acid rain on larger animals. For example, they believe that some deer in Poland are less healthy because of acid rain. If deer are hurt by the rain, what about people? This is the question many people are beginning to ask. No one knows the answer yet. But it is an important question for us all.

Starting time _____

Finishing time _____

Reading time _____

Turn the page and answer the questions.
Don't look back at the passage.

Circle the best answer.

1. This passage is about
   a. fishing.
   b. air pollution.
   c. acid rain.
   d. scientists.

   1. ☐

2. Every year in the Adirondack lakes there
   a. are more fish.
   b. are fewer fish.
   c. are more factories.
   d. is less rain.

   2. ☐

3. Acid rain comes from
   a. factories that burn oil or gas.
   b. the northern part of New York State.
   c. the water in lakes.
   d. science laboratories.

   3. ☐

4. Factory smoke
   a. stays over the factories.
   b. turns into air.
   c. is usually clean now.
   d. can travel hundreds of miles.

   4. ☐

5. Acid rain
   a. makes lake water acid.
   b. is good for flowers.
   c. falls mostly in the Midwestern states.
   d. is natural and clean.

   5. ☐

6. Plants and animals
   a. prefer acid water.
   b. like vinegar and lemon juice.
   c. can't live in acid water.
   d. are becoming more acidic.

   6. ☐

7. Scientists think acid rain
   a. is killing people.
   b. may be good for the trees.
   c. helps kill bugs.
   d. is killing trees.

   7. ☐

8. No one knows if
   a. deer are hurt by acid rain.
   b. people are hurt by acid rain.
   c. fish are dying because of acid rain.
   d. acid rain is a problem.

   8. ☐

Go back and answer the questions a second time. You may look back at the passage. Write the answers in the boxes on the right.

Check your answers in the Answer Key. Number correct _____
Find your Reading Rate. Fill in the Progress Chart.

Diamonds Return From Europe

Yesterday afternoon Susan and Sam Diamond returned to Rosebud after almost two months in England and Scotland. Sam Diamond is a dentist and he is also the president of the Rosebud Fishing Club. While he was in Scotland, he had a heart attack and stayed in the hospital for three weeks. However, the heart attack was not serious. Dr. Diamond's patients and friends will be glad to know that he is now in good health.

Susan Diamond also has some good news that may interest people in Rosebud. There is a lot of talk these days about the problem of acid rain. No one knows what acid rain is really doing to our world or to us. Next month Susan's laboratory in New York will begin an important study of acid rain. The money for the study will come from the United States Government. Susan and the other scientists at the laboratory hope they will find out more about the causes and effects of acid rain. We are lucky to have people like Susan Diamond studying this very serious problem.

Susan and Sam Diamond were met at the airport yesterday by their son Ted. He and Maria, his wife, returned from Italy this spring. Last month they had their first child, a daughter named Elena. Ted is a reporter for *The New York Times*, and he is writing about the United Nations. He is also working on a book about living in Italy. Maria, an artist, recently had a show of some of her paintings in New York. An article in *The New York Star* reported on Maria's paintings and said that she is a very talented artist.

And finally, we also have good news from the youngest member of the Diamond family. Many of us remember Jane Diamond as a person who likes excitement and change. In high school, she was always busy with sports, theater, music or other activities. She lived in California for several years and she moved to New York a few months ago. Now we hear she is going to get married. She met Dr. Andrew Campbell while she was in Scotland visiting her father. The wedding will be here in Rosebud in October. Jane and her husband plan to live in Edinburgh.

Congratulations to Jane, Ted and Maria, and welcome home to Susan and Sam!

Starting time _____

Finishing time _____

Reading time _____

Turn the page and answer the questions.
Don't look back at the passage.

Circle the best answer.

1. This passage is about   1. ☐
   a. Rosebud.
   b. Sam's heart attack.
   c. Susan and Sam.
   d. the Diamond family.

2. The person who wrote this passage   2. ☐
   a. probably lives in New York.
   b. probably lives in Rosebud.
   c. is a member of the Diamond family.
   d. does not know the Diamonds very well.

3. Susan and Sam Diamond.   3. ☐
   a. are still in Scotland.
   b. are coming back soon.
   c. came back yesterday.
   d. are not coming back from Scotland.

4. This writer probably   4. ☐
   a. saw the Diamonds and talked with them.
   b. did not talk with the Diamonds.
   c. will talk with the Diamonds tomorrow.
   d. does not want to talk to the Diamonds.

5. People in Rosebud think   5. ☐
   a. acid rain does not matter.
   b. there is no acid rain.
   c. acid rain is a serious problem.
   d. acid rain is only in Scotland.

6. This writer thinks Susan is   6. ☐
   a. a rich scientist.
   b. a good scientist.
   c. not a good scientist.
   d. not a scientist.

7. Susan and Sam Diamond were met at the airport by   7. ☐
   a. Sam's patients and friends.
   b. Jane.
   c. Ted.
   d. Dr. Andrew Campbell.

8. This writer thinks Jane always liked   8. ☐
   a. excitement and activities.
   b. a quiet life.
   c. children.
   d. painting.

Go back and answer the questions a second time. You may look back at the passage. Write the answers in the boxes on the right.

Check your answers in the Answer Key. Number correct _____
Find your Reading Rate. Fill in the Progress Chart.

Exercise 1

1. It used to take months to cross the Atlantic Ocean in a ship. But now a plane can cross the Atlantic in
   a. a few months.
   b. a long time.
   c. a few hours.
   d. more time.

2. The easiest way to travel is to walk. You don't need anything special. All you need is
   a. two feet.
   b. to hurry
   c. a car.
   d. gasoline.

3. Cars are a problem in big cities. There are too many cars in the streets. Most city streets are noisy and
   a. safe.
   b. large.
   c. parking.
   d. crowded.

4. Alexander Graham Bell made the first telephone in 1876 in the United States. Now the telephone is international. You can use it to talk to someone anywhere
   a. in the city.
   b. in the world.
   c. in history.
   d. on time.

5. Henry went to the doctor because he could not see well. The doctor told him he should get a new pair of
   a. shoes.
   b. pants.
   c. gloves.
   d. glasses.

Exercise 2

1. New York is one of the biggest cities in the world. It has about seven million people. But Peking is much larger. It has almost
   a. a million people.
   b. thousands of people.
   c. as many people.
   d. 15 million people.

2. Plants grow faster in the spring. The weather is usually warmer and the days are longer. It is a good idea to start a garden in the spring. Then plants will get more
   a. air.
   b. sunlight.
   c. water.
   d. leaves.

3. Some plants grow in very dry places. These desert plants can live for a long time with no
   a. flowers.
   b. sun.
   c. food.
   d. water.

4. People used to wake up when it was light. They went to bed when it was dark. The sun was their
   a. star.
   b. time.
   c. clock.
   d. bed.

5. What is your favorite color? If you like red, you may be full of life. If you like blue, you may want peace. Your favorite color tells something about
   a. colors.
   b. life.
   c. you.
   d. peace.

Exercise 3

1. Sometimes children get sick because of problems at home. So doctors like to meet with the children's
   a. friends.
   b. parents.
   c. teachers.
   d. patients.

2. Dentists think that eating candy is bad for the teeth. If children eat candy, they will probably have tooth trouble
   a. before.
   b. in the past.
   c. someday.
   d. now.

3. Some birds fly many miles every year. In the fall they leave countries in the north. They fly south to warmer places. Then, in the spring, they leave their winter homes and go back
   a. north.
   b. south.
   c. around.
   d. away.

4. Many farmers in Florida grow oranges. They also grow lemons, limes, and grapefruit. Florida is famous for its
   a. apples.
   b. vegetables.
   c. weather.
   d. fruit.

5. Some people prefer warm climates. They enjoy the heat and feel happy in the sun. They do not like cold weather or
   a. climate.
   b. sun.
   c. snow.
   d. night.

Exercise 4

1. Some people enjoy the winter. They like winter sports such as skiing and skating. They enjoy ice and
   a. weather.   b. snow.   c. sun.   d. rain.

2. Jazz is the only kind of music started in the United States. It began around 1900. Even today, the best jazz musicans are
   a. English.   b. dead.   c. European.   d. American.

3. In very hot countries, the sun can hurt your eyes. It is a good idea to wear a hat when you go outside. You may also need
   a. shoes.   c. a swimsuit.
   b. sun glasses.   d. gloves.

4. Last week Mr. Thomas rented a new apartment. He does not have a table, chairs or any other furniture yet. The apartment looks very
   a. comfortable.   c. empty.
   b. full.   d. crowded.

5. On special days, the whole family has dinner at our house. Everyone came last week for my father's
   a. parents.   b. family.   c. house.   d. birthday.

Exercise 5

1. The police stopped a man. They said he took some money from a store. They found the money in his pocket. So they took him to
   a. the hospital.   c. the bank.
   b. the police station.   d. his home.

2. People used to learn the news from the newspaper. But today many people do not read the paper. They prefer to learn the news
   a. in a movie.   c. in books.
   b. on television.   d. from friends.

3. The whale swims like a fish and lives in the ocean. But it is not a fish. Fish stay under water all the time. But whales must have air. They can go down deep in the ocean for many minutes. But they always need to
   a. find a fish to eat.   c. act like a fish.
   b. swim a long way.   d. come up again for air.

4. Whales are the largest animals. But they eat very tiny fish and sea plants. That means they must
   a. eat larger fish.   c. drink a lot of water.
   b. eat a lot.   d. travel far.

5. Curtains on the windows can make a room cooler in the summer. They let air come into the room, but they
   a. stop the wind.   c. are dark.
   b. keep out the sun.   d. are light.

Exercise 6

1. Coffee grows in places with warm climates. In some parts of the world, the land is good for growing coffee. But the winters are too
   a. cold.   b. dry.   c. short.   d. cloudy.

2. In Sweden, the summer days are very long. The sun shines for many hours. But the winter is very dark. The days are short because the sun sets
   a. very late   c. at midnight.
   b. are beautiful.   d. very early.

3. In every country there is a different kind of money. For example, you may plan to go from Japan to the United States. Then you must change yen to
   a. cash.   b. dollars.   c. money.   d. airplanes.

4. In New England, the weather changes often. It may be sunny in the morning. Then it can be very cold and rainy in the afternoon. That is why a famous writer said: "If you don't like the weather in New England,
   a. go home."   c. bring an umbrella."
   b. wait a few hours."   d. listen to the radio."

5. My favorite book is about the life of Charles Dickens. He was a famous English writer. It is a very interesting story. The best part is about
   a. airplanes.   c. his childhood.
   b. the economy.   d. the mountains.

Exercise 7

1. Clocks were first made in Europe in about 1500. Before then, people looked at the sun
   a. to tell the time.   c. in the morning.
   b. to get places.   d. to read.

2. The piano is a popular instrument because it is easy to play. The violin is less popular because it is more
   a. fun.   b. beautiful.   c. boring.   d. difficult.

3. In California, the time is three hours earlier than the time in New York. If it is 11 o'clock in New York, it must be
   a. 3 o'clock in California.
   b. 8 o'clock in California.
   c. 11 o'clock in California.
   d. later in California.

4. Glassmaking is a very old art. The Romans and the Egyptians made glass many years ago. Now we can make special kinds of glass in many different colors. But the art is
   a. the same.   b. very new.   c. beautiful.   d. not old.

5. Thousands of years ago, people loved gold. They wore gold rings, earrings, and bracelets. Today, people still like to wear jewelry made of
   a. rings.   b. gold.   c. bracelets.   d. wood.

Exercise 8

1. Some people like history. They like to look at old buildings and old streets. They like to know that many others lived there before them. These people have a strong feeling for
   a. cities.   b. people.   c. buildings.   d. the past.

2. Other people prefer new cities. They like to see modern buildings and clean streets. They feel that new things are exciting. These people don't think much about the past. They are interested in
   a. the present.   c. history.
   b. cities.   d. old times.

3. The best way to learn about a new city is to walk around. You can watch people and listen to their conversations. You can look at things in the shop windows. This way you will get to know
   a. the price of food.   c. how the people live.
   b. the language.   d. the history of the city.

4. Denver, Colorado, is very close to the mountains. In fact, it is partly in the mountains. That is why it is called the
   a. "low city."   c. flat city.
   b. "mile-high city."   d. city of dreams.

5. Every year more people move to cities. They think they will find better jobs in the city. They do not want to work on farms and live in small towns. So cities are growing larger all the time. And
   a. more people are living on farms.
   b. people are more interesting.
   c. there are no jobs in small towns.
   d. fewer people are living on farms.

Exercise 9

1. Every country has its favorite beverage. Italians like to drink coffee after dinner. The English prefer tea. Americans often drink
   a. ideas.   b. soda.   c. food.   d. dinner.

2. You can tell a horse's age by looking at its teeth. You can learn about its health by looking at its eyes. So before you buy a horse, look carefully at its
   a. chest.   b. feet.   c. tail.   d. head.

3. Summer sports are popular even in northern countries with short summers. For example, in Sweden, sailing is an important national sport. So is
   a. tennis.   c. cooking.
   b. ice skating.   d. skiing.

4. Reading is a very good way to learn a new language. You can learn new vocabulary. You can also learn to think in that
   a. book.   c. comprehension.
   b. language.   d. word.

5. "April showers bring May flowers." People say this because April is the time for planting flowers. It is usually a very
   a. rainy month.   c. long month.
   b. dry month.   d. hot month.

Exercise 10

1. When people get older, their eyes get weak. They need to wear glasses to see close things. They especially need glasses for
   a. driving a car.   c. reading a book.
   b. watching a movie.   d. looking out the window.

2. People used to think that the sun moved around the earth. They thought the earth stayed in one place and the sun
   a. never rose.   c. never moved.
   b. moved across the sky.   d. also stayed in one place.

3. One hundred years ago, there were no radios or record players. If people wanted to hear music, they had to
   a. read a book.
   b. find someone to play music.
   c. change the station.
   d. stay home.

4. Josef Haydn wrote music in the 1700s. He lived to be 77 years old. Many younger musicians loved him and they learned a lot from him. To them, Haydn was like
   a. a son.   c. other old men.
   b. a father.   d. a violinist.

5. Many Italian people are great singers. Singing is very popular in Italy. Some people say that even the Italian language sounds
   a. like English.   c. different.
   b. like music.   d. the same.

Exercise 11

1. Siberia is the coldest part of Russia. When Russians talk about a Siberian wind, they mean
   a. a warm wind.   c. a strong wind.
   b. a soft wind.   d. a cold wind.

2. Some kinds of trees are always green. They do not lose their leaves. So they are called
   a. flowers.   c. evergreens.
   b. lifeless.   d. leafless.

3. Years ago, corn was grown only in South and North America. But now it grows in many places, even
   a. in South America.   c. on farms.
   b. in China.   d. in the United States.

4. People used to think tomatoes were not good to eat. They believed that tomatoes made you
   a. live longer.   c. fatter.
   b. hungry.   d. sick.

5. Every country has a national holiday. This holiday usually is a very important date in the history of
   a. the United States.   c. the world.
   b. the summer.   d. that country.

Exercise 12

1. In the United States, many children do not read books. They watch TV many hours every day. These children are not good readers because they
   - a. have no books.
   - b. go to school.
   - c. read books all day.
   - d. watch too much TV.

2. You lose 60% of your body heat through your head. So on cold days you will feel warmer if you
   - a. wear two sweaters.
   - b. put on your boots.
   - c. cover your ears.
   - d. wear a hat.

3. New Yorkers love city life. They like noisy places and bright lights. They are not happy in the country. The country is too
   - a. noisy.
   - b. loud.
   - c. bright.
   - d. quiet.

4. Cooking is different in the mountains. You have to cook things longer. For example, it usually takes an hour to bake bread. But in the mountains, it may take
   - a. an hour and a half.
   - b. half an hour.
   - c. less time.
   - d. forty-five minutes.

5. In Tokyo, the subway station is like a small city. You can shop, eat, or get a haircut underground. You can be in Tokyo and never see
   - a. the subway.
   - b. the sky.
   - c. the station.
   - d. the driver.

Exercise 13

1. Seagulls are birds that live near the ocean. But you can also find seagulls near garbage dumps. Their favorite food is fish, but they will eat
   - a. at the beach.
   - b. only fish.
   - c. near the ocean.
   - d. almost anything.

2. Penguins are unusual birds. They can swim very well. But they have very small wings, so they can not
   - a. sing.
   - b. talk.
   - c. fish.
   - d. fly.

3. Penguins are funny-looking birds. They look like little men with black suits and white shirts. They are very friendly, and they are not afraid of people. In zoos, penguins
   - a. hide from people.
   - b. are very popular.
   - c. sometimes wear clothes.
   - d. never eat.

4. In a civil war, people in the same country fight each other. This can be the most terrible kind of war. Sometimes even people from the same family
   - a. work together.
   - b. fight each other.
   - c. live near each other.
   - d. move to another country.

5. New ideas travel from one country to another very quickly. Businesses try to sell new things in other countries. TV carries new ideas everywhere. Soon the countries of the world will be
   - a. crowded.
   - b. different.
   - c. more alike.
   - d. empty.

Exercise 14

1. The idea of flying is very old. Many years ago, people watched birds in the air. They studied the birds' wings, and they made wings with bird feathers. Then they
   a. flew.   c. will fly someday.
   b. tried to fly.   d. told stories.

2. The Wright brothers are famous in the history of flying. In 1903, they flew 120 feet in the world's first
   a. automobile.   b. machine.   c. airplane.   d. wings.

3. Sputnik was the first space ship. The Russians sent it up into space in 1957. Soon after that, the Americans sent a space ship up, too. That was the beginning of the
   a. Scientific Age.   c. Nuclear Age.
   b. Space Age.   d. Industrial Age.

4. Some scientists believe that we will have cities in space some day. Space cities may be the answer to our problem of
   a. crowded cities.   c. technology.
   b. travel.   d. farms.

5. In 1785, two men flew from England to France in a balloon. They began to have trouble with the balloon. It went lower and lower. They threw out everything they had. It went even lower. It almost touched the water. Finally, they took off their clothes and threw them out, too. So when they arrived in France, they were safe, but
   a. wet.   b. happy.   c. unhappy.   d. cold.

Exercise 15

1. Sometimes distant mountains look blue. But when you look closer, you see that they are not blue. They just look blue when they are
   a. near the sky.   c. large.
   b. under the clouds.   d. far away.

2. On windy days, the clouds are thin and high in the sky. And on rainy days, the clouds are heavy and dark. Clouds can tell you a lot about the
   a. sky.   c. weather
   b. air.   d. temperature.

3. In Los Angeles, there are no subways. And there are very few buses. But there are highways everywhere. Most people get from one place to another in Los Angeles by
   a. bus.   b. train.   c. car.   c. plane.

4. Cars are one important cause of air pollution. In Los Angeles, most people drive their cars to work. This is one reason why Los Angeles
   a. has such clean air.
   b. is such a large city.
   c. has little air pollution.
   d. has a problem with dirty air.

5. Before the 1800s, Italy was not really a country. It was many small countries with different governments. In 1870, all these small countries came together. Then
   a. modern Italy died.
   b. modern Italy was born.
   c. the old Italy was born.
   d. they started a war.

Exercise 16

1. The Hebrides Islands are in the northwest of Scotland. The sea is beautiful there. But the water is cold, even in summer. It is not a good place to go
   a. fishing.
   b. swimming.
   c. shopping.
   d. walking.

2. Tweed is a special kind of cloth. The Scottish island of Harris is famous for its tweed. All around the world, people pay a lot of money for
   a. Scotch bread.
   b. cloth.
   c. the island of Harris.
   d. Harris tweed.

3. Fishermen today have large boats and special nets. They can catch thousands of fish in a short time. But this may be a problem. Some scientists are afraid
   a. there will be too many fish soon.
   b. the boats will not be large enough.
   c. the fish will swim away.
   d. there soon will not be any fish.

4. Violins are made from special kinds of wood. The wood is very important for the sound of the violin. A violin made from the wrong wood will
   a. sound better.
   b. sound the same.
   c. not sound as nice.
   d. have no sound.

5. Some birds travel long distances. They may fly thousands of miles to a winter home. Then they fly back to their old home in the spring. They always return to the same place. But no one knows how they do it. Scientists think these birds have some kind of
   a. language in their heads.
   b. map in their heads.
   c. special wings.
   d. special food.

Exercise 17

1. In New England, the worst winter storms come from the northeast. So it is important to plan where you put your windows. To stay warm, put your windows
   a. on the south side of the house.
   b. on the northeast side.
   c. on all sides of the house.
   d. on the second floor.

2. Some scientists used to have strange ideas about the size of a person's head. They thought that people with large heads were the smartest. And they thought that people with smaller heads were
   a. not as smart.   c. the smartest.
   b. also smart.   d. even smarter.

3. A strong heart is necessary for a long life. People with weak hearts usually
   a. live longer.   c. get better.
   b. die at a younger age. d. do not die young.

4. Doctors say they can tell that some people will get heart trouble. These people are too heavy. They work too hard. They smoke cigarettes. Some doctors get heart attacks. Maybe they do not
   a. smoke cigarettes.   c. do what they say.
   b. work too hard.   d. eat too much.

5. The weather report says rain is coming tonight. Before we go out, we should
   a. watch the news.   c. lock the door.
   b. close the windows.   d. read the newspaper.

Exercise 18

1. On weekends, people in Boston like to go away. They go to the country, to the mountains, or to the sea. Every Friday night, the roads going out of Boston are
   a. empty.   b. crowded.   c. wet.   d. wide.

2. The American Civil War was a difficult time. The North was fighting the South. People did not agree about which side was right. Even members of the same family sometimes disagreed. Many times, one son was fighting for the North and another
   a. was fighting for the South.
   b. moved to another state.
   c. stayed home.
   d. had more children.

3. Chinatown is a neighborhood in New York City. Every year people move to New York from China. Most of them go to live in Chinatown. So Chinatown is
   a. near New York.   c. not changing.
   b. getting larger.   d. getting smaller.

4. Every year the Italian neighborhood in New York has a special day. There is Italian food. There are Italian songs and dances. There are games and exciting rides. The streets are full of people and noise.
   a. No one is happy.
   b. Few people enjoy themselves.
   c. Everyone has a good time.
   d. Many people do not have fun.

5. World War I ended in 1918. It was a very bad war. Many Europeans believed there would be no more wars. They called World War I
   a. "the first of many."
   b. "the war to end all wars."
   c. "only the beginning."
   d. "a war to be proud of."

Exercise 19

1. Two thousand years ago, the Romans ruled much of the world. The city of Rome was in the center. Writers like to say that in those days
   a. no roads led to Rome.   c. all roads led to the west.
   b. all roads led to Rome.   d. all roads led to the east.

2. A map of Italy looks just like a boot. It seems to have
   a. a heel and a toe.   c. shoes.
   b. feet.   d. many mountains.

3. The violin, viola, and cello all belong to the same family. They are musical instruments. The violin is the smallest, with the highest sound. The viola is larger, with a lower sound. The cello is largest, with the lowest sound. In this family,
   a. larger instruments have lower sounds.
   b. the size makes no difference to the sound.
   c. large instruments have higher sounds.
   d. the sizes are all the same.

4. Some people say that photographs are not art. They say that a photograph is just a copy of the real world. A photograph does not tell you what the artist was thinking. These people believe that art
   a. is a true picture.
   b. must be the same as what we see.
   c. must show you what someone thinks.
   d. must not show you what someone thinks.

5. Most European languages came from one language thousands of years ago. So in some ways they are alike. But Hungarian is very different from the other European languages. No one is sure
   a. who they are.   c. why it is the same.
   b. who speaks it.   d. why it is different.

Exercise 20

1. One hundred years ago, the British Empire was very strong. It sent ships and soldiers to North and South America, Africa, and Asia. There were British ships all around the world. The British were very proud of this. They liked to say "The sun never sets
   a. in England."
   b. in our hearts."
   c. on the far side of the world."
   d. on the British Empire."

2. In some movies, there are only good cowboys and bad cowboys. The good cowboys are great men who help everyone. The bad cowboys are robbers and killers. But in real life, most cowboys were not so special. They worked hard in the American West. The idea of cowboys we get from movies is
   a. true.
   b. not true.
   c. good.
   d. robbers and killers.

3. Scientists say that Americans move often. The average American moves to a new home every seven years. But some Americans never move. They live all their lives in the same place. So there must be other Americans who
   a. move to new homes.
   b. move more than once in seven years.
   c. never move.
   d. move every seven years.

4. It is harder to learn some things when you get older. Your brain does not work as quickly. That is why we sometimes say, "You can't teach
   a. a young dog anything."   c. a young dog old tricks."
   b. an old dog new tricks."   d. a dog when you are old."

5. The "Potato Famine" happened in Ireland in the 1830s. The Irish people were very poor. Meat was too expensive, so everyone ate mostly potatoes. Then a disease killed many of the potato plants. With no potatoes to eat, the people
   a. were happier.   c. died of hunger.
   b. ate meat instead.   d. were ill.

Exercise 21

1. A beaver is a small animal that lives in northern forests. It cuts down trees with its teeth. It puts the trees in a small river. Then the beaver makes a nice home in the water. This is hard work, and it takes a lot of time. We sometimes say that someone at work is
   a. as lazy as a beaver.   c. as small as a beaver.
   b. as big as a beaver.   d. as busy as a beaver.

2. "An apple a day keeps the doctor away." This means that eating apples is
   a. good for your health.
   b. bad for your teeth.
   c. unhealthy.
   d. good for your doctor.

3. Some people like to dream about things that are not possible. They plan wonderful vacations, but they have no money. They think of getting married to someone they do not even know. These people, we say, are
   a. building a solid future.
   b. making a new life for themselves.
   c. building castles in the air.
   d. telling tall tales.

4. A few days ago, Sarah found a chair. It was lying on a pile of garbage outside her house. She did not understand why it was there. It was not broken or old. In fact, it was quite new. She needed a chair, so she
   a. left it there.   c. took it home.
   b. sat on it.   d. looked at it.

5. Many Americans like to keep dogs as pets. Some dogs help with work on a farm. Others may help hunt wild animals. And many dogs are just nice to have in the house. Dogs are often called
   a. bad names.   c. farmers and hunters.
   b. man's worst enemies.   d. man's best friends.

Exercise 22

1. In many countries, jogging is a very popular sport. Some people jog to lose weight. Others jog because it feels good. But the best reason for jogging is for your health. Doctors say it
   a. makes your heart stronger.
   b. makes your heart weaker.
   c. makes you go faster.
   d. makes you eat a lot.

2. England is famous for its runners. Many young English people want to become famous runners. They work very hard at it. That is why English runners
   a. are not very good.
   b. are young.
   c. win so many races.
   d. travel a lot.

3. Today people can run much faster than they could in the past. In 1950, the time for running a mile was over four minutes. But in 1954, Roger Bannister ran a mile in
   a. ten minutes.
   b. five minutes.
   c. more than four minutes.
   d. less than four minutes.

4. Many words in English came from Greek. For example, the Greek word for "star" is *aster*. So the scientists who study the sky are called
   a. philosophers.
   b. sky-gazers.
   c. astronomers.
   d. archaeologists.

5. In the last few years of his life, Beethoven could not hear. When he wrote his music, he could not try it on the piano. He had to
   a. listen to an orchestra.
   b. play the violin.
   c. sing the music to someone.
   d. think the music in his head.

Exercise 23

1. Many New Yorkers prefer to live in tall apartment buildings. Everyone wants the apartments near the top. So these are usually
   a. empty.
   b. the most expensive.
   c. the least expensive.
   d. the last ones to be rented.

2. There is a very large apartment building in New York. In fact, it is like a small city. You can shop for food in the building. You can meet friends, go for a swim, or get a haircut. Everything you need is
   a. far away.
   b. at home.
   c. in the next town.
   d. in New York.

3. Strange things happen when there is a full moon. More babies are born. Cats and other pets become restless. Some people cannot sleep. So it is not surprising that when the moon is full
   a. people can sleep well.
   b. there are more car accidents.
   c. the sky seems darker.
   d. dogs are quiet.

4. In the country, it is very dark. If you look at the sky at night, you can find many stars and the Milky Way. Sometimes you can also see planets. But in the city, it is different. You can not see many stars.
   a. There is not enough light.
   b. There is not enough time.
   c. There are no stars near cities.
   d. The city lights are too bright.

5. Elephants and whales are a lot alike. Elephants are the largest animals on land. Whales are the largest animals in the sea. People hunt and kill both whales and elephants. This is too bad. Someday
   a. elephants will not be large anymore.
   b. there may be more whales and elephants.
   c. there may not be any more whales or elephants.
   d. whales will move to different parts of the sea.

Exercise 24

1. The most expensive apartments are at the top of tall buildings. These apartments are called penthouses. People like to live in penthouses because they can
   a. see the whole city from their windows.
   b. save money.
   c. have many neighbors.
   d. have trees in their garden.

2. There are not enough apartments in New York City. More than 20,000 poor people have no place to live. The city government tries to help. It gives some poor people money to live in hotels. The people can stay in the hotels
   a. because hotels are cheaper than apartments.
   b. with penthouse apartments.
   c. because they do not want apartments.
   d. until they find apartments.

3. In England, tea does not mean just something to drink. Teatime is a special part of the day. With their cup of tea, English people like to eat. They eat beautiful little sandwiches, sweet breads, and cake. When you have tea in England, be ready for
   a. a hot drink.   c. a quick sandwich.
   b. a nice meal.   d. breakfast.

4. Tea is a popular drink in many countries. In Russia, the people use a special pot to make tea. It is called a *samovar*. This pot is very important to Russian families. Even the poorest family
   a. has a *samovar*.
   b. drinks milk.
   c. does not drink tea.
   d. makes tea.

5. People who live alone sometimes feel ill and unhappy. Their doctors may tell them to get a pet. Their "medicine" can be a dog, cat, bird or goldfish. They are not sick. They just need
   a. some medicine.   c. something to love.
   b. a new doctor.   d. to find a new job.

Exercise 25

1. All living things change because of where they live. For example, there are fish in rivers deep underground. There is no light there, so these fish have no

   a. food.　　　b. eyes.　　　c. eggs.　　　d. babies.

2. A bicycle is very useful in the city. It can go more places than a car. And it is faster than

   a. a car.　　　b. a plane.　　　c. visiting.　　　d. walking.

3. In the past, people did not know much about faraway countries. News traveled very slowly around the world. Nowadays, TV and computers make countries seem very close together. People know a lot about every part of the world. A famous writer says that the world is becoming

   a. far apart.　　　　　　　c. larger.
   b. a big village.　　　　　 d. a strange place.

4. What happens in one place is important all over the world. A factory makes the air dirty in one country. Then the air of the whole world is changed. We are all part of the same world. We all travel around the sun together. In fact, we can call the world

   a. space ship earth.　　　　c. strangers in strange lands.
   b. many separate islands.　　d. a big, round ball.

5. People around the world are trying new foods. In New York, they eat Japanese food. In Tokyo, they love Italian food. Maybe someday people will

   a. eat Italian food in Tokyo.
   b. eat the food they do now.
   c. eat Japanese food in New York.
   d. eat every kind of food in every country.

Appendix

Appendix

ANSWER KEY FOR INTRODUCTION

How to Read Faster

A. 1. c
   2. a
   3. d
   4. c

B. 1. c
   2. c
   3. b
   4. a

C. 1. d
   2. d
   3. b
   4. c

How to Think in English

1. c
2. a
3. d
4. b
5. d
6. d

ANSWER KEY FOR PART II

Unit 1: Previewing and Predicting

Previewing

Passage A.
1. b
2. b
3. d
4. c

Passage B.
1. b
2. b
3. c
4. b

Passage C.
1. a
2. b
3. c
4. c

Predicting

Exercise 1.
1. d
2. e
3. a
4. b
5. c

Exercise 2.
1. b
2. a
3. a
4. b

Exercise 3.
1. no
2. yes
3. yes
4. no
5. no
6. yes
7. yes
8. no
9. yes
10. no

Predicting

Exercise 4.
1. no
2. yes
3. yes
4. no
5. yes
6. yes
7. yes
8. no
9. yes
10. yes

Exercise 5.
1. c
2. b
3. b
4. b
5. b
6. c
7. c
8. b
9. a
10. b

Unit 2: Scanning

Example.
1. Chapter 5
2. Chapter 3
3. page 46
4. 3.10
5. yes, on p. 191

Exercise 1.
1. 132
2. 53
3. v, 12, 28, 29, . . .
4. 63
5. 75, 76, 131, . . .
6. 9, 14, 53
7. 118
8. 127, 128, 132
9. 159
10. 66

Exercise 2.
1. "D.A.R.Y.L.", "Secret Admirer", "Code of Silence", and "Nine Deaths of Ninja"
2. 1 Beacon St.
3. 536-2870
4. Two
5. "Police Academy 2"
6. No
7. Copley Place
8. Cinema 57
9. "Falcon and Snowman"
10. Village Cinemas, Allston Cinemas, and Beacon Hill
11. Friday at 1:30, 3:30, 5:30, 7:30 and 9:30 p.m.
12. no

Exercise 3.
1. Yes.
2. $379.
3. Susan or Mrs. Young
4. Yes.
5. Yes, small pets are allowed.
6. Yes.
7. Brighton, East Boston, Concord, Brookline, Newton, and Watertown.
8. 914-2811.
9. Watertown ($800)
10. Waltham ($225)
11. $300.
12. $295.

Exercise 4.	Exercise 5.	Exercise 6.	Exercise 7.
1. 14	1. 515	1. Two	1. Horatio
2. shoestore	2. Monday	2. Nov. 12	2. Software package
3. 4:40 p.m.	3. 445,000	3. 1200 pounds	3. Data Systems
4. Yonkers (or	4. Panay Island	4. 224 miles	International (DSI)
Westchester County,	5. Agnes	5. Allen	4. over 40
or on the Cross	6. more than 400	6. Rick Hauk	5. Paqcomp
County Road)			6. $2195.

Unit 3: Guessing Word Meanings

Exercise 1.	Exercise 2.	Exercise 3.			
1. coat	1. runs	A. 1. N	6. N	B. 1. books	6. she
2. boots	2. cooks	2. V	7. V	2. traveled	7. became
3. book	3. likes	3. V	8. V	3. is	8. loved
4. bus	4. calls	4. N	9. N	4. woman	9. they
5. window	5. plays	5. V	10. N	5. was	10. parents

Exercise 4.		Exercise 5.	
1. years	6. to	1. wanted	6. family
2. they	7. teacher	2. she	7. beautiful
3. but	8. find	3. be	8. they
4. not	9. wrote	4. what	9. not
5. something	10. a	5. to	10. teach
	11. is		

Exercise 6.		Exercise 7.	
1. eat	6. thought	1. mother	5. teach
2. noises	7. could	2. that	6. of
3. her	8. know	3. not	7. Helen's
4. ran	9. to	4. take	8. Annie
5. it	10. not		

Exercise 8.		Exercise 9.	
1. they	8. hand	1. Helen	8. was
2. very	9. Annie	2. learned	9. time
3. in	10. on	3. to	10. She
4. cup	11. water	4. then	11. go
5. was	12. became	5. to	12. in
6. then	13. name	6. with	13. good
7. finger	14. Helen	7. went	14. graduated

Exercise 10.		
1. about	7. part	13. good
2. was	8. wanted	14. loved
3. many	9. people	15. a
4. the	10. help	16. That
5. and	11. tried	17. Helen
6. countries	12. believed	18. of
		19. in

Exercise 11.		Exercise 12.	
A. 1. c	B. 1. c	A. 1. g	B. 1. c
2. k	2. d	2. f	2. b
3. d	3. b	3. a	3. c
4. h	4. b	4. i	4. b
5. j	5. d	5. h	5. c
6. a		6. j	
7. i		7. b	
8. l		8. c	
9. f		9. k	
10. b		10. d	
11. e		11. e	
12. g			

Unit 4: Topics

Examples.
2. color
4. head

Exercise 1.
1. family
2. number
3. animal
4. house
5. kitchen
6. city
7. furniture
8. food
9. party

Exercise 2.
1. drinks
2. clothes
3. money
4. travel
5. car
6. water
7. class
8. hospital
9. feeling

Exercise 3.
Students write their own answers.

Exercise 4.
Students write their own answers.

Exercise 5. (Any similar topic is acceptable.)
1. countries
2. buildings
3. parts of a book
4. languages
5. sciences
6. foods made from milk

Exercise 6. (Any similar topic is acceptable.)
1. things to read
2. times of day
3. states in the United States
4. feelings
5. Presidents of the U.S.
6. world problems

Exercise 7. (Any similar topic is acceptable.)
1. people on an airplane
2. electronic things
3. mathematics
4. rivers
5. people in hospitals
6. sports
7. places for driving

Exercise 8.
1. Topic: American cities (Paris does not belong)
2. Topic: school (ice cream does not belong)
3. Topic: clothes for cold weather (bathing suit does not belong)
4. Topic: months (Tuesday does not belong)
5. Topic: desserts (carrots do not belong)
6. Topic: paid jobs (husband does not belong)

Exercise 9. (Any similar topic is acceptable.)
1. Topic: parts of the body (top does not belong)
2. Topic: colors of the rainbow (black does not belong)
3. Topic: parts of the head (elbow does not belong)
4. Topic: what you can put things in (table does not belong)
5. Topic: parts of a house (tree does not belong)
6. Topic: sports using balls (swimming does not belong)

Exercise 10. (Any similar topic is acceptable.)

1. Topic 1: countries in Africa
   Zimbabwe
   Nigeria
   Kenya
   Zambia
   Ethiopia

   Topic 2: religions
   Catholic
   Buddhist
   Muslim
   Christian
   Jew

2. Topic 1: parts of the face
   nose
   chin
   mouth
   ears

   Topic 2: colors
   blue
   red
   yellow
   purple

3. Topic 1: animals
   dog
   horse
   cow
   camel
   elephant
   cat

   Topic 2: bodies of water
   stream
   ocean
   canal
   lake
   sea
   river

4. Topic 1: English-speaking countries
   Ireland
   Scotland
   Australia
   England
   Canada

   Topic 2: states in the western United States
   California
   Washington
   Arizona
   Oregon
   Nevada

5. Topic 1: time
   hour
   year
   minute
   month
   day
   second
   century

   Topic 2: sounds
   tick
   bang
   boom
   meow
   thud
   screech

6. Topic 1: kinds of
   transportation with
   wheels
     bus
     motorcycle
     taxi
     bicycle

   Topic 2: clothes
   pajamas
   socks
   pants
   shirt
   shoes
   dress

7. Topic 1: drinks
   milk
   cola
   coffee
   water
   tea

   Topic 2: school
   subjects
     science
     math
     reading
     writing
     history

8. Topic 1: kinds of
   winter weather
     cold
     windy
     ice
     sleet
     snow

   Topic 2: geography
   mountain
   river
   lake
   hill
   valley

Exercise 11. (Any similar topic is acceptable.)

1. Topic 1: furniture
   chair
   desk
   table
   bed
   bookcase
   chest

   Topic 2: things to
   read
     magazine
     newspaper
     book
     letter

2. Topic 1: grammar
   noun
   adjective
   verb
   pronoun
   article

   Topic 2: astronomy
   planet
   sun
   moon
   stars

3. Topic 1: medicines
   aspirin
   tetracycline
   quinine
   penicillin
   valium

   Topic 2: parts of the
   body
     chest
     arm
     hip
     neck
     leg
     shoulder

4. Topic 1: kinds of
   cloth
     cotton
     silk
     linen
     nylon
     rayon
     wool

   Topic 2: parts of the
   atom
     proton
     nucleus
     neutron
     electron

5. Topic 1: kinds of
   music
     jazz
     folk
     rock
     blues

   Topic 2: musical
   instruments
     violin
     trumpet
     drum
     clarinet
     piano

6. Topic 1: senses
   see
   hear
   touch
   smell
   taste

   Topic 2: sweet
   things
     sugar
     honey
     maple syrup
     candy

7. Topic 1: kinds of
   summer weather
     sun
     breeze
     heat
     warm
     showers

   Topic 2: forms of art
   painting
   print
   photograph
   drawing

8. Topic 1: things to
   write with
     pencil
     chalk
     pen
     brush
     marker
     typewriter

   Topic 2: food from
   animals
     chicken
     lamb
     pork
     beef

9. Topic 1: people in
   government
     president
     prime minister
     mayor
     chancellor

   Topic 2: things
   built by engineers
     tower
     skyscraper
     bridge
     dome

Unit 5: Topics of Conversations

1. What: a new car
   Where: a place where cars are sold
   Helpful words: miles, belonged to, use it, price, you should get it

2. What: Someone is arriving at the airport
   Where: at the airport
   Helpful words: will be late, Air India, Airline agent

3. What: a hurt leg
   Where: at the doctor's office
   Helpful words: happen, fell down, can you move it, can you walk on it, x-ray

4. What: going to a movie
   Where: at a movie theater
   Helpful words: long line, get in, tickets, first show, $2.50, popcorn

5. What: buying some new clothes
   Where: at a store
   Helpful words: the color, style, look on me, it looks great

6. What: a language class
   Where: at school
   Helpful words: understand, test, language lab, practice

7. What: taking a taxi to the train station
   Where: in a taxi
   Helpful words: where, train station, hurry, what time

8. What: getting a table at a restaurant
   Where: at the restaurant
   Helpful words: how many, reservation, tables

9. What: changing jobs
   Where: at work
   Helpful words: last day, leaving, nervous, different, change, more pay

10. What: how traffic is a problem in the city
    Where: in a car
    Helpful words: working in a big city, every day, late, run out of gas, radio

Unit 6: Topics of Paragraphs

Exercise 1.
A. 1. a. too specific
      b. too general
      c. topic
   2. a. topic
      b. too specific
      c. too general
   3. a. too general
      b. topic
      c. too specific
B. Mexico City's problems

Exercise 2.
A. 1. a. too general
      b. too specific
      c. topic
   2. a. too specific
      b. topic
      c. too general
   3. a. topic
      b. too specific
      c. too general
B. Television in the United States

Exercise 3.
A. 1. a. too general
      b. topic
      c. too specific
   2. a. too general
      b. too specific
      c. topic
   3. a. topic
      b. too specific
      c. too general
B. Forests

Exercise 4.
A. 1. a. too general
      b. too specific
      c. topic
   2. a. topic
      b. too specific
      c. too general
   3. a. too general
      b. too specific
      c. topic
B. Kinds of drinks

Exercise 5.
A. 1. fog
   2. lightning
   3. kinds of clouds
B. Weather

Exercise 6.
A. 1. where drinking water comes from in the United States
   2. problems with drinking water
   3. ways to use less water
B. Water

Exercise 7.
A. 1. getting ready to look for a job
   2. a doctor's job
   3. how to keep a job
B. Jobs

Exercise 8.
A. 1. Why Galileo was an important scientist
   2. Galileo's study of how things fall
   3. Galileo's problems with religious people
B. Galileo's life and work

Unit 7: Main Ideas

Exercise 1.
1. b. Clothes tell a lot about a person.
2. b. Clothes are important when you travel.
3. c. Clothes today are different from the clothes of the 1800s.

Exercise 3.
1. c. Cats are nicer than dogs in some ways.
2. b. Pets may be good for children.
3. c. Cats are not just pets.

Exercise 2.
1. c. Alchemists studied chemicals in strange ways.
2. a. Lavoisier learned important facts by doing experiments.
3. c. Lavoisier was a great man in many ways.

Exercise 4.
1. c. Erosion changes the earth.
2. b. The Mt. St. Helens and Mt. Vesuvius volcanoes both caused trouble.
3. c. Scientists still have many questions about the earth.

Note: The main idea must be a complete sentence. You may use different words. But your answer should have the same idea as the answers below.

Exercise 5.
1. People use newspaper ads in many ways.
2. Ads tell a lot about the people in a country.
3. Sometimes people write personal ads for bad reasons.

Exercise 6.
1. "Black Thursday" was a terrible day for many Americans.
2. The Great Depression was very serious and surprised many people.
3. The Great Depression ended because of Roosevelt's government and because of World War II.

Exercise 7.
A. 1. Population growth is a serious problem around the world.
   2. In some countries the population is not growing.
   3. In other areas, the fast population growth is causing problems.
   4. China found a way to slow down population growth.
B. 1. Population growth.
   2. Population growth is a serious problem around the world, but there is some hope for change.

Exercise 8.
A. 1. Many people moved out of American cities after World War II.
   2. American businesses also moved out of the cities in the 1950s and 1960s.
   3. Cities began to have money problems.
   4. Many people believed American cities were dying.
B. 1. American cities after World War II.
   2. Changes in American cities caused many problems.

Unit 8: Patterns of Organization
Listing

Exercise 1.
1. a. computers
   b. Computers are helpful in many ways.
   c. many

Signals	Details
first	computers are fast
second	they can work with lots of information at the same time
third	they can keep information for a long time
also	they are almost always correct.

2. a. computers
   b. There are a number of ways to learn about computers.
   c. a number of

Signals	Details
some	some companies have computer classes
also	most universities offer classes
another	you can learn from a book
or	you can learn from a friend

Exercise 2.

1. a. computer programs
   b. There are many kinds of computer programs.
   c. many

Signals	Details
first	programs for doing math problems
second	some programs are like fancy typewriters
third	programs for courses in schools and universities
other	programs for fun
finally	

2. a. computer language
   b. Computer language can be funny at times.
   c. at times

Signals	Details
for example	computers have a "memory"
also	many computer programs have a "menu"
another	there is a "mouse" in some computers

Exercise 3.

1. a. computers
   b. Computers come in all shapes and sizes.
   c. all

Signals	Details
also	small personal computers for the home
other	special computers for factories
even	computers for telephones, televisions, cars

2. a. computers
   b. Computers can cause problems.
   c. problems

Signals	Details
one	computers can lose information
another	they can break down and erase information or stop doing anything
and another	they may be bad for your health

Exercise 4.

1. a. computers
   b. Computers are used for all kinds of work.
   c. all kinds of

Signals	Details
for example	scientists use computers
so	mathematicians and economists
(no signal)	business people
also	doctors
too	writers
finally	people at home

2. a. computers
   b. There are many reasons to like computers.
   c. other

Signals	Details
some	the sounds computers make
also	the lights and pretty pictures
and	computers have personalities

Time-order

Example A. Events:
Einstein was born.
He graduated from the University of Zurich.
He did some of his most famous work in physics.
He won the Nobel Prize.
He lived in Germany and traveled a lot.
He left Germany.
He lived in Princeton, New Jersey.
He died.

Example B. The answers are the same as the answers for Example A.

Exercise 1.

1. Topic: The first part of the Vietnam War
     1946 — The beginning of the war
     1953 — The French army was in trouble.
     1954 — The French army left Vietnam.

2. Topic: The second part of the Vietnam War
     1954 — The beginning of the second part of the war
     1954-1960 — North Vietnam and South Vietnam were fighting all the time.
     1965 — The North Vietnamese were winning the war.
     March, 1965 — The United States began to help the South.
     July, 1965 — There were 75,000 American soldiers in Vietnam.

Exercise 2.
1. Topic: How the Vietnam War became an
   American war
   1965 — The Vietnam War became an
   American war.
   that year — The United States bombed North
   Vietnam.
   each year — The United States used more
   bombs and sent more soldiers.
   the end of 1967 — There were almost
   510,000 Americans in Vietnam.

2. Topic: How the Americans stopped fighting in
   Vietnam
   the early 1960s — A few Americans did not
   want the war.
   the late 1960s — Many people did not want
   the war.
   May, 1968 — The United States and North
   Vietnam began to talk about stopping the
   war.
   for the next few months — There were fewer
   bombs.
   by the end of the year — The bombing
   stopped.
   1970 — American soldiers started to go
   home.
   three years later — The last Americans left.

Exercise 3.
1. Topic: Anh Ngyen's early life
   1960 — Anh was born.
   when she was four years old — Her family
   moved to Saigon.
   1972 — She finished grammar school.
   in the fall — She won a prize.
   that winter — She decided she wanted to
   study in France.
   in the spring — She did very well on her
   French exams.

Exercise 4.
2. Topic: How Anh's life changed because of the war
   1973 — Life in Saigon was changing.
   1974 — The North Vietnamese army moved
   into Saigon.
   that year — New troubles began for the
   people.

Exercise 4.
Topic: How Anh decided to leave Vietnam
   the next few years — Anh had an unhappy and
   difficult time.
   at first — She continued to go to school.
   after a while — She stopped going to school and
   started working.
   at last — She decided to leave.
   the day came — Anh said good-bye.
   at night — The boat left Vietnam.
   for several days — They sailed with no trouble.
   finally — A large Japanese ship picked them up.
   right away — Anh wrote to her cousin Pho in
   Boston.
   next — She showed his letter to the immigration
   office.
   finally, almost one year later — She got her
   American visa.

Exercise 5.
Topic: What happened when Anh arrived in the
   United States
   December, 1979 — Anh arrived in Boston.
   that evening — She talked with Pho and
   To-Van.
   that night — She made a decision.
   the first winter — Boston seemed very cold.
   in January — She started studying at the high
   school.
   by summer — The worst times were over.
   for the next two years — She studied very hard.
   at the end of her last year — She won a
   scholarship.
   finally — Anh had a plan.

Cause and Effect

Exercise 1.
1. Cause: exercise
   Effect: you are hungry and
   thirsty
   Signal words: can make

2. Cause: ice and snow on the
   road
   Effect: car accidents
   Signal words: because of

3. Cause: bad food and not
   enough sleep
   Effect: bad health
   Signal words: reasons for

4. Cause: smoking cigarettes
   Effect: cancer
   Signal words: lead to

5. Cause: drinking coffee
   Effect: some people become
   nervous
   Signal words: because of

6. Cause: careless smokers
   Effect: fires in homes
   Signal words: due to

7. Cause: eating too much
   Effect: heart disease
   Signal words: the result of

8. Cause: very bright sunlight
   Effect: your eyes are hurt
   Signal words: can cause

9. Cause: car accidents
   Effect: high insurance costs
   Signal words: result of

10. Cause: serious family
       problems
    Effect: illness
    Signal words: can cause

Exercise 2.

1. Topic: some of the effects of coffee

Causes	*Signals*	*Effects*
coffee	can help	stay awake
coffee	can keep	awake at night
coffee	makes	some people feel alive
coffee	—	other people feel nervous
coffee	can help	your stomach
coffee	can cause	a stomachache

2. Topic: the effects of aspirin

Causes	*Signals*	*Effects*
aspirin	can stop	a headache or earache
aspirin	helps take away	pain
aspirin	can stop	fever
aspirin	can make you	feel better
aspirin	can result in	a healthy heart
aspirin	may stop	heart disease

Exercise 3.

1. Topic: why many Americans are fat

Causes	*Signals*	*Effects*
the kind of food	one cause	many Americans are fat
the way they eat	another cause	many Americans are fat
not enough exercise	a third cause	many Americans are fat
health problems	because of	many Americans are fat

2. Topic: what can happen to your health if you are too fat

Causes	*Signals*	*Effects*
being too fat	cause	the heart
being too fat	lead to	a heart attack or other problems
being too fat	cause	diabetes
being too fat	is a result of	high blood pressure
being too fat	can be a result of	cancer

Exercise 4.

1. Topic: the reasons why some people become unhappy and ill in the winter

Causes	*Signals*	*Effects*
winter	does cause	problems
not enough light	may cause	illness and unhappiness

2. Topic: the reasons why poor city children are often ill

Causes	*Signals*	*Effects*
poor diet	because of	children are ill
bad housing	caused by	poor health
dirty water	result of	poor health
crowded apartments and schools	may be caused by	poor health

Comparison

Exercise 1.

1. What Peter and Joe like to cook	*Signals*
Differences:	
Peter — lots of simple food	
Joe — special dishes	but
Likenesses:	
they like to cook good meals	both

2. Poland and Italy	*Signals*
Differences:	
Poland — in the north of Europe	
Italy — in the south of Europe	but
Poland — a communist government	
Italy — a democratic government	but
Likenesses:	
Catholic religion	both
history is important	both
friendliness and good spirit	both

Exercise 2.

1. the cooking of India and China	*Signals*
Likenesses:	
rice is important	both
spicy	both
use many vegetables	both
meat is not always important	both
many different kinds of cooking	both

2. the way people eat in Europe now and the way they used to eat a thousand years ago	*Signals*
Differences:	
now — forks, knives and spoons	
before — no forks	but
now — do not use fingers	
before — picked up food	but
now — glasses	
before — bowls or wooden cups	instead

Exercise 3.

1. English breakfasts and American breakfasts	*Signals*
Likenesses:	
Large	both
several dishes	both
meat	both
Differences:	
English — do not like cake for breakfast	
Americans — sweet bread or cake	but

2. American breakfasts and Italian breakfasts	*Signals*
Differences:	
American — larger	
Italian — bread and coffee	but
American — meat	
Italian — no meat	but
American — no strong coffee	
Italian — strong, dark coffee	but

Exercise 4.

1. the old neighborhood market and today's supermarket	*Signals*
Differences:	
the old markets—small, friendly places	not the same
people went there to talk or hear the news	different
supermarkets today — very large	however
not very friendly	
not good places for meeting	
people are tired, in a hurry, not polite	

2. Medical care in England and the United States	*Signals*
Differences:	is very different
England — national	
U.S. — private	but
England — free	
U.S. — expensive	but
England — everyone gets it	
U.S. — poor people sometimes do not get it	not like this

Using All Four Patterns

Exercise 1.
1. d
2. b
3. a
4. e

Exercise 2.
1. a
2. c
3. d
4. b

Unit 9: Using Reference Words
Pronouns

Example B: jogging

Exercise 1.
1. Running
2. Runners
3. long races
4. Boston Marathon
5. winners
6. people

Exercise 2.

they	people
this	Boston Marathon
It	Boston Marathon
They	runners
them	runners
it	the Marathon
It	the race
them	runners
they	runners
They	crowds of people
them	runners

Exercise 3.

it	jogging
it	the weather
This	Central Park
them	New Yorkers
They	dogs
them	joggers
them	dogs
They	dog owners
They	park police

Exercise 4.

They	Mary Simms and Jim Fuller
It	large white dog
them	Mary and Jim
They	Mary and Jim
She	Mary
it	the dog
her	Mary
It	rock
she	dog's owner
it	the dog
you	Mary and Jim
It	the dog
she	the dog's owner
He	park police officer
them	Mary, Jim, and the dog's owner
this	the fighting
he	park police officer

Example B.

These	people need homes and jobs
	buildings and street need to be fixed
	schools are old
	streets are dangerous
them	problems

Exercise 5.
1. Running on a very hot day
2. shoes, socks, shorts, and shirts
3. joggers, dogs, bicyclists, many people

Exercise 6.
1. make the air hot
2. raise and lower the balloon to find a good wind direction
3. carry film and heavy equipment
4. deaf, blind, could not speak
5. blow over cars, destroy houses, kill people
6. dust and dirt in the air, a cone shape in the sky
7. tornadoes
8. destroy a street of homes and stores, kill people
9. Kansas, Arkansas, Nebraska, Iowa, and Missouri
10. wind in the center

Related Words

Exercise 1.

	1	2	3
2. Mount Fuji, Japanese mountain, mountain
3. water pollution problems, pollution problems, problems
4. pine tree, evergreen tree, tree
5. Michael Jackson, popular musicians, musicians
6. Nicaragua, central American country, country
7. Dr. Diamond, dentist, man
8. Boston, city, place
9. *The New York Times*, newspaper, reading material
10. Diamond family, group, people
11. tornado, wind storm, storm
12. president, political leader, person
13. white shirt, shirt, clothing
14. flute, wind instrument, musical instrument
15. IBM corporation, company, organization

Exercise 2.
1. Paris
2. stringed instrument
3. president
4. storm, winds
5. lemons, limes, and oranges; citrus fruit
6. breakfast, food in the morning
7. gasoline
8. lion and three cubs; animals
9. season, that time of year
10. motion sickness; problem

Exercise 3.

2. violin
   string instrument

3. president
   leader

4. tornado
   storm
   winds

5. lemons, limes, and oranges
   citrus fruits
   source of vitamin C

6. breakfast
   food in the morning
   meal

7. gasoline
   fuel

8. lion and three cubs
   cats
   animals

9. winter
   season
   time of the year

10. motion sickness
    illness
    problem

Unit 10: Skimming

Skimming for Point of View

Example B. Yes
       Nicer, happy, cooler in the summer

Exercise 1.
1. Against
2. Against
3. For
4. Against
5. Against
6. For
7. Against
8. For

Exercise 2.
1. Against
2. Against
3. Against
4. For
5. Against
6. For
7. Against
8. For

Skimming for the Pattern of Organization

Exercise 1.
1. c
2. list
3. t-o
4. c-e
5. list
6. c
7. t-o
8. c

Exercise 2.
1. t-o
2. list
3. c
4. c-e
5. list
6. t-o
7. c-e
8. list

Skimming for Ideas

Example:
1. d
2. d
3. b

Exercise 1.
1. c
2. d
3. b

Exercise 2.
1. d
2. b
3. d

Exercise 3.
1. b
2. a
3. c

Exercise 4.
1. c
2. c
3. b

Exercise 5.
1. a
2. c
3. c

ANSWER KEY FOR PART III

Faster Reading Passages 1-20

QUESTIONS

	1	2	3	4	5	6	7	8
1	c	a	a	a	b	d	b	d
2	c	b	d	a	b	d	d	c
3	a	b	a	b	b	b	d	a
4	c	a	c	b	a	d	b	d
5	b	b	a	d	b	c	a	d
6	b	d	b	c	b	a	a	b
7	c	c	b	c	b	a	b	c
8	c	a	c	c	b	d	d	a
9	b	c	d	b	a	a	c	b
10	c	b	c	a	c	b	d	b
11	b	c	d	b	c	b	b	b
12	d	b	a	c	c	d	c	c
13	d	b	c	a	a	b	c	d
14	d	b	c	a	d	d	d	c
15	b	c	b	d	a	b	b	c
16	d	c	b	a	b	c	d	c
17	c	c	d	d	c	d	c	a
18	d	a	c	b	d	a	c	d
19	d	b	c	d	a	b	c	b
20	d	b	a	d	a	c	d	c

PASSAGES

Faster Reading Passages 21-40

QUESTIONS

	1	2	3	4	5	6	7	8
21	d	d	a	b	c	c	c	c
22	d	c	a	c	d	b	a	c
23	c	b	d	d	b	a	c	c
24	b	c	c	c	a	d	b	c
25	d	c	a	d	c	a	c	c
26	d	b	b	b	d	a	b	a
27	c	b	c	b	a	c	c	d
28	d	c	b	c	a	c	b	b
29	d	b	d	b	a	b	a	c
30	d	a	c	d	b	d	a	d
31	b	d	b	d	c	c	b	c
32	c	d	c	c	b	c	b	b
33	c	a	a	c	b	d	d	c
34	c	d	d	a	a	b	d	c
35	d	d	a	b	a	a	c	b
36	b	c	a	a	c	c	a	a
37	d	b	d	a	c	b	d	c
38	d	b	d	c	a	b	c	b
39	c	b	a	d	a	c	d	b
40	d	b	c	a	c	b	c	a

P
A
S
S
A
G
E
S

ANSWER KEY FOR PART IV

Thinking Skills

QUESTIONS

	1	2	3	4	5
1	c	a	d	b	d
2	d	b	d	c	c
3	b	c	a	d	c
4	b	d	b	c	d
5	b	b	d	b	b
6	a	d	b	b	c
7	a	d	b	a	b
8	d	a	c	b	d
9	b	d	a	b	a
10	c	b	b	b	b
11	d	c	b	d	d
12	d	d	d	a	b
13	d	d	b	b	c
14	b	c	b	a	d
15	d	c	c	d	b
16	b	d	d	c	b
17	a	a	b	c	b
18	b	a	b	c	b
19	b	a	a	c	d
20	d	b	b	b	c
21	d	a	c	c	d
22	a	c	d	c	d
23	b	b	b	d	c
24	a	d	b	a	c
25	b	d	b	a	d

(Row labels at left: E X E R C I S E S)

Reading Rate Tables for Faster Reading Passages
Passages 1-20 (200-word passages)

Reading Time (minutes)	Reading Rate (words per minute)
:30	400
:45	266
1:00	200
1:15	160
1:30	133
1:45	114
2:00	100
2:15	89
2:30	80
2:45	73
3:00	67
3:15	62
3:30	57
3:45	53
4:00	50
4:15	47
4:30	44
4:45	42
5:00	40

Reading Rate Tables for Faster Reading Passages
Passages 21-40 (400-word passages)

Reading Time (minutes)	Reading Rate (words per minute)
:30	800
:45	533
1:00	400
1:15	320
1:30	267
1:45	229
2:00	200
2:15	178
2:30	160
2:45	145
3:00	133
3:15	123
3:30	114
3:45	107
4:00	100
4:15	94
4:30	89
4:45	84
5:00	80
5:15	76
5:30	73
5:45	70
6:00	67
6:15	64
6:30	62
6:45	59
7:00	57

Reading for Pleasure Progress Chart

Book Title _____

Author _____

SPEED

in wpm

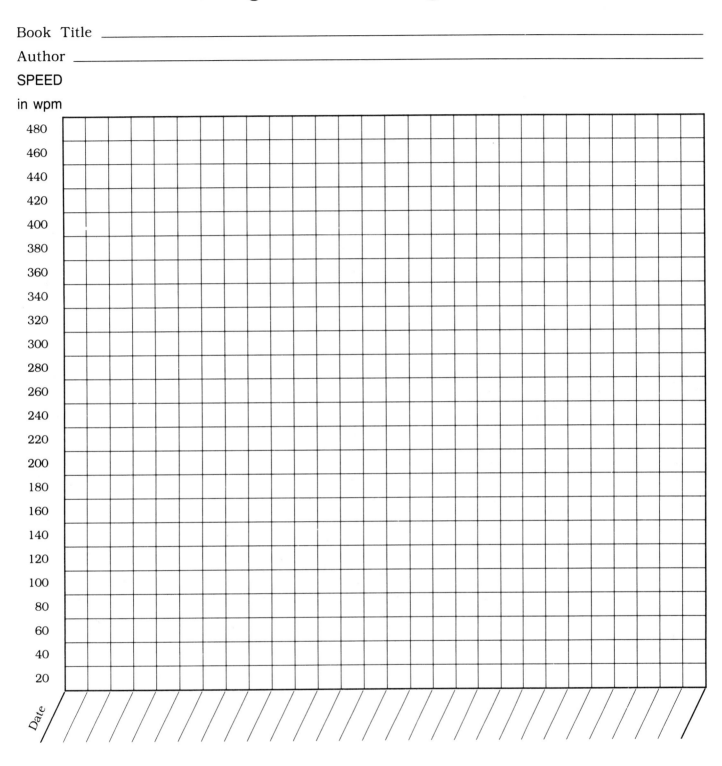

Progress Chart for Faster Reading
1 – 20

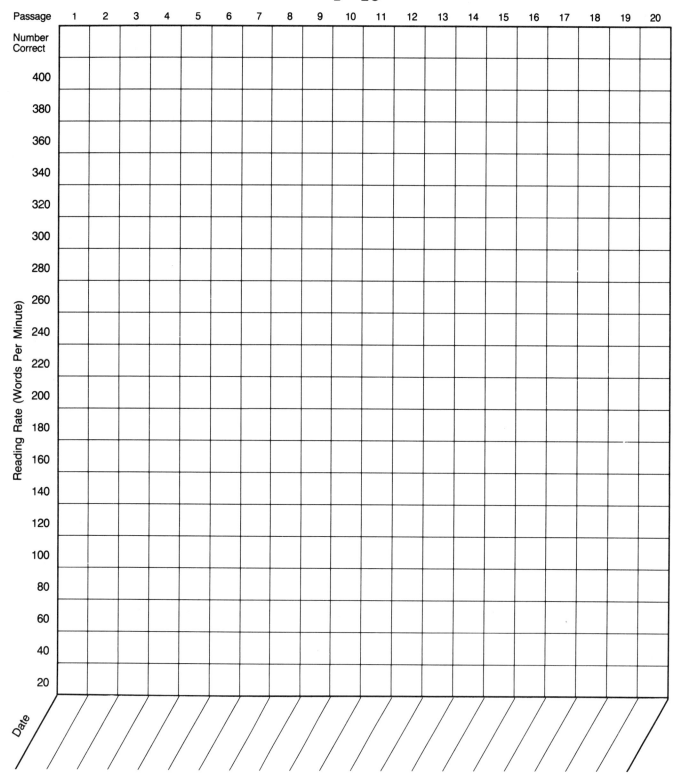

Progress Chart for Faster Reading
21 – 40

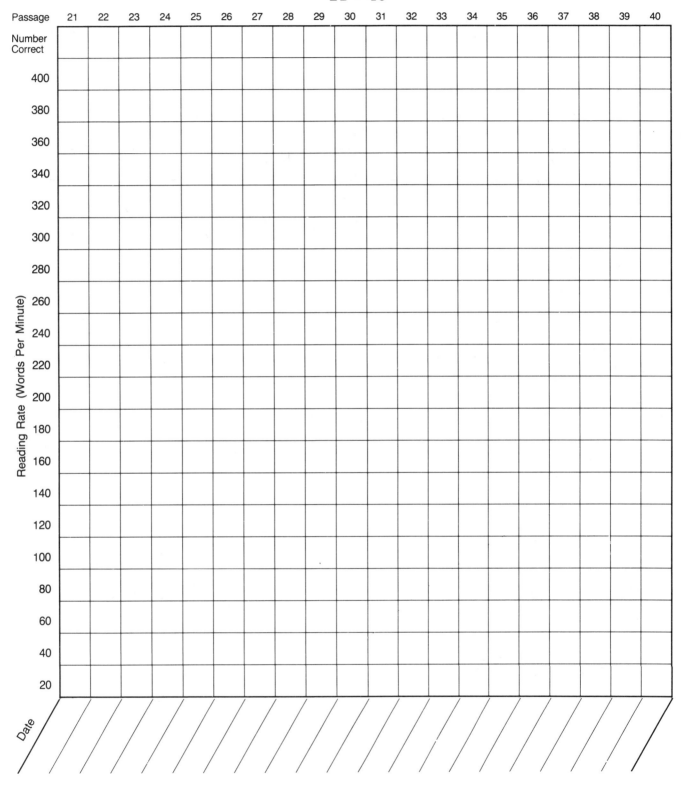

Thinking Skills Progress Chart

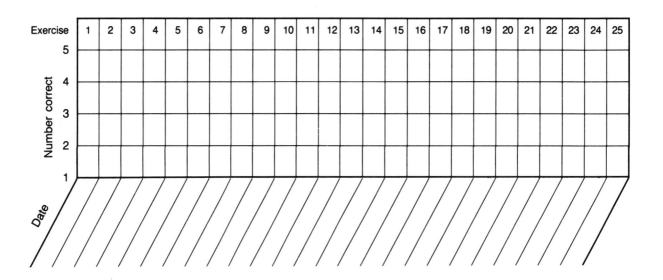

Teacher's Supplement

Teacher's Supplement

Using *Reading Power* in Your Class

The materials in this book are designed to take approximately 35 hours of class time. This can be accomplished in different ways, depending on the structure of your class and the amount of homework assigned. Here are some suggestions for using this book in different class situations:

★ In an integrated skills class which meets for two to three hours per day, five days a week, plan to use this book for about twenty minutes every day. For example:

Monday	— Two *Faster Reading* passages
	One page of *Thinking Skills* exercises
Tuesday	— Two or three pages from a *Comprehension Skills* Unit
Wednesday	— *Reading for Pleasure* and *Book Conferences*
Thursday	— Two or three pages of *Comprehension Skills* exercises
Friday	— Two *Faster Reading* Passages
	One page of *Thinking Skills* exercises

★ In an integrated skills class which meets for three hours per week, plan to use this book for about one third of the class time. For example, in one week of class time students can complete:

- Four *Faster Reading* passages
- One page of *Thinking Skills* exercises
- Six pages of *Comprehension Skills* exercises

Homework assignments can include:

- *Reading for Pleasure*
- *Faster Reading* passages
- *Thinking Skills* exercises
- Selected *Comprehension Skills* exercises

★ In a reading class which meets two hours per week, use this book and the pleasure reading books in every class. Each hour the class can do:

- Two or three pages of *Comprehension Skills* exercises
- Two *Faster Reading* passages
- One page of *Thinking Skills* exercises
- *Reading for Pleasure* and *Book Conferences*

★ In a reading lab, where students work independently, the lab supervisor should explain how to use this book. As in a classroom, the students should work regularly in all four parts of the book. If students go to the reading lab three hours per week, each hour they can do:

- Two or three pages of *Comprehension Skills* exercises
- Two *Faster Reading* passages
- One page of *Thinking Skills* exercises
- *Reading for Pleasure* and *Book Conferences*

General Guidelines

This supplement will give step-by-step guidance in using *Reading Power*. But first, here are some general principles for teaching reading with this book:

- Reading should become enjoyable for the students. The reading class must engage them fully and never turn into "busy work."
- Students should be encouraged to work in pairs as often as possible, especially on the skills exercises in Part II. Talking about the exercises will facilitate language acquisition.
- Teachers should focus on the thinking process. The "right answer" is not important here. What matters is *how* the student arrives at an answer.
- The use of a dictionary should be discouraged. Instead, students should be encouraged to guess the meanings of words.
- Awareness of the purpose of their work will increase the students' efficiency and involvement in learning.
- Students should check their answers in the Answer Key at the back of the book and should try to analyze their own mistakes.
- Some exercises can be assigned for homework as reinforcement after similar exercises have been done in class.

Page 1   INTRODUCTION

In order to encourage students to begin thinking about reading, the first reading class should start with a questionnaire like the one below.

Reading Questionnaire

True or False?

1. It is important to read every word if you want to understand.
2. You will learn more if you look up every new word in the dictionary.
3. Reading stories and novels is not important.
4. If you read fast, you will not understand.
5. You should be able to say every word you read.
6. Reading class is the same as vocabulary class.
7. Books for ESL students must be simple. ESL students cannot read books for English speakers.
8. You should write the words in your own language above the English words in a book.

(All of these statements, of course, are false.)

A discussion of the results of this questionnaire will increase the students' awareness of the reading process, the value different cultures place upon reading, and the role of reading in their own culture. Finally, it will help clarify for the students their objectives in the reading class. Page 1, *How to Become a Better Reader* is intended for the students' information.

Page 2   HOW TO READ FASTER

This section gives the rationale for learning to read faster and establishes the procedures for reading and timing the passages, and for answering the questions. Students will use these same procedures in Part III. It is essential that the teacher read and understand these procedures before working on them with the class.

The passages tell the story of Susan and Sam Diamond and their family. The forty passages must be read in order. None should be skipped. As the students read the passages, they build background knowledge, which enables them to read with increasing speed and fluency.

The students will have much more success with the *Faster Reading* passages if, from the very beginning, they

- learn to time themselves.
- answer the comprehension questions *twice.*

(Allowing the students to answer the questions twice will encourage them to take risks and to guess answers. Knowing they can look back the second time, they are more willing to take those risks.)

Passages A, B, and C introduce the timing procedures. If possible, use a wall clock with a second hand for timing. A typical routine for timing follows:

1. When the class is ready to begin Passage A, the students should write the starting time on the line at the top of the passage. They should then start reading and read as quickly as possible with understanding.
2. As soon as they have finished reading, they should write the finishing time on the line at the end of the passage.
3. Then tell the students to turn the page and circle the best answers to the questions, without referring back to the passage.
4. After they have answered the questions once, the students should go back and answer them a second time. This time, they may look at the passage. They should write their answers in the boxes to the right of the questions.
5. After they are finished, they can check the answers in the boxes. The Answer Key is on page 259. They should write down the number correct.
6. Show the students how to determine their reading rate, using the directions on page 9.

Page 10   # HOW TO THINK IN ENGLISH

This is the introduction to Part IV. In these exercises the students will learn to recognize synonyms, comparatives, definitions, analogies, opposites, and classifications. They will practice using syntactic clues, guessing word meanings, and drawing conclusions.

The *Thinking Skills* exercises require little outside knowledge. The students should be able to guess the right answer from the context of the exercise.

The students should learn to do the *Thinking Skills* exercises without using a dictionary. As the class goes through the practice example on page 10, ask the students to explain their answers. They should be able to tell which words in each example helped them to guess the answer.

Page 13   # PART I—READING FOR PLEASURE

Rationale

Reading Power is based on the belief that the best reading practice materials are the ones which the student selects. If your class uses a standard reader — a collection of stories or articles — it should be used *in addition* to student-selected materials.

The reason for this is simple: When students select a book which interests them, they usually already have some knowledge about the subject, so their understanding will be greater. They will also find the reading more enjoyable.

Books are preferable to short articles or stories because reading a book is more likely to improve reading fluency. It allows the reader to adjust to the writer's style and to build a context for the vocabulary and concepts.

Where to Find Books

Teachers often ask where the students can find books which are interesting to them and easy to read. This may be a problem at the beginning level. The lists in this supplement (page 283) and in Part I (page 19) offer some suggestions. These books are not skills books, with questions at the end of each chapter. They are meant to be read solely for pleasure. (Additional suggestions can be found in an excellent article in *Reading in a Foreign Language*, volume 2, number 2, Autumn, 1984: "Extensive Reading by Means of Graded Readers" by Julian Bamford.)

If there is a library or book store near the school, you can also take your students there during a reading class, to encourage them to develop the habit of browsing for books.

Setting Up a Class Library

Setting up a classroom library is not difficult. If you begin with a dozen or so books, in a few semesters you will have a decent collection. Friends often are willing to donate used paperback books. Students may buy books and then give them to the class library after they have finished reading them. The school might be willing to purchase some books for you, also.

The reading classroom should appear full of tempting materials, with books displayed prominently. Since most books for beginning readers are fairly short and thin, it is a good idea to display them with their covers showing.

Book Conferences

The teacher should meet regularly with individual students for conferences on the students' pleasure reading books.

There are many advantages to such informal oral reports over the traditional written reports. First of all, written reports often turn into drudgery for the students, which can take all the pleasure out of reading. Book conferences, on the other hand, are usually both rewarding and enjoyable for both teacher and student. Also, by giving the "pleasure reading" component of the course more status, they encourage students to take their reading more seriously.

A further advantage of oral conferences is that they provide an opportunity for more interaction between teacher and student with the book as a focus. More specifically, book conferences provide the following benefits:

1. Teacher and student can get to know each other better.
2. The teacher can find out if the student enjoyed and understood the book.
3. The student has an opportunity to express perceptions of the book and how the book relates to their own experience. The teacher's interest and questions can help the student develop these ideas further.
4. The teacher's questions can lead the student toward a more critical view of the book and eventually toward a more critical kind of reading.
5. These conferences help the students develop the habit of talking about reading, a habit which will enhance their comprehension and motivation.

Book conferences can be scheduled by appointment whenever the student has finished a book. The day before the conference, the student should give the book to the teacher. Since the books are usually short and easy to read, the teacher should be able to skim them in time for the conference. And often, students read many of the same books, so the teacher gets to know them.

If a student does not finish a book within a few weeks, however, the teacher should discuss the book in progress and check for any possible problems with the level or subject matter of the book the student has selected. If the book does seem inappropriate or is simply uninteresting, the student should be free to move on to another.

Rate Improvement Practice in Student-Selected Books

Included in Part I are instructions for finding reading rate in the students' self-selected "Pleasure reading" book. This use of the students' books adds to their motivation for improving their reading rate. The Progress Chart (on page 276) is intended as an additional incentive to work on reading faster.

The directions for calculating their rate in words per minute also provide meaningful practice for the students in following directions.

Book List

Graded Readers:

The Jamestown series and the Scott, Foresman series were *not* specifically designed for ESL/EFL students. They were intended for use with English-speaking students in Adult Basic Education classes.

Jamestown Adult Learners Series
(Jamestown Publishers, Providence, R.I., 02940)

A City for Ransom	
Dr. Valdez	
Murder By Radio	
The Man Who Stopped Time	by Judith Andrews Green
The Man with the Scar	
The Secret of Room 401	

Scott, Foresman Adult Readers Library
(Scott, Foresman and Co., Chicago, Ill. 60025)

All the Way Back, A Story of Courage	by Anne V. McGravie
Becoming a Supervisor	by Peggy Simonsen
Cargo	by A. B. Poole
Carlotta's House	by Amita Malin
Dona Eleanora and Lord Edward	by Barbara McGraw
Getting and Keeping a Job	by Peggy Simonsen
Images of Courage	by Catherine Podojil
Mary Ellen and Ida, Portraits of Two Women	by Stephen Beal
Mother Teresa	by Catherine Podojil
Night Prowlers	by Barbara Malin
Stages in Adult Life	by Mary Charuhas
Those Who Dared, Adventure Stories from the Bible	by Barbara McGraw
Truth is Stranger than Fiction	by Betty Burns Paden
Your Body in Health and Sickness	by Merle T. Coughlin

For other suggested books, see page 19 in Part I.

Page 21   PART II—READING COMPREHENSION SKILLS

General Guidelines

1. The purpose and utility of the exercises in each unit should always be discussed with the students before doing the unit.
2. The whole class should work togther on the introduction and examples at the beginning of each unit.
3. Students should enjoy these exercises. The teacher can introduce competitions or other game-like activities to increase the involvement and fun for the students.
4. Whenever possible, students should work in pairs in these units. The exercises lose much of their effectiveness when done individually.
5. The units and the exercises within each unit should be done in order and at a steady pace. If students have already covered similar exercises in class, some exercises can be assigned for homework. However, students should not try new exercises on their own.
6. In some of the exercises, where students write their own answers, their wording may vary from the wording in the Answer Key, but the meaning should be the same.

Page 21   Unit 1: Previewing and Predicting

Previewing

Previewing is a high-speed reading activity. Therefore, the previewing exercises should be timed, or in some way limited in time to encourage the students to work rapidly.

Students should be encouraged to preview everything they read for the following reasons:

1. It allows the reader to place the text in context or mental framework.
2. It helps the reader to judge the level of difficulty of a text and the extent of their background knowledge of the subject.
3. It demonstrates to ESL/EFL students in particular that they can extract information from a text without reading every word.
4. It sets the groundwork for improvement in reading rate and eventually for learning how to skim.

Note that on the first page of this unit (page 21), the students should not turn the page until they have read the passage and had some time to discuss it. They may or may not be able to guess what the passage is about (learning to ride a bicycle), but it is important for them to try. This exercise shows:

- How the establishment of context is crucial to comprehension;
- How a simple picture can help establish that context.

The next exercise, "A Busy Student" on page 23, is intended to show students how to establish context by a very brief look at the text. In this exercise, students should realize that they can learn something about a text without reading every word.

Predicting

These exercises (beginning on page 29) are designed to make the students more aware of the thinking processes involved in drawing inferences. The exercises show students how to locate the evidence for their inferences. The emphasis here is on guessing as a legitimate part of reading.

The predicting exercises follow the previewing exercises because the two activities together will develop the students' ability to tap background knowledge before reading. In the predicting exercises, as in previewing, it is *essential* that the students work in pairs.

Page 34   ## Unit 2: Scanning

Scanning is a high-speed reading skill used when a reader wants to find specific information. The reader already has a question in mind and is simply looking for the answer.

To ensure that students work at high speed in these exercises, they should be timed. Any of the following methods for timing may be used:

1. Students can time each other, working in pairs.
2. The teacher can divide the class into two teams and make the exercises competitive. The winning team will have the highest number of right answers in the shortest amount of time.
3. The teacher may turn the exercises into a race for the whole class. The students get a point for each time they find the right answer first. The student with the highest total points wins.

Page 47   ## Unit 3: Guessing Word Meanings

ESL/EFL students are often unwilling to guess words they do not recognize. These exercises are designed to show them how and when to guess. Be sure that students understand this before doing the exercises.

Notice that the directions for exercises 1–10 in this unit all require the students to work in pairs. This is very important because working with another student makes the exercises less intimidating and increases their value as language acquisition activities.

In the cloze exercises in this unit (exercises 3–10), students should read the entire passage first. Then they can go back and try to write in the missing words. Exercises 3–10 form a complete story. The students can use their knowledge of previous episodes to help them guess the missing words later in the unit.

Exercises 11 and 12 include words the students may not recognize, but should be able to guess from context.

Unit 4: Topics

Note: The exercises in Units 4, 5, 6 and 7 should be worked on sequentially. They are designed to lead the students through the following sequence of skills:

1. Finding topics of lists.
2. Stating topics of lists.
3. Stating topics of longer passages (dialogues).
4. Finding topics of paragraphs.
5. Stating topics of paragraphs.
6. Selecting the best main idea.
7. Stating the main idea.

Unit 4 trains students to distinguish between generalization and details and to develop semantic networks in English. More specifically, in these exercises students will learn to:

1. Identify the general topic by sampling from the list and noticing relationships among the items.
2. Predict and look for a word which matches their inner notions of the category for the words on the list.
3. Ignore words they do not recognize and which are not necessary for establishing the category.
4. Learn new words and reinforce vocabulary and classifications they may already know.
5. Read with a question in mind.

These exercises should be done in pairs. Students usually catch on quickly to the game of finding the topic. The class should move through this unit rapidly.

Unit 5: Topics of Conversations

This unit gives students practice in the following skills:

1. Drawing inferences from clues.
2. Reading with a question in mind.
3. Finding the topic of a longer passage.

These dialogues are not intended to be read aloud by students to the class. Oral reading requires a different set of skills. It may even interfere with comprehension because students tend to concentrate instead on pronunciation.

The class should first do the practice exercise (page 76) together, so the teacher can emphasize using clues to guess the topic and location of each conversation. Then the students should work in pairs on the rest of the unit.

Unit 6: Topics of Paragraphs

Students continue to practice zeroing in on a topic in this unit, but the task becomes more challenging here. The teacher should go through the examples on page 80 with the whole class.

In the first set of exercises students are given three possible topics and asked to select the one which fits the paragraph best and is neither too specific nor too general. A visual representation may help clarify for the students the meaning of specific and general, terms they will need to understand.

The teacher may draw this diagram on the board:

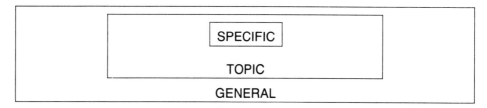

Note that each page of exercises includes a question about the topic for the entire page. Be sure students do not overlook this question.

Page 91 **Unit 7: Main Ideas of Paragraphs**

Students are by now well-trained in finding the topic by asking the question, "What is the topic?" Unit 7 teaches them how to find the main idea of a passage by asking, "What is the author saying about that topic?" The teacher should go through the examples on page 91 with the whole class.

The main idea of any passage should be stated in a complete sentence, to ensure that it is really an idea and not just a topic. All the exercises in this unit require students to form main idea sentences. At first, in Exercises 1 and 2, the students simply complete the best main idea sentence with the topic. Exercises 3 and 4 give students a choice of main idea sentences. The final exercises, 5-8, require students to write out the main idea sentence themselves.

Page 101 **Unit 8: Patterns of Organization**

This unit focuses the students' attention on the organization of the text. They learn to:

1. Recognize four of the most common patterns of organization in English discourse.
2. Identify signal words for each pattern.
3. Use the signal words and the patterns they indicate as tools for better comprehension.

These exercises should help students develop the habit of always asking "What is the pattern?" whenever they read.

The exercise on the first page of the unit is meant to be a whole class activity. After the students try to draw the pictures from memory, the class should discuss the results, and the teacher should then immediately introduce them to the four types of patterns they will learn about in Unit 8.

For each kind of pattern mentioned on page 102, the teacher should ask students to think of other examples. Here are some possibilities:

Listing:
Courses you can take at college
Kinds of holidays
Sports

Time order:
Daily schedule of a student
Getting ready for a party
Steps in applying for a visa

Cause-effect:
Causes of a headache
Effects of a headache
Causes of a war
Effects of a war

Comparison:
Two governments
Two TV shows
Two cars
Two people in the class

Each of the four patterns is introduced by a set of examples. Be sure to do the introduction and examples for each pattern with the whole class. The students need to understand the importance of the signal words used with each pattern.

Using All Four Patterns, Exercises 1 and 2, allow the students to practice identifying the patterns they have learned in this unit.

Page 129   Unit 9: Using Reference Words

ESL/EFL students often run into comprehension problems because they cannot identify the referent for a pronoun. They also often fail to notice the way hyponyms can connect ideas. These exercises will train the students to become more aware of the way writers commonly use these words in English and how important they are for understanding a text.

Pronouns — The whole class should work together on the examples on page 129. Exercises 1–4 give students practice in identifying simpler pronouns. The next exercises, 5 and 6, include some pronouns which serve to summarize earlier facts or ideas.

Related Words—The whole class should work together on the examples on page 135. The exercises on hyponyms are designed to alert students to their function in connecting ideas and also to the way the related words usually are used progressively: a specific noun is used first, then a less specific one, and then a more general term.

Page 139   Unit 10: Skimming

In this unit students will use many of the reading skills they have just learned. Successful skimming requires making guesses from partial evidence, and quickly drawing conclusions about some of the general ideas in the text. This is a complex task — for both native speakers and second language learners — and teachers should not be surprised if their ESL/EFL students find it difficult.

Speed is the key to skimming. It should be stressed from the beginning, even though students are likely to resist. All the exercises in this unit should be timed or limited in time in some way to force the students to work quickly.

Skimming for Point of View. The whole class should work together on the examples on page 139.

Skimming for the Pattern of Organization. The whole class should work together on the examples on page 142.

In Exercises 5–9, they will practice using this skill, and their knowledge about the organization of English paragraphs, in skimming longer passages. The questions following the passages are intended only to check their grasp of the *general* nature and ideas of the text. Be sure that students really do skim the passages. They need to read only the first line and a few words of each paragraph in order to answer the questions.

Page 152 PART III—PASSAGES FOR READING FASTER

Passages 1 to 20 are all 200 words long. Most of these are simple narratives, with a few dialogues and expository passages included. Passages 21 to 40 are 400 words long, and include more expository passages.

The class should start to use these passages as soon they have completed the introductory section at the beginning of the book. They should do two passages each time they practice faster reading, whether at home or in class. It is a good idea to use these passages at least once a week in class. You can monitor the students, timing procedures and try to encourage them to speed up.

The teacher should make sure that the students are timing themselves accurately, using the rate table on page 274 for converting their reading time into reading rate (words per minute), and recording their rate on the Progress Chart on page 275. The teacher's interest in the Progress Chart will encourage the students to work on improving their reading speed.

Page 241 PART IV—THINKING SKILLS

These exercises are designed to provide practice in grasping logical thought patterns in English and guessing the meanings of words from the context. The exercises present problems in logical thinking which the students can solve by using synonyms, comparatives, opposites, analogies, negation, syntax, part/whole relationships, and definitions, and by drawing conclusions based on evidence.

Thinking Skills begins with very simple problems, but each exercise increases in complexity. The students should do them in order.

Students should work independently, at their own pace, in this part. They should check their answers in the Answer Key (page 273), and then record their scores in the Progress Chart (page 278). The students should try to understand their mistakes. Encourage the students to ask the teacher's assistance in figuring out the logic of the answers.

Index of Skills

Skill	Part	Unit	Exercise/Passage
Building concentration ability	II	2, 10	All
	IV		All
Developing awareness of thinking processes in English	II	1	3, 4
	II	3	3-10
	II	4, 5, 6, 9	All
	IV		All
Developing vocabulary	II	3,4,8,9	
Drawing inferences	II	1	
	II	3, 4, 5	
	III		At least one question for each passage
Following directions	I		All
Guessing word meanings from the context	II	3	
	IV		All
Identifying discourse connectors	II	8, 9, 10	
Identifying macro level organization	II	8	
	II	10	3, 4
	III		11, 17, 18, 21, 22, 24, 25, 26, 28, 32, 35, 36, 39
Identifying point of view	II	10	
Increasing reading speed	II	1, 2, 10	
	III	All	
Identifying the main idea	II	7	1-4
Identifying the topic	II	4, 5, 6, 7, 8	
	III		First question for each passage
Previewing	II	1	
Reading with a question in mind	II	2, 4, 5, 6, 7, 10	
Scanning	II	2	
Skimming	II	10	
Stating the main idea	II	7	5-8 Listing section
Using a diagram to aid comprehension	III		33